I0128534

RADIATION AND REVOLUTION

THOUGHT IN THE ACT *A series edited by Brian Massumi and Erin Manning*

RADIATION AND REVOLUTION

Sabu Kohso

DUKE UNIVERSITY PRESS   DURHAM AND LONDON   2020

© 2020 Duke University Press All rights reserved
Text designed by Amy Ruth Buchanan
Cover designed and illustrated by Skillet Gilmore Typeset
in Arno and Trade Gothic by
Copperline Book Services

Library of Congress Cataloging-in-Publication Data
Names: Kōso, Iwasaburō, [date] author.
Title: Radiation and revolution / Sabu Kohso.
Other titles: Thought in the act.
Description: Durham : Duke University Press, 2020. |
Series: Thought in the act | Includes bibliographical
references and index.
Identifiers: LCCN 2019055652 (print) |
LCCN 2019055653 (ebook)
ISBN 9781478009948 (hardcover)
ISBN 9781478011002 (paperback)
ISBN 9781478012535 (ebook)
Subjects: LCSH: Fukushima Nuclear Disaster, Japan,
2011. | Nuclear energy—Social aspects—Japan. | Nuclear
energy—Political aspects—Japan.
Classification: LCC HV623 2011 .F85 K67 2020 (print) |
LCC HV623 2011 .F85 (ebook) | DDC 363.17/990952117—dc23
LC record available at https://lccn.loc.gov/2019055652
LC ebook record available at https://lccn.loc.gov/2019055653

It may be that believing in this world,
in this life, becomes our most difficult task,
or the task of a mode of existence still to be
discovered on our plane of immanence today.
—GILLES DELEUZE AND FÉLIX GUATTARI,
What Is Philosophy?

I'm not referring here to the microapocalypse
of death: everybody dies, and even if everybody
dies at the same time (I mean everybody),
what's the problem? The earth becomes a
cleared tape and why should the angels grieve?
—GEORGE CAFFENTZIS, *In Letters of Blood and Fire*

Emancipate yourselves from mental slavery
None but ourselves can free our minds
Have no fear for atomic energy
'Cause none of them can stop the time
—BOB MARLEY, "Redemption Song"

CONTENTS

Nine years have passed since March 11, 2011. The subsequent period of turmoil seems to have been eclipsed in collective memory. The images circulating through the media environment gradually shifted from progressing devastation to invisible degeneration, from the catastrophe to the apocalypse: coastal towns being washed away, mushroom clouds spewing from the reactors, and men in nuclear, biological, chemical (NBC) suits undertaking lethal operations were replaced by endless piles of black plastic bags, roaming domestic animals in the deserted countryside, and medical examinations of children. This transition is concomitant with the process through which the cataclysmic event that shook the nation of Japan has been subsumed into the reconstruction of capitalist/state apparatuses while the environment with radioactive debris and soil is left to remain and even to expand with the unpredictable mutations of vital activities. In the sense of endurance and expansion, the Fukushima nuclear disaster is perceived as an epitome of the dystopian world.

This book is an assemblage of thoughts on the Fukushima disaster I have conceived during these years. The disaster is grasped here both as a singular event and as a series of events, as the process that prepared it and continues to live on. The following chapters thus comprise personal narrative, empirical description, theoretical analysis, and metaphysical speculation on both the event and the process, extending from shorter to longer spans of time and nearer to farther stretches of space. The basic premise is that the disaster is not over; it continues in the unsettled disposition of powers (pronuclear regime and popular struggles in and against it) vis-à-vis the chaotic permeation of radioactivity. In confrontation with this developing situation, it is imperative for us to revise the idea of changing the world.

A couple of months after the wake, I began translating Japanese texts on the devastating situation into English and elaborating my own accounts based on them.[1] These early interventions arose from the utter shock of the unprecedented disaster and the urge to digest the thoughts and acts of Japanese friends in the midst of the conjuncture. Through these projects I came to believe that the disaster, which delivered irreversible damage to the people, must metamorphose into an irreversibility in another sense; that because it was the apparatuses of the postwar regime that caused the disaster, this should be the moment for people to give up their society and rise up for its radical change. However naive the logic linking the disaster to a revolution may be, such aspiration was manifestly conceived in common among many in Japan and elsewhere for about two years, and still is by some of us.

Eventually, the worst-case scenario of Armageddon was suspended, but the disaster has endured to this day, increasingly obscured by the issue of radioactive contamination in small doses—unresolvable debates on the threshold and nonthreshold models—which has been tacitly playing the main role for the reconstitution of the pronuclear regime. Affecting economy, society, culture, and everyday life, this issue of contamination also engenders new initiatives of the people. Meanwhile, the event of the disaster itself has been buried under more spectacular affairs (i.e., the 2020 Tokyo Olympics) and imminent crises (i.e., increasing disasters and violence by the global business/military regimes), to the extent that it is almost forgotten. The same landscape of consumerist society has returned as if nothing ever happened. This general obsolescence has nurtured a fathomless pessimism in many of us. My senses have since been fluctuating between a will to radical change and a resignation to the world dying its long, slow death by irreversible degradation. In this fluctuation, it has become clear that the catastrophe itself would not necessarily create a revolutionary process. The catastrophe did disrupt the maintenance of the status quo, and it did trigger people's rage and protest. But for the radical break of catastrophe to nurture true metamorphosis, its bifurcations should be developed in synchronicity toward innumerable dimensions and with unknown intensity. Through this awareness, my writings came to focus on the contexts that engendered the disaster, namely, what the disaster has been *revealing*: the role of nuclear power in the formation of Japan's postwar regime as well as global capitalism, and the horizon of people's lives and struggles against it. These writings thus sought to set flight from the fluctuation, toward another horizon.

///

This book is less about the nuclear disaster per se than it is about its revelations. It does not, as such a book may be expected to do, propose how to solve nuclear problems in and of themselves.

The notion of solution is tricky vis-à-vis the nuclear problematic. In the first place, the best we can do with nuclear power is clear and simple: stop it once and for all. Nothing more, nothing less! But then the question is always raised from the standpoint of policy making: how can we sustain enough electricity without it? The answer is by replacing it with safer sources of energy or, better still, by learning to live with less energy. In either orientation, the voices commanding solutions belong exclusively to those most apparently implicated in power—policy makers, bureaucrats, and corporate executives—or to those specialists with access to scientific knowledge and technological means who participate in projects sponsored by states, corporations, or international organizations. Nuclear policy operates within the international society of authorities, wherein the voices of the majority—those who actually live with and fight against its hazards—are hardly accounted for. Authoritarianism is the essence of nuclear apparatuses, and it precludes collective engagement.

In the second place, even if nuclear production is stopped, tasks will remain for decommissioning 449 reactors and containing and decontaminating the radioactive waste that has already accumulated and still continues to accumulate. There has been no answer as to how such tasks could be undertaken or by whom. So far, all decommission and decontamination treatments have been monopolized by private and public enterprises as highly specialized, costly, and secretive projects, more or less under the premise of nuclear proliferation. Sustaining and expanding already existing enterprises—regardless of consequences—is the modus operandi of capitalism and states, be they nuclear or otherwise.

In the third place, therefore, nuclear power is far from a mere source of energy that could be replaced by a better one were everybody enlightened about its perils. The most demoralizing fact is that, even after Hiroshima and Nagasaki, Three Mile Island, Chernobyl, Fukushima, and countless other incidents, those superpowers that have access to nuclear production hardly nurture intentions or develop techniques to give it up. This is due to the monstrosity of nuclear fission: its Janus-faced functions provide conflicting states with the maximal potency of destruction and competing capitals with the most privileged apparatus of energy. It is too good to be true for the men reigning in our world with their will to power: money and violence. Nuclear power is the most substantial means of ensuring an upper hand in the world order. It is the most guaranteed and deadly scheme to accumulate profit and to govern the populace at once.

In this manner we are cornered, and thereby bump into the real question—how to decompose the network of powers (military–industrial complex) assembled around nuclear production/consumption while collectively creating new forms of life outside this network—before the idea of a solution can ever be reached. This leads us to the ultimate problematic concerning all environmental destruction: what should we do with the World as the expanding and totalizing movement of capitalist nation-states, from the vantage point of the Earth as the assemblage of the *lives-as-struggle* of planetary beings? The nuclear problematic thus conceives the questions of power, life, and revolution within an unending catastrophe. These questions are at the crux of what the Fukushima event is revealing to us.

The core ideas here have been conceived not so much at my cubicle as by thinking and acting together with friends in Japan and elsewhere, especially in the United States, Canada, France, South Korea, Greece, and Turkey. The ways Japanese friends felt, thought, and acted in the wake of the catastrophe provide the text with its body while the passion of foreign friends to tackle the Fukushima problematic as their own gives the book its affective and intellectual extensions. Orientations to approach the problematic are inspired by the two questions most frequently raised by non-Japanese: Why did Japan dare to introduce nuclear power after the experiences of Hiroshima and Nagasaki? Why wouldn't the Japanese people rise up to oust the nuclear state? These straightforward and honest questions touch a sore spot in the historicity of Japan's convoluted relationship with nuclear power as well as call attention to enduring issues for Japanese oppositional movements. While the first makes us confront the substance of postwar capitalism, the second implicates the closure of the revolutionary uprisings of the 1960s and the difficulties of the attempts to create popular, antiauthoritarian, and radical movements thereafter. These are now contextualized in the ongoing lives-as-struggle of people under the catastrophe. So it is that attempts to think through these questions form the basso continuo of the following narrative.

/ *Disaster/Catastrophe/Apocalypse*

Around the year 2011, two series of events were set in motion that came to embody the epitomes of our planetary reality today: revolution and disaster. In December 2010, a new cycle of global uprisings began with the Arab Spring; the following March, a new type of catastrophe unfolded in the Fukushima nuclear disaster. The wave of uprisings inspired rebellions across both hemispheres, including the square phenomena in Europe, the post-Fukushima struggles in Japan, and the Occupy movements in the United States, among many other insurgencies rising in reverberation. Fukushima was the beginning of an as-yet-interminable radiation leak affecting people in Japan and the world over. From August to September, while the cosmopolitan public was dreading possible planetary contamination, Occupy Wall Street (OWS) reinvigorated New Yorkers, inspiring them to act. It activated new associations among friends within the city and abroad, creating a *metropolitan crowd* in rebellion against finance capitalism, urban development, and police violence at once.

Born in Japan and living at the time in New York, I was radically affected and deeply perplexed by the crossing of these two events—that is the main incentive of this project. Though seemingly unrelated or even antithetical, their commingling conveyed a limit experience for those of us who aspire to a planet without capitalist nation-states and who are concerned with the apocalyptic situation spreading from the Far Eastern archipelago.

These instances emerged as manifestations of the intensifying interconnectivity of events on Earth and opened fissures in the world order on different ontological registers: one as an unprecedented catastrophe and the other as the new becoming of a *planetary crowd*. While one was a collision between infrastructure and planetary activity that inflicted upon us a maximal disquiet, the other was a synchronic reverberation among lives and struggles in numerous locations, encouraging us by flashing prospects for revolution in a transnational space. Mirroring each other, together these epitomize the global condition in which we are living today: while the World as *logos*, or the ecumenical order based on nation-states, has begun to annihilate our desire and potency for creating life, relations, and the environment, the Earth as *nomos*, or the assemblage of all forces, has begun to express itself in its overwhelming complexity of entanglements and frictions.[1] While belief in the World is collapsing, the expectation of life of permanent struggle permeates the Earth.

///

In the history of nuclear calamities, Fukushima stands out in the sense that its liquidation has so far been beyond the reach of any existing power, knowledge, and technology. It is a catastrophe without end. It manifests the irreversible tendency of man-made apparatuses to expand over the planetary body and trigger more and more accidents, the impacts of which affect all vital activities. Though slowly and minutely, the invisible flow of radionuclides is still merging into our environments. In response, a new regime has come into place that takes the populace hostage. Rather than neutralize unending contamination, this new regime manages it. By scheming programs to commodify accumulating wastes through public and private enterprise, it extends its previously underestimated prospects. In opposition, a *radioactive crowd* has arisen with its will to live the event by resisting the governance of the regime and creating new forms of life. This is the figure of the affirmative power of people—beyond passive victimhood—rising against the physical influence of radioactivity and the policy of nationalizing it. Their practices unfold a resistance that exceeds that of the limited frameworks of antinuclear movements by expanding the struggle to living itself. The lives-as-struggle of this radioactive crowd involve all existential territories: mind/body, social relation, and environment.[2]

The new cycle of global uprisings comprises waves of enraged and life-affirming hordes confronting multifaceted injustice, oppression, and expropriation. Following the Global South, then the Middle East and North Africa, the Global North has also seen a dramatic upsurge of popular movements corresponding to the intensifying immiseration of all-front crises (economic, political, environmental). These uprisings have nevertheless begun to conform to a pattern that involves both limit and potency. Following historical precedent, the revolt of each and every locality is either crushed immediately or quelled gradually, by measures as varied as violent crackdown and institutional tampering—that is, when it does not lead to endless civil war. At the same time, however, these impetuses continue to emerge in synchronicity, as if their impacts reverberated and traveled from place to place—what George Katsiaficas suggests in terms of the "eros effect."[3] Even if this mysterious and unexplainable phenomenon might be easily ignored, it embodies the positive aspect of the conjuncture we are now facing across the world.

Impetuses of revolt today interchange along multiple flows of memes over electric signals and through vital energy via personal and local connections rather than under the unilateral command of international organizations. Speaking climatologically, heat waves do not originate by heavenly commandment but in earthly struggles; in the convergence of winds with varying temperatures, speeds, and orientations, virtual currents are created in reality. The crux of the convergence of struggle is that, no matter what oppression awaits, people will never stop revolting as an extension of their life activities. The interconnectivity of singular struggles is in this sense *planetary*, more concretely so than any spectacle of international politics distributed through the media. It is thanks to the mutual recognition of today's intensifying uprisings that this interconnectivity has been gradually made visible. Thus, the climatological cartography of two planetary impetuses—environmental mutation and global uprising—is preparing the present and future of our political ontology: namely, the battleground of our lives-as-struggle.[4]

///

In the following pages, the Fukushima event plays dual roles: it is the subject of narration and analysis and, at the same time, a zoom lens for the revelation of powers (power over and power to) operating in varying spatial and temporal dimensions. Thereby we will have macro- and microviews of people's life experiences and struggles in a society that has been given shape by a postwar regime—shaped in some respects since the wake of modernity or even further back. In turn, Japanese experiences are employed as filters through which to sieve experiences of the wrecked world and the struggling Earth. These roles point to the singularity of Fukushima, which enfolds three conceptual strata embodying the haecceity of the event: Disaster, Catastrophe, and Apocalypse.

Political reason is quick to reject the eschatology implicit in these terms because it tends to either incapacitate us with fatalism or induce a short-circuited association between end and emancipation. Such reason would warn us that eschatology nullifies the political by reducing its operative dimensions to sublimity and opportunism.[5] Certainly, the incitation of the impending end for all can provide convenience to the concentrated interventions of governance and massive infrastructural reconstruction before it could empower our collective projects. The call for powerful leadership would take place as the reminder of the Hobbesian proposition of a social contract and rule by an absolute sovereign vis-à-vis Leviathan. And nuclear scares, whether by accident or war, would certainly provide such instance.

However, there is something about eschatology that cannot be easily dismissed as a mere irrationality subservient to the ruling power. Historically, it has conveyed the vital perception of crises by both the ruling power and by people: while the formation and restructurings of capitalism were triggered by such moments, people's uprisings unequivocally aspired to end their present hells and envisioned the birth of new heavens: that is, millennialist uprisings. They are two sides of a coin, as it were. In today's global condition, wherein the interminable expansion of infrastructural development synchronizes with the catastrophic destruction of social and environmental processes, it is impossible for us not to conceive the eschatological bent to the course of capitalist civilization itself. With the Fukushima event in particular, this sense has been deeply inscribed in our affective drives, which needs to be taken not only as a vacuum for new governance to sneak in but also as an opening for our critical thinking and transformative action.

In the present context, three concepts function in the following manner, with the above implication. Disaster is the real experience of people the world over. Catastrophe is the synergetic disruption of social and environmental processes, increasingly appropriated by the modus operandi of contemporary capitalism and states. Apocalypse is a metaphysical, imaginative, and affective device for us to confront the world in degeneration and to envision its radical change. These are considered as the conceptual components of what the singular name *Fukushima* implies for us today.

The Fukushima event was a disaster that is epitomic today, as tectonic and atmospheric movements and human activities increasingly merge into one and the same planetary interconnectivity: in Fukushima, the disaster was doubly articulated by the death and destruction by earthquake and tsunami followed by nuclear calamity. One of the innumerable devastations that people all over the world experience today, its fatal aspect lies in the irreversible radiation contamination that will affect innumerable people for uncountable years to come. The outcome is really unknown to us; we would need an unparalleled patience to observe and act on it. But one thing we could say is that, although the primary cataclysm caused by tectonic movement was monumental, a relatively straightforward recovery could have been expected by mutual aid projects (i.e., the "paradise built in hell" of Rebecca Solnit) or even capitalist development (i.e. the "disaster capitalism" of Naomi Klein)—if, that is, the secondary disaster had not introduced the nanoactivity of radionuclides into the environment.[6] But it did, and this worst possible merger began to generate "a land without a people and a people without a land."[7] Land and people were severed in and around radioactive zones across northeastern Japan, where residents can no longer enjoy a nature of innocence. The historic loss of that promised accord has destroyed the subsistence of farmers and fishermen and produced innumerable refugees while at the same time provoking a dramatic return of nationalism, eager to mobilize society in order to accelerate redevelopment. The catchphrase word *fukko* (revitalization) has been propagated by the status quo, following the many historical examples through which the nation-state forged its apparatuses of capture in response to catastrophe. This loss also means a new challenge for the "paradise built in hell," or for any antiauthoritarian movement based on the promise of natural resources to be shared as commons. Growing counter to redevelopments are the autonomous projects of people to protect their reproduction. Extending beyond political protest, these include do-it-yourself (DIY) radiation monitoring, studying the nature of radionuclides and their hazards, creating information networks, introducing medicinal diets, evacuating irradiated zones, experimenting with off-grid ways of living, and building community in new territories. Although each of these projects initiated by the radioactive crowd is inconspicuous and their coordination has not been fully established as a new impetus, they internalize a potency to open up territories of life-as-struggle and decompose the polis of the new regime.

The Fukushima event is a catastrophe that has triggered a few pivotal bifurcations toward conflicting orientations. It has severely damaged institutions, infrastructures, and the environment, and at the same time it has critically revealed their compositions and induced their recompositions. It has created a vacuum in the previously existing arrangement of powers—of governance, capitalism, people, and the environment—which gives people occasion to test their potency for living and struggling autonomously, even as it paves the way for inertia and the degeneration of that potency. Evidently, this has been one of the most radical junctures that the nation has ever experienced. This is the liminal situation into which the regime and the capitalist/state mode of development intervene, in order to turn the vacuum into a fulcrum for their own reinforcements. And their success so far has made us feel as if it comes from their own initiative or invention. Empirically, the disaster was experienced as pure contingency for everyone, especially for the immediate victims. However, what we discovered ex post facto was that even a calamity of this magnitude and knottiness could be taken as a mere opportunity for larger developments. As Paul Virilio points out:

> If, in fact, *invention is just a way of seeing*, of grasping accidents as signs, as opportunities, it is high time to open up our galleries to the impromptu, to that "indirect production" of science and the technosciences that is the disaster, the (industrial or other) catastrophe. If, according to Aristotle, "accident reveals the substance," the invention of the substance is also the invention of the "accident." Seen this way, the shipwreck is indeed the futuristic "invention" of the ship, the air crash the invention of the supersonic plane, and the Chernobyl meltdown, the invention of the nuclear power station.[8]

So too can the Fukushima event be seen as an invention. This invention should not be attributed, however, to science, technology, civilization, or humanity in general, as anthropocentrism tends to do, but to specific interests and the powers that implicate them in a specific society at a specific historical moment. It is an invention of the capitalism/state conglomeration, which has long persisted in its mode of development wherein accident and destruction indefinitely assimilate each other, equally employed as methods for larger redevelopments. It took place as an event and continues as a process in a highly mediatized and consumerist society of control, crystallized in Japan's postwar regime as a client state of the United States, the fountainhead of "nuclear exceptionalism."[9]

The Fukushima event is apocalyptic in terms of its power to affect our feeling, thinking, and acting. Its affectivity contains both passive and active modalities, manifest in the complexity of emotions that emerged from within the bodies and minds of people: grief for losses, despair and anxiety for the future, rage against the regime that invented the disaster, and even a glimmer of exhilaration for the unknown. The Fukushima event was perceived by many as the end of the world they had known in their economically flourishing and war-free enclave after World War II. This eschatological feeling was inexorably accompanied by a vexing sense of recurrence. Why for us again? While the first instance, in Hiroshima and Nagasaki, was a tragedy inflicted by an enemy of war, the second (if not a mere farce of the original tragedy) was tragicomical, "a war of a peaceful nation against itself," in the words of a Japanese friend.[10] In this repetition, people have undergone in their bodies and minds—the *collective soul*—the Janus-faced function of nuclear fission: weaponry and energy. Meanwhile, the *national spirit* is eager to forget the revelations of both events as it quickly short-circuits them by provoking the sentiment of the national bond (*kizuna*) that functions as facilitator for further control and development. After Fukushima, the collective soul nurtured a critical function of Revelation—in the biblical sense of the Apocalypse—of the substance of its society: sustained under the control and protection of its original assailant, the United States, and driven by the catastrophe qua invention. Accordingly, it was this collective soul that prepared the projects of the radioactive crowd.

///

Throughout the ages, eschatology has appeared in different places and in varied forms. We find an illustrious example in the Apocalypse of John (of Patmos) in the New Testament. What stands out in this text is its maniacal programming of stages and its elaborate symbols for good/ evil, culminating in radical rupture (judgment) and messianic moment (emancipation). Today, the most trivial and unsound interpretation comes from the fanatical sects of evangelical Christians who wait for or even wish to fabricate Armageddon to settle the battle between God (Christians) and Satan (infidels). In contradistinction, our secular minds have long aspired, for good reason, to create the programming of the total collapse of capitalism as the ultimate revolution. Indeed, when we plan to change our reality for its betterment, a radical discontinuity is inexorably assumed, whether as a singular event or as a long-lasting process.

Meanwhile, in the East, the idea of the end appeared in the predestination of Dharma's decline as the third stage of Buddhist universal history. In contrast with the event of the biblical Apocalypse, the cyclical process of Dharma's decline internalizes an unthinkable temporality of suffering and degeneration for all, lasting some ten thousand years. For Buddhists, this functioned as a moral admonition against unprincipled behaviors and decadent ways of life. In China, after the idea of Dharma's decline was introduced in the sixth century, it came to be seen in correspondence with the real historical ages, through the degeneration of dynasties, while in the case of Japan, its application was rejected by the state-backed Buddhism, around the mid-eleventh and into the twelfth centuries. It influenced newly rising schools as a way to view sociopolitical realities—as *mappo* (the end of Buddha's law)—and act on them, resulting in either aristocratic pessimism or religious war (mass uprisings).[11] In contradistinction to the Christian Apocalypse, the emancipatory doctrine of eschatology internalized a radically antiauthoritarian idea of salvation, prioritizing the bad people (or the social outcasts) who were destined by caste to break Buddhist precepts (for their subsistence) before the good people who were not.[12]

Despite their differences, both examples speak to the fact that throughout the age of "civilization," commoners, who are unequivocally oppressed and dispossessed, have identified the present—more or less—as a time of decline or of revolutionary change. Both interpretations of the end of the world seem to be bound by sets of moral judgment, the fatalism of decline, and the programming of time. That is, people have always been expecting either the end or the rebirth of the world. Then, in capitalist civilization, the sense of time has been articulated by the recurrence of its fundamental crisis, whereby capital endlessly seeks its rebirth and expansion. Today, the material limit of the World, whose expansion is driven by capital's critical reproduction, is exposed more catastrophically than ever.

If the Fukushima event itself is interpreted as an eschatological sign, it does not seem to indicate the immediate end/rebirth of the world. It gets even nastier in a sense. Fukushima materializes the inaccessibility of a singular moment of end/rebirth, as the catastrophe of its event is absorbed into an endless process of radioactive contamination and its management. This seems to fit more, if we are to choose, with the long-lasting and all-inclusive downfall of Buddhist fatalism than the selective judgment of Judeo-Christianity. Here, apocalypse is perceived as an unending process toward the predetermined future (or return) of a radioactive planet.

As a Japanese friend has voiced acutely, what this fatalism is about to take away from us is not necessarily hope or a promised future but difference, or the future as an unknown and undetermined temporality from which we can create new planetary experiences. At the same time, he has also spelled out a few points that pull us back to the political, unaffected by the sublimity of all-inclusive fatalism. First, though the apocalyptic effects of radionuclides on our bodies and minds can potentially be all-inclusive, they are also always uneven according to class, subsistence, gender, age, and locality. Second, the event nurtured two other moments: critical revelation and the will to live the event. These two pillars ground people's initiatives beyond passive victimhood.

Another friend has reflected on her will to confront and live the event as follows: during the heyday of the global justice movement, she used to single-mindedly embrace the slogan "another world is possible," but after Fukushima she chants "staying with the trouble" because now it is the regime that seeks to avert people from confronting radioactive threats and to mobilize them with its "utopian vision" for an everlasting industrial reconstruction and security state while taking advantage of the apocalyptic power of nuclear fission—the sublimity of destruction and the imperceptibility of contamination—that incapacitates our thinking and acting.[13] Because, in an ontometaphysical sense, the strongest weapon of the nuclear regime is this incapacitation of our thinking and acting, she suggests that we must dare to face events in all their trouble if we are to confront the Fukushima process and to create difference or other worlds therein. What she intends to do is to gaze at and to live the Fukushima event full-heartedly as it materializes the breach of World History and all its progressivist promises, through which full experiences of life and death on Earth are surfacing. This is dreadful, but it is necessary for action.

Radionuclides travel along with the planetary *becoming* or heterogenesis that implicates everything—tectonic activities, atmospheric movements, human traffics, and all other forces/events on Earth—while mutating vital activities throughout the entire ecosystem. This permeation reveals an invisible, imperceptible, and unrecognizable connectivity between human activities and naturing nature (*natura naturans*). The dreadful turn of event is nevertheless sending us a cue: with the Fukushima event, the time has come for us to affirmatively confront the complexity of planetary becoming that has been revealed through the breaches of the endlessly expansive World by which we are existentially captured. Now the crux for the lives-as-struggle of our mass corporeality lies in the *extensiveness* of what we must do for reproduction and the *unknownness* of what we can do for happiness. In these senses, the Fukushima nuclear disaster is just beginning; it is undeterminable how long life-as-struggle continues and how far it extends.

For about two years after the onset of the disaster, an anarchy of heterogeneous actions shook Japanese society. This included both the political spectacle of street demonstrations and the osmosis of autonomous projects based on everyday reproduction. Thus, the radioactive crowd arose. In fact, this rise occurred in interaction with the two epitomic planetary impetuses of radioactive contamination and global uprisings. On the one hand, the radioactive crowd's sine qua non for survival was to develop the technopolitics of life-as-struggle to keep away from and/or live with the virtual flow of radionuclides—the unthinkable temporality of their half-lives, the invisible complexity of their traveling and accumulating patterns, their ungraspable physical effects (varied radionuclides vis-à-vis varied physical conditions). On the other hand, it was at the very moment when many of my friends were talking excitedly about the Arab Spring that the Fukushima disaster intervened and disrupted the ongoing course of their struggles. Therefore, for them, it became a crucial point of bifurcation, whether they would contextualize their subsequent struggles as part of the reverberation of the planetary crowd or isolate themselves in the national politics for economic and industrial recovery.

Notwithstanding their ontological difference, the dissemination of radionuclides and the reverberation of struggles share the common attribute of belonging to an *antiworld*: neither of them can be properly confined to national territories, nor registered in the arenas of political and judicial institutions. They both slip not only through political rationality—institutional and geographical—but also through causal logic in the positivist sense. At the same time, they connect invisible forces and events via atomistic flows that decompose the logos of the World.

In interaction with the forces of the antiworld, the radioactive crowd unveils the horizon of a new political ontology by reminding us of the situation we are thrown in, where everything in everyday life is interconnected via flows. For this reason, we who are evicted from the house of being in the World are vulnerable in uncontrollable manners, but we also have an unknown potency to live the Earth. Precisely in these ambiguous senses, the political must now follow a climatological assemblage of forces and events on Earth. Although the epochal potentiality of the radioactive crowd has been unnoticed, ignored, or marginalized by the media spectacle of national politics in Japan, it sustains itself as the premise for all thinking and acting on the Fukushima event.

///

Along the line of metaphysical investigation of the apocalypse running from D. H. Lawrence to Gilles Deleuze, we can trace a passage of transposition from fatalism to action via the critical function of revelation. Echoing Friedrich Nietzsche's critique of Christianity, this line of thinking affirmatively confronts the messy complexity of power—involving both *power over*, or the power of rule based on nature as passive object (*natura naturata*), and *power to* / *power with*, or our potency to live, struggle, and create together in interaction with nature as active creativity (*natura naturans*)—in which we are implicated existentially in all respects. This treatment of power illuminates the real battleground of our lives-as-struggle in the post-Fukushima age, or the age of the antiworld.

D. H. Lawrence begins his enigmatic book *Apocalypse* with a clarification: "Apocalypse means simply Revelation, though there is nothing simple about this one."[14] Revelation here is no longer a postponed moment of salvation but the materiality of psyche—the physical or biological psyche—that *knows* the forgotten connectivity that makes us, our society, and the universe as the union of spirit and body through life energy. This is the moment at which we are to discover what forces make us and what potencies we have—to accept limit and engage in survival.

In an essay touching on Lawrence's book, Deleuze pushes for an ethical reading of the Apocalypse: "The gospel is aristocratic, individual, soft, amorous, decadent, always rather cultivated. The Apocalypse is collective, popular, uncultivated, hateful, and savage . . . John of Patmos deals with cosmic terror and death, whereas the gospel and Christ dealt with human and spiritual love. Christ invented a religion of love . . . whereas the Apocalypse brings a religion of Power (*Pourvoir*)."[15] If the gospel is an apparatus that captures the individual spirit in the name of salvation by humanly love, the Apocalypse embodies desire stripped bare, as affects of body and mind. This desire drives crowds to penetrate, multiply, judge, and destroy power by and for themselves, in interaction with the cosmic forces of the antiworld. The Bible's dark and final book functions as a radical critique of its piteous opening, by way of revealing the complexity of power in the name of a collective soul that distinguishes itself from individual spirit. The conceptual shift from individual spirit to collective soul involves a bifurcation of potential mutation: either positive with mass empowerment or negative with mass degeneration. After all, the collective soul is the drive of mass corporeality to survive in crises, and as such it persists in its will to power as counterpower.

In this articulation, it is hard for us not to make an association with the trouble of political organization that is increasingly observed today, both in the twilight of compassionate leadership or vanguardist organization (Christ) and the rise of anarchic and horrifying crowds (horned lambs), which, unleashed from the logos of the World, become an uncontrollable counterpower, eager to penetrate, multiply, judge, and destroy the sovereign power. Yet the crowd's own forces can be quickly captured by a new kind of priest—the most vulgar caricature of their desire—as we see today in the global permeation of nationalist populism or fascism. In any case, it is true that political representation—be it by government, political party, or social movement—can never contain, manage, and orient mass corporeality satisfactorily. In *The Eighteenth Brumaire of Louis Napoleon*, written in 1852, Karl Marx initiated the critical analysis of this essential problem of political representation, after his observations of the social unrest that followed the coup of Louis-Napoleon Bonaparte, the vulgar caricature of people's desire, and the farcical or confusing repetition of the dramatic situation that created Napoleon the Great. The trouble of political representation is manifest more than ever in the present epoch. But it seems today that the age of tragedy has long gone and that all troubles, no matter how intense and devastating, will appear only as absurdity.

In another register, Deleuze describes the distinctive sign of today's apocalypse in its direct relation to the modus operandi of capitalist/state development: it appears as the future that we are now being promised "not only in science fiction, but in the military-industrial plans of an absolute worldwide state."[16] The apocalyptic project is figured in the New Jerusalem or ecumenopolis, with its system of management of life by programmed installations of ultimate judiciary/moral authority and everlasting infrastructure. This power appears to us increasingly as acephalic, hiding behind its personified face or mask—be it Louis-Napoleon, Adolf Hitler, Emperor Hirohito, or Donald Trump—as it pushes endless planetary urbanization, reinforcing the polis of business/military states and leading ecosystems to exhaustion. Thereby our lives are exposed to the uncontrollable mutations of genetic activities, engulfed in the automatic expansion of techno-industrial-metropolitan networks and domesticated throughout the vital/machinic process—through the phases of working (living), malfunctioning (illness), broken and wasted (dying and dead)—by the necropolitical management of energy, information, medicine, and security businesses. Our implication in the messy complexity of mutating power is what the promised progress of World History has ultimately delivered to us—far from its promise of dialectic sublimation in the unity of human society and original nature.

Over the mutation of power from individual spirit to collective soul, Deleuze polymerizes two more conceptual shifts: from *the ego* to *relations* and from *the world* to *flows*. In ensemble, these three shifts embody the collapse of the existential protection that used to be promised to the people as the citizenry of a nation; now people are thrown out and exposed to the dreadful chaos of all forces. As such, these shifts reveal in ensemble the decomposition of the metaphysical principles holding the logos of the World together and the physical rise of planetary becoming. Relations make us confront the composition of the ego by its decomposition: to conceptualize relationality is to treat the problematic of political subjectivity from the vantage of interactivity and heterogeneity rather than individuality and identity while observing the individual body mutating in interaction with transmuting life chains. The concept of flows finally addresses the way the World expands and totalizes itself as an interaction among circulating powers—capital, labor, information, military, pollutants, epidemics, . . . —which themselves circulate within a climatological assemblage of all the Earth's forces and events. Meanwhile, the multidimensional frictions among all powers are unilaterally intensifying. These shifts thus reveal the real battleground of our lives-as-struggle in planetary becoming.

In this precise manner, those Japanese friends who are developing ways to protect themselves from radionuclides and confronting the power over that seeks to control their distribution are also telling themselves: "Stop thinking of yourself as an ego in order to live a flow, a set of flows in relation to other flows, outside of oneself and within oneself... The soul as the life of flows is the will to live, struggle and combat."[17] This command announces the advent of life-as-struggle after Fukushima, which is the most radical break from the idea of life nurtured within the nuclear family in the postwar consumerist society.

Outside Japan, as the physical limit of the World's expansion has become manifest in the ecological and reproductive crises of our existential territories, the mutation of power has also begun to manifest itself in affirmation, that is, in the antiauthoritarian impetuses to change the world—from indigenous peoples, immigrants, feminists, and anarchists, among others—that constitute a broad horizon for projects to create "dual power" through autonomous zones of reproduction and new forms of collective living. These territorialities resist the confinement of national borders within and traverse them from community to community without, outside, or on top of political projects to take over state power—namely, those of socialist or social democratic governments operating within the expansive World toward internationalism. This is the advent of a *planetary community* in correspondence with the reverberation of global uprisings.

Along these lines, we consider the Fukushima event to be an epitomic moment, wherein antiauthoritarian and ecological struggles could converge to embody the shift of our main battleground from the politics of the World to lives-as-struggle on Earth. Philosophically, this is an ontological shift from dialectics to immanence—from totalization by capitalism and the state to the omnipresence of singular events. In this shift lies the prospect of planetary revolution to be grasped in the *decomposition of the World* and the *rediscovery of the Earth*. However, it is imperative to acknowledge a proviso here in the introduction. This shift is neither smooth nor complete; we do not even know if it will ever end. Meanwhile, we continue to confront both the politics of historically driven territorial wars among the empires and nation-states of the World together with the politics of the climatological interactions of all the ever-mutating powers/forces on Earth.

///

Before the disaster narrative begins, let us share a glimpse of the program: the arrangement of this book's concepts and the composition of its contents. The use of concepts here is inspired by the geophilosophy of Gilles Deleuze and Félix Guattari, with the conviction that all thoughts—as much as actions—occur in relationship with the Earth: "Thinking is neither a line drawn between subject and object nor a revolving of one round the other. Rather, thinking takes place in the relationship of territory and the earth."[18] Accordingly, in this context, the Earth is the assembly of all movements and events, of which we are just a part; even the World is just a part. The Earth is the ontological index of immanence and omnipresence. In distinction, the World is the global order, or the assembly of all human societies and activities, that has been driven by the totalizing impetus of the capitalist nation-state; it is the ontological index of totalization and expansion. As a tacit premise, Marxism is considered a tendency to think and act vis-à-vis the World, while anarchism is deemed a tendency to think and act vis-à-vis the Earth.[19] While the former tends to tackle structures, the latter tends to intervene in flows. We have been oscillating in between these approaches for a long time. In this project, all things happen in between the World and the Earth.

Therefore, all this work's other concepts, more or less echoing geology and climatology, will appear in relationship with both the World and the Earth, in between them, as the narrative progresses from event (chapter 1) to context (chapter 2) to mechanism (chapter 3) to struggle (chapter 4). In other words, the following four chapters are rendered in correspondence with the revelations of the Fukushima event in variable spatial and temporal extensions. In the beginning is the catastrophe. Thereafter, every word is uttered in repercussion from the epicenter of the earthquake or from ground zero of the hydrogen explosions.

Chapter 1, "Transmutation of Powers," narrates the disaster as event. Based on my own observations, stories from friends, and reports published in Japan, this chapter describes the event of the catastrophe and the social process through which the event was subsumed. These heterogeneous anecdotes concerning post–nuclear disaster lives, struggles, society, and governance provide the subsequent chapters with raw materials for their theoretical analyses.

Chapter 2, "Catastrophic Nation," details the catastrophe, in response to which the nation was geohistorically constituted as an insular territory over an archipelago. The geopolitical form of the insular nation plays a pivotal role in the fabrication of Japan's postwar regime, as it constituted a laboratory for the US global strategy to create an ideal client state. In consequence of this experimentation, the regime realized an unprecedented prosperity, which, however, lasted for only a limited moment in between two nuclear calamities: Hiroshima/Nagasaki and Fukushima. Outside US control, the regime became an economic giant thanks to Tokyo as an expansive and contractive movement, absorbing and mobilizing tremendous amounts of desire for the developments of the capitalist nation-state that ended up spreading nuclear power plants across the earthquake-prone archipelago.

Chapter 3, "Apocalyptic Capitalism," describes the apocalypse that today's capitalism ensures by assimilating itself to the nuclear industry, which, spatially, stretches its industrial sectors—mining, transportation, energy, research, and military—across the planet and which, temporally, grants it zombie life through the endless demand for the managements of its wastes (negative commons). This analysis of the global nuclear regime illuminates the theoretical juncture where the problematics of ousting capitalism and stopping nuclear power must merge, in confrontation with the totalizing expansion of the World.

Chapter 4, "Climate Change of the Struggle," compares the struggles of 1968 to those of the post-Fukushima present via the struggles that arose in between. The difference is considered as a shift in political ontology that is provoked by increasing catastrophes: from the unification (dialectic synthesis) of the World to the reverberations (immanence) of planetary complexity. Thereby, it seeks to grasp the horizon of planetary revolution as an existential metamorphosis beyond regime change, by a dispersion of the World constituted by capitalist nation-states.

The epilogue, "Forget Japan," poses questions about the end. What does the end of Japan mean to the people in Japan? What does the end of the human world mean to us? As a final gesture, it seeks to undo the haunt of rationalist thinking whereby a big problem can only be solved by a big power, and to propose an empirical/pragmatic thinking toward reverberations among small powers.

EVENT AND PROCESS

We shall follow how the singularity of the Fukushima event—condensed in the state of emergency—prefigured a subsequent process of transmutations of regime, society, people, and movements as the melees of powers within Japan. We observe roughly three phases of development in the ongoing disaster: the first three weeks in a state of emergency, the next two years with people's indignation overwhelming the regime, and the subsequent reinforcement of the status quo. The premise is that the disaster is not over. It continues in the repercussions of the event, like quakes spreading multidimensionally from an epicenter or devastations multiplying themselves from ground zero.

What event implies here is an insistent break in the smooth continuity of social reproduction, in opposition to psychoinformatic operations that gloss over this discontinuity to register it in the social narrative of national recovery. By process we mean to treat the shifting junctures of the melees of powers as phases that unfold sequentially, whether toward that successful recovery proclaimed by the status quo or toward an unknown sensed by the people. These powers include equally the forces of *physis* and *nomos*: those of the generative potency of nature (natura naturans) and those of the struggle between post-Fukushima governance (power over) and people (power to / power with). The crux is how both the mutation by radionuclides and the transmutations of reaction thereby and of action therefrom together affect individual, society, world, and, most crucially, people's struggles for survival and autonomy and their ideas for change.

The catastrophe erupted as an inexorable consequence of nuclear development on an earthquake-prone archipelago stretching over the

Ring of Fire, an archipelago already congested with infrastructure and population. Its impacts live on in an entanglement of varying impetuses. Technically, the crippled reactors have neither been liquidated nor contained; though the amount of contamination has been significantly diminished since the time of the hydrogen explosions, the reactors are still releasing small doses of radionuclides into the environment. Socially, divergent attitudes toward the catastrophe—either confront it fully or negate it into oblivion—have occasioned conflicts between people and the pronuclear state as well as frictions within the populace.

The first phase was witness to the all-encompassing collapse of the apparatuses of hyperconsumerist society in the midst of destruction by earthquake, tsunami, and radioactive fallout. This collapse revealed to the populace the social, political, economic, and environmental composition of their reality, a reality that had always been there but mostly in their inattention. It was a radical education—a revelation. In the second phase, a state of anarchy flared up from the soup of emotions experienced through the disaster—grief (for losses), despair (for the future), rage (against the authorities), anxiety (over uncertainty), excitement (of volatility), and even aspiration (for the possibility of change)—which opened up space for radically questioning the postwar regime and for wildly imagining unknown futures. At the same time, crowds took to the streets in numbers unprecedented since the 1960s to protest the government and the Tokyo Electric Power Company (TEPCO) while various DIY projects were initiated by commoners to protect their everyday reproduction from radiation. The third phase saw the reaction of the status quo toward normalization, whereby the opening created by the event was gradually glossed over by business as usual and the name *Fukushima* was recapitulated as a slogan for industrial recovery. Although we live in the third phase now, it is crucial that we perceive the ongoing existence of conflictual impetuses within which the opening toward the unknown remains open, in order to note that popular initiatives persist despite their marginalization by the narratives of national unity propagated by government and media. The three phases that appear to have proceeded chronologically are in fact present synchronically. It is only that the visible stratum alternates.

Incalculable numbers of people, in different manners and varying intensities, have been influenced by Fukushima's double disaster of tectonic cataclysm (earthquake/tsunami) and nuclear accident. In crude estimation, we can categorize three kinds of impact: primary (immediate), secondary (collateral), and potential (future). Those who were impacted primarily include the direct victims of the earthquake, tsunami, and/or high radioactivity and its related symptoms. Secondary impacts affect those who have had to evacuate to safer environments and whose subsistence is threatened by industrial devastation. Potential impacts refer to the unknown dangers of exposure to small doses of radiation. The number of those potentially impacted, whose symptoms are not yet but may eventually become manifest, is creeping up to an incalculable majority. These potential impacts go on expanding beyond the confines of the Japanese archipelago.

From primary to secondary to potential, as the affected zone enlarges and the quantity of those impacted increases, the quality of those real impacts shifts from actual to virtual. But across these categories cuts a common denominator: radioactive exposure in small doses. In this regard, political and legal divisions between victim/nonvictim or insider/outsider are ultimately irrelevant. Radiation does not discriminate in principle (even if, as we shall later see, discrimination takes place politically through the management of radiation for sustaining business as usual). For all the potential victims, living everyday life is the struggle in and of itself, as they are forced to contend with the invisible threat of radiation, invent new techniques of reproduction under its influence, and confront both national and global regimes that prioritize the maintenance and expansion of nuclear apparatuses over the well-being of vital activities. After Fukushima, living is becoming equal to struggling against such hazards and the regimes that impose them: this is one of the common conditions of all planetary inhabitants.

Though legal accountability for the nuclear accident at Fukushima has finally been ascribed to TEPCO and its negligence of safety and security measures, another question has been raised in the context of the larger dimensions of society and world: whose political, social, and economic interest—or class interest—caused the disaster? A nationalist would insist that all Japanese share the benefits of advanced technoindustrial consumerist society, and that therefore all are responsible for the disaster that was inextricable from those benefits. But, as is evident, the political, social, and economic beneficiaries of nuclear power are limited to particular groups within society, in distinction from the general public. The conflict between the interests of nuclear promoters and those of the rest of the populace is embodied by the different attitudes each have taken in response to the disaster. It is not surprising that those who have reacted most sensitively, eagerly, and passionately to radioactive contamination have been those who take care of everyday reproduction in families, communities, and society—so-called reproductive workers, most of whom are women. Meanwhile, the main priority of those in charge of sustaining political, social, and economic order—the authorities—has been to exempt themselves from responsibility for the unimaginably difficult and costly aftercare necessitated by the disaster; as the authorities ignore or even deride reproductive workers' efforts, they tacitly take advantage of their shadow works. In this sense, the disaster epitomizes power conflicts that have been continuous throughout modernity between patriarchal authority and the common caretakers of life; between industrial-technological-economic ambition and the most basic desire to live a healthy life; and between production-centrism and everyday reproduction. In other words, the disaster is an assault on commoners by the men in power who lead the emperorist-nuclear-capitalist nation-state.

Ever since the disaster rendered radical discontinuity as a singular event, many have been striving to live that event by fully confronting its devastation for the sake of survival. Meanwhile, economic and political interests have intervened to reinforce their bonds and to collaborate on sustaining their industrial operations and the social order: their main objective is to normalize living environments with more or less radioactivity and to make the event invisible. Those who share the interests of authorities have behaved as if nothing ever happened. This is an unending process—what Rob Nixon calls "slow violence"—politically, socially, and economically imposed upon the everyday life of the masses.[1] The crux of this slow violence is the imposition of industrial waste—waste created in the first place by the exploitation of human and natural resources for commodification. Instead of being recycled within productive and reproductive systems, this waste is pushed back directly on our bodies and environments, always with unevenness or discriminatory concentration (imposed, for example, by advanced capitalist nation-states on underdeveloped peripheries). Unfortunately, such violence does not often induce immediate action for justice against the assailants. The imposition of small doses of radiation is an ultimate form of slow violence. In distinction from the impacts of imminent and spectacular violence, the effects of radiation are gradual, out of sight, dispersed across time and space, and often not even perceived or conceived of as violent. Confronting the invisible and incalculable impacts of radioactivity—radio-onto-metaphysics—we have difficulty thinking consistently and acting promptly.

Furthermore, the effects of radioactivity are psychologically made doubly invisible by political, social, and economic mechanisms or schemes that urge the nation to forget the ongoing catastrophe and move on to the revitalization of productivity and development. Observing the "politics of invisibility" at work after Chernobyl, Olga Kuchinskaya emphasizes the culturally produced perceptions that embody the challenges and the possible systematic problems of seeing and learning about imperceptible environmental risks.[2] The troublesome experiences post-Chernobyl have been repeated post-Fukushima within Japan's seductive atmosphere of hyperconsumerism. Facing the invisible threats of radiation, people must deal with their everyday lives technopolitically for the sake of their well-being, not only in negotiation with the collective psychologies of family, community, workplace, school, and society that, under the influence of master discourses, dismiss concern about radiation, but also against governmental policy that is intentionally negligent of its threats. Thus, the complications confronted by peoples' lives-as-struggle are both *technopolitical* and *ontometaphysical*. In what follows, we shall see the political, social, and economic devastations that caused these complications.

DISASTER

Beginning on March 11, 2011, two disasters unfolded as a chain reaction: a magnitude 9 earthquake followed by a thirty-nine-meter tsunami and a nuclear calamity. The primary cataclysm was already colossal, with 15,899 deaths, 6,157 injuries, and 2,529 missing persons.[3] It triggered the devastation of infrastructure across the Tohoku and Kanto regions, including the total blackout of the Fukushima Daiichi Nuclear Power Plant, which caused the meltdown and melt-through of nuclear cores, hydrogen explosions, and radioactive plumes and fallout.

In the wake of this double disaster, systemic malfunctions within emergency management—provoked mainly by authorities' conflicting priorities and interests—resulted in significant shortcomings in rescue operations and accident control. All these created a "parallel chain crisis," wherein a failure in dealing with one kind of crisis provoked a chain of crises in other dimensions that multiplied and intensified the disaster.[4] The event revealed to witnesses around the world the fissures running through the organization of Japan's postwar regime—in the government, social milieus, and everyday life as well as in international relations. By the end of March, the worst-case scenario was evaded: eastern Japan did not become uninhabitable by Armageddon, as most of us had dreaded. However, the calamities of the reactors have not been resolved. While the phase of emergency has shifted to a phase of unending management, the catastrophe continues.

The state of emergency lasted for about three weeks. As learned from many testimonials, the response by authorities exhibited significant shortcomings.[5] It was a historical moment when TEPCO, leader of the most influential sector (energy) of all key industries in Japan, failed comprehensively. And so Fukushima, the name of one prefecture, came to show the limits of Japan's postwar constitution to its populace, though reactions to this revelation as well as ways of responding to the situation diverged radically.

Rescue operations in the disaster area were tremendously strained due to the devastation of key infrastructure: transportation, communication, and electricity. In addition, the situation was worsened by failures in the chain of command and information sharing. Conflicting orders from the central government and Fukushima Prefecture delayed evacuations and the distribution of iodine tablets to people affected by high doses of radiation. Some residents in the "crisis management district" were even left behind.

Life and death decisions had to be unequivocally made by the leaders of local municipalities near Fukushima Daiichi who risked accusation by higher authorities and even illegality.[6] The radicality of the event surpassed that normal condition wherein the command of a central authority functions regardless of geographic distance. But the locals were lacking necessary information and the sophisticated technology needed for radioactivity detection, that is, equipment for dust sampling, space dose monitors, and data analyses from the System for Prediction of Environment Emergency Dose Information (SPEEDI) for predicting radiation fallout patterns. In the center, a scandalous mystery unfolded: though the data from SPEEDI was available and in the hands of the Nuclear Safety Commission, for unknown reasons it was not shared with the office of the prime minister. Instances amassed where crucial information did not reach those who needed it when it was needed. Disruptions in information pathways drew a graphic map of power conflicts within the status quo, between ministries, political parties (the Democratic Party in power and the Liberal Democratic Party in contestation), government advisory agencies (Japan's Nuclear and Industrial Safety Agency and Nuclear Safety Commission, America's Nuclear Regulatory Commission and the International Atomic Energy Agency), self-defense forces, police departments, fire departments, TEPCO, Toshiba (a nuclear apparatus supplier), and, finally, the US Armed Forces.[7] All authorities nevertheless shared one concern: that should they be forthright with an honest scenario of real and present threats, mass hysteria would cause social unrest. Thus the government spokesperson repeatedly announced, "There is no immediate health hazard."

Operations to fix or confine the crippled reactors were forestalled one after another by ever more complicated situations. Judgment regarding how to deal with each critical phase was paralyzed most graphically by the conflicting priorities of nuclear advocates and safety advocates. Even facing the possibility of Armageddon, TEPCO executives hesitated to take the determinant measure of sacrificing the plant, in favor of saving their assets (the reactors) for future use. This taught us an ultimate lesson: the nation's leading capitalists—personifications of capital—care for their business over anything and everything, including the safety of the people and environments that make their business possible in the first place.

The organization of TEPCO, epitomic of Japan's corporate society, is based on hierarchies. The managerial class (legal and business experts) is markedly superior to the engineering class (technical experts); while the operation of highly mechanical devices is handled by TEPCO employees, the most dangerous work is assigned to the employees of subcontractors, who are not provided with sufficient information or protection; the employees at the reactors are strictly subservient to Tokyo headquarters. These hierarchical divisions put tremendous pressure on those trying to resolve the critical conditions at the Fukushima plant while exposing their bodies to high doses of radiation. It was they who were forced to respond, to decide when and how to act, with such tragicomically pathetic and desperate measures as attempting to cool melting radioactive fuel with seawater.

At the most critical moment, faced with the possibility of Armageddon, TEPCO executives asked the government's permission to evacuate all their workers from the site. As some commentators claim, this was TEPCO's desperate gesture to transfer the command of their "mission impossible" to state power, aware as they were of the essential fallaciousness of a commercial enterprise being committed to a project that endangers the lives of the masses as well as of its own workers.[8] Common sense dictates that the task of mending or liquidating nuclear reactors on the verge of explosion should go beyond the limit of wage labor—such should only be a mission for a suicide squad, if any. But Prime Minister Kan Naoto issued an executive order that TEPCO remain at the site to quell the critical phase. If not, he said, "Japan will end." He also called for a voluntary suicide corps among the members of his administration; some responded and went to the site. This was the exceptional instance in the postwar period that the state of Japan issued an imperative order to the private sector.

Meanwhile, all sectors of the authorities agreed that the last resort to confront the apocalyptic situation would be the military: Japan's Self-Defense Forces and, after all, the US Armed Forces, the ultimate guardian and controller of Japan's capitalist regime with its superior technology and manpower. However, there was reluctance in the Japanese government to invite a full foreign intervention, particularly by the United States. With the memory of the post–World War II occupation, they feared that Japan would be occupied again. This insistence on sovereignty became another occasion for the fatal delay of disaster measures.

The US government was increasingly losing faith in the Japanese government and TEPCO in terms of their willingness, might, and determination to confront the situation. But it chose not to abandon its most successful client state of all time. While it ordered all American citizens living in Japan to evacuate a fifty-mile radius from Fukushima Daiichi, it sent its forces, including the Chemical Biological Incident Response Force, to support disaster control and relief operations. In consequence, some US Navy personnel have developed radiation illnesses.[9] Most other countries instructed their nationals to leave Japan immediately.

In terms of culpability, TEPCO and the Nuclear and Industrial Safety Agency (NISA) insisted that the Fukushima disaster was the consequence of an "unexpected" natural cataclysm and that therefore TEPCO should not be held accountable, citing the Atomic Energy Damage Compensation Law (1961), which states that in the case of an accident caused by an unexpected large natural disaster or social upheaval, the electric company is exempt from responsibility. In mid-2012, however, a Japanese parliamentary panel determined that the meltdown was a "man-made disaster" caused by TEPCO's negligence, and that the company was responsible.[10] Thereafter, both TEPCO and the Japanese government have been the target of innumerable lawsuits in civil trials. In 2018 the Tokyo District Court sentenced ex-TEPCO executives to five-year jail terms.[11]

Notwithstanding all this, we have learned that the use of nuclear power will never cease. Our hope in the darkness was miserably betrayed. Those superpowers with access to nuclear development do not have any intention of giving it up. Before the accident, 442 nuclear power reactors in thirty countries produced 14 percent of the world's electricity. This number dropped to 11 percent in 2012. But by 2014, 435 reactors were operating in thirty-one countries, and sixty-eight more were under construction.[12] Apparently, Fukushima's influence was no more than a momentary blip. After the disaster, Japan ordered large-scale inspections and introduced new safety regulations, and in December 2011, the Noda administration of the Democratic Party, under pressure from intensifying antinuclear protests, declared denuclearization in "future Japan." But within a year, the Shinzō Abe administration of the Liberal Democratic Party undid the proclamation and revived the nuclear proliferation policy. By August 2016, three nuclear power plants—Sendai 1 and 2 in Kagoshima Prefecture and Ikata 3 in Ehime Prefecture—were back online for commercial services.[13] And at no point during the disaster did the Japanese government give up its project of boosting civilian nuclear exports to countries with nuclear ambitions such as Vietnam, Jordan, South Korea, Turkey, and the United Arab Emirates. In December 2011, the House of Representatives approved the export of nuclear plants to Jordan and Vietnam, and then in 2015, the Abe administration established a specifically nuclear-based industrial treaty with India.[14] Via the interests of nuclear industries, capitalism and the state continue to secure their marital status.

All this is to say that radioactive waste will go on accumulating endlessly on the planet. Its treatment is too immense a task for any mortal being, but global nuclear industries and states insist on enterprising it in ultimate gestures of vanity.[15] As friends tend to stress, capital's utopia is always our dystopia.

From the vantage point of statecraft, the lesson from the event was clear: Japan needed a stronger central command system, abundant resources and supplies, troops with highly advanced equipment and fearless manpower, and, finally, a strong national bond (*kizuna*).[16] The reflections of men in power on the failure of disaster control seem to have revived an old slogan from the Meiji Restoration at the wake of Japan's modernization: *fukoku kyōhei* (wealthy nation and strong soldiers). Seen under this light, the political reforms of the present Abe administration that have been suffocating civil liberties step by step—that is, the act to protect specially designated secrets, the right of collective defense, and the conspiracy crime bill—are simply logical responses.[17]

In terms of the economy, it is the primary industries that have been affected most substantively by radiation contamination. While, roughly speaking, the destruction of primary industries was inflicted by the secondary sector, there is no ready-made expression for the particular devastation experienced by farmers and fishermen. This devastation has been both economic and psychological, as they are forced to face a most difficult question, which will never go away: what to do with potentially radioactive products? The situation is especially painful for organic farmers, who now have to confront a new type of inorganic substance that is impossible to avoid: namely, the invisible, minute, and overall permeation of radionuclides in the soil.[18] As many of us feel, the Fukushima nuclear disaster has announced the end of the era when the connection between humans and land could be taken for granted.

In dark prospect, accident remediation will necessitate a myriad of endangered workers and endless costs. The deficit of TEPCO will be limitless, beginning with the 4.2 trillion yen (estimate from August 2016) to be paid off by the populace via electricity bills and taxes. This will exhaust human and natural resources for years to come. Many countries have stopped importing food products from Japan.[19] Excessive oil and liquefied natural gas importation has caused a trade deficit for the first time in thirty-one years. So-called Abenomics intervened with a double standard: to save the national economy in an unprecedented crisis, it reintroduced the neoliberal reforms of the Shinjirō Koizumi administration (2001–6). The basic schemes of these reforms are public spending cuts, deregulation, and deflation via a weaker yen. By aiming at nominal economic growth, they seek to cover up losses in real economic growth and, claiming to increase employment (especially for women), they accelerate the informalization of work forces in toto. All these measures transfer the waning national wealth to a handful of ruling elites, allowing the immiseration of the populace to intensify.

Meanwhile, earthquake "special procurements" increased the gross production of the three prefectures most severely affected by the disaster. General contractors in Iwate, Miyagi, and Fukushima prefectures were fully engaged in the business of reconstruction, including decontamination work. Amid this construction bubble, the waste of radioactive debris and soil was accumulating endlessly, and there was a necessity to somehow enterprise its treatment. The central government began to demand that local municipalities share the waste by incinerating it at local facilities. The Ministry of Environment considered mixing contaminated soil into compounds to be used in nationwide construction projects.[20] The Ministry of Agriculture, Forestry and Fisheries started a campaign called "Eat and Support Fukushima" to encourage the recovery of Fukushima's primary industries.[21] Through such policies, postdisaster governance initiated the nationalization of radiation. From the commoners' standpoint, this is nothing but a secondary and everlasting disaster. The politically imposed sharing of radiocontamination has been the most dystopic aspect of the Fukushima process.

The intensive period of parallel chain crises passed, but what happened during that time prefigured what has been happening since. While the nuclear disaster has not been resolved, postdisaster governance has created a regime of disaster management that goes on imposing its dystopian projects in every corner of the social system and everyday life. It continually seeks to reinforce national endurance to its process of management by covering the fissures opened up in the postwar regime by the event of the catastrophe.

MUTANT

I visited my native country, Japan, in early June 2011. This was the first of many trips I have made since the eruption. I assumed everything would be different in an unimaginable way; I was anxious to find that out for myself. More than anything, I was eager to meet friends and ask their whereabouts, observe their everyday lives, share their feelings, and learn if they were developing any new projects in confrontation with the event. These friends were mostly close associates from the antiglobalization movement since the first decade of the twenty-first century, with whom I had collaborated on a number of actions and publications.

Beforehand, I had been informed about the radical transmutations of people's everyday lives and the rise of a broad antinuclear movement. Most extraordinary were the stories from the intense days of the initial exodus. The explosions, leaks, and melt-through of the reactors came to affect not only a large part of northeastern Honshu but also the Tokyo metropolis with its 13.62 million residents. In addition to those living in the immediate vicinity of the reactors who were forced to leave their homes for shelters, an unknown number from the entire Tohoku and Kanto regions also evacuated, in threat of the imminent danger of more explosions and plumes. In fact, most of my friends living in Tokyo fled to Nagoya or other western cities, where they shared communal living for a few weeks or a few months. Some stayed away for good and began to build new lives. While the majority returned to their homes when they found out that the worst-case scenario had been avoided, many of them came to nurture the sense that Tokyo was no longer a permanent residence and that they would leave it sooner or later. This was a revolutionary break from the nationalized consensus that Tokyo should be the pivot of the country. Thus the first wave of evacuations was followed eventually by a second, quieter, slower, and longer current of exodus to western Japan or Hokkaido.[22]

By March 22, 2011, radioactive substances had been detected in Tokyo's tap water.[23] In response, people rushed to buy extra bottles of water for their families. In the media, they were accused of being "antisocial." Meanwhile, nationalist campaigns started labeling the screams of concerned people as "rumor-mongering." The term *fūhyō higai* (rumor hazard) began to circulate in the media, representing the government's interest in silencing the screams.

In early April, the highly radioactive water that had been used to cool the reactors overflowed its tanks and was released into the ocean. Subsequently, marine products began to show radioactive contamination. In many areas across the Tohoku and Kanto regions, cesium-137 was found in everyday environments. Hotspots appeared in Tokyo.[24]

Beginning in April, an alternative neighborhood community based in Koenji, Tokyo, called Amateur Riot organized a series of antinuclear demonstrations that turned out to be a dramatic success, mobilizing thousands of people of varied social backgrounds.[25] I heard from friends that these crowds were differently composed than those of the old sociopolitical movements. They were no longer aligned with political parties, labor unions, and new left sects but with individuals and affinity groups of heterogeneous political orientations, mostly in antiauthoritarian veins. The demonstrations were conceiving a potency for developing creative forms of action. I was eager to see the rising power of this *metropolitan crowd* on the street, something that had been missing since the 1960s, a time of insurrection across the country.

///

As I arrived at Narita Airport, located midway between Fukushima and Tokyo, it was emptier than ever, and the highway from Narita to Tokyo was totally deserted. From the bus window, overlooking the same old landscape consisting of a mishmash of small houses, shrines and temples, factories and farmland, I suddenly realized that the green zones no longer offered comfort: now there was an invisible radioactivity. The monstrous nanoactivities that mutate all vital forms could be hiding in any spot. As the bus entered the metropolitan zone, the urban space was the same, but the atmosphere appeared somber, inactive, and darkened by planned phased blackouts.

Throughout my stay, while walking in strolls and demonstrations, friends would point out in detail which urban spots were prone to accumulating radioactive substances: roofs, eaves, drains, the leaves of trees, and playground sandboxes. An increasing number of people were purchasing affordable radiation-monitoring equipment. Many neighborhood communities were being organized, as an immediate DIY measure, to monitor the radioactivity in their living environments, especially those inhabited by children. What I found most catastrophic was that the places we normally cherish and enjoy without hesitation—the green parks where children play, the countryside where farmers farm—were the most deadly in terms of radioactivity because of their spatial complexity. Here things were inverted. Adjectives like green, natural, or organic that figure motherly resources could no longer embrace us with their good intentions, but internalized the invisible threat of radiation. On the other hand, artificial constructions and foods—cold, ugly, distasteful, and unhealthy as they could be—came to give us a minimum sense of security. I felt that in the inversion, the dystopian imagery of cyber punk had been materialized.

I was told that in order to live a safer life, one should avoid inhaling dust, being exposed to rain, drinking tap water, eating numerous categories of food, and should even refrain from enjoying the celebrated tea of Shizuoka Prefecture, located southwest of Tokyo farther away from Fukushima. People obsessively listed mutant items: fish caught in the Pacific Ocean, all kinds of mushrooms that readily absorb radionuclides, milk in which contamination tends to be concentrated, on top of almost everything from the Pacific side of the Tohoku and Kanto regions. The mortification is hard to share with nonnatives: Fukushima was known for the quality of its rice, sake, and seafood, all central to the Japanese diet.

Those activists whose concern centered on the protection of health suggested that going to demonstrations on windy or rainy days was inadvisable; a few moralists even scolded it as politically incorrect. This hypersensitivity toward the threat of radioactivity created a totally new ecopolitical position. Accordingly, the "antiradiation movement" diverged from the traditional antinuclear movement by prioritizing safety measures above anything else.

Many felt Tokyo as the capital was beginning its slow death. But this tacit acceptance was veiled by the same everyday scenes of high consumerist society. It was surreal how urban flourishment continued amid the catastrophe. Reactions to the probable decline of commercial activities appeared in a fanatical manner. For instance, food chains and restaurants proudly advertised their use of products from Fukushima, encouraging clients to join them in support. Campaigns to encourage heroic consumption professed the rise of a new patriotism. What could we make of this? Some friends interpreted it as a consumerist version of the historically nurtured death drive for the nation, the epitome of Japanese machoism once embodied in the ritualistic suicide of *seppuku* and the death mission of Kamikaze fighters.

Transmutations were thus progressing in every process of social reproduction. At the fountainhead of these transmutations was the *virtuality* of radiation, in the sense of its mutant attributes that slip through our perception and causal logic. It appeared that the virtual nature of radiation was the most intense focus of my friends' discussions as they considered its ontological effects on people's everyday lives and, accordingly, their politics and actions. Although, as we shall see again and again, radiation is very real, the actualization of its effects on vital activities is blurred in multiple dimensions. First, the half-lives of radionuclides are unimaginably long. That of plutonium-239 lasts more than twenty-four thousand years. For a shorter example, common discourse explains that the half-life of iodine-131 is eight days, and this gives us relative relief. But technically speaking it never disappears; its effects just get infinitely smaller, diminishing by one half, one quarter, one eighth, one sixteenth, and so on. In the strictest sense, there is no threshold between safe and unsafe. Second, radionuclides travel in complex mosaics driven by all planetary forces, including both atmospheric movements (wind and rain) and human traffic (flows of bodies and commodities).

In the wake of the accident, the government demarcated a hazardous zone according to a radial distance from the nuclear plant, but it had to withdraw this fixed model within a month, having confronted the reality of radionuclides' complicated and fluctuating patterns. Third, the nuclear fission of radionuclides is invisible and does not always affect our senses. We do not feel exposure (internal or external) to it in small doses, and yet it can inflict deadly effects.[26] People especially emphasized the threat of internal exposure by drinking water, eating food, and breathing dust, and cautioned that radionuclides remain in the body and mutate the genetic activities of generations to follow. Finally, these effects are incalculable. They may not manifest immediately: though symptoms will appear at some point, their appearance is unpredictable and varied. They are likely to come in three-, five-, and fifteen-year cycles, which differ also according to the type of nuclides and the condition of the body.

Herein intervenes the lingering issue of compensation for the victims of exposure to radiation. Because its effects do not always appear in accordance with the logic of proof authenticated by judicial and political institutions, the medical recognition of nuclear victims eligible for compensation is often troubled. A friend announced that she had begun cutting strands of her hair and sealing them in plastic bags with dated labels in order to sample the radioactivity to which she was exposed in everyday life. *Prepare for unending measures!* Many associate their present difficulties facing the virtual flow of radiation with the longtime struggles of those who survived the initial blasts at Hiroshima and Nagasaki.

The Fukushima event was inevitably felt to be a historical repetition of Hiroshima and Nagasaki, a second nuclear catastrophe. This time it was not inflicted by an enemy of war but by a capitalist/state project of the nation. To be precise, however, the events of the Hiroshima and Nagasaki nuclear attacks are not over. Some casualties and their offspring still suffer and are still fighting for compensation. Moreover, the postwar constitution that made Japan what it is today—a war-free enclave equipped with "atoms for peace"—was ironically designed by the United States to benefit its global power contestation, backed, of course, by its "atoms for war." Therefore, Fukushima is not only a repetition of Hiroshima/Nagasaki but also its twisted continuation; the operative dimension of nuclear power simply shifted from weapon to energy, both of which ended up exposing innumerable lives to radiation. The nation has thus been entrapped between two faces of nuclear catastrophe: instantaneous destruction and the slow process of internal exposure.

These dual catastrophes have resulted so far not in the end of the world but instead in a process of the profound transmutations of life-world. These transmutations involve a complexity of existential dimensions both virtual and actual, with which people interact ontometaphysically in their affectivity while seeking to develop methods to interact technopolitically.

In the first place, such transmutations are expressed not by rational language (discourse) but by screams and affective expression (enunciation). They involve all the body's senses, feelings, and emotions (grief, dread, anxiety, and rage) vis-à-vis the catastrophe and governance as well as the imagination of the unknown. As Svetlana Alexievich wrote after Chernobyl, "The simple fact, the mechanical fact, is no closer to the truth than a vague feeling, rumor, vision."[27] A new history of feeling has begun wherein the politics of sensibility takes over the primary position from the politics of rationality. Thus, a collective soul has begun to think and act. Although these expressions appear to be sheer noise and are often dropped from the main discourses of political theater, they are orienting people's lives-as-struggle as their basso continuo.

Increasing numbers of people have come to distrust the authorities in terms of their words and conduct regarding the catastrophe. Under their entitlements, the men in power derided and neglected people's enunciations while exempting themselves as much as possible from their responsibilities. While government and industries veiled their irresponsibility and lied about imminent threats, the media flooded the airwaves with confusing spectacles and discourses. In its dismissal of commoners' concerns, academia acted as a proxy for government and industry. All took full advantage of radiation's virtuality, pulling their robes of authenticity tighter around themselves in an attempt to discredit the screams and experiments of the commoners. But in the light of day, their pathetic beings were fully exposed, and emboldened commoners waged a heated information and intellectual war in the shadows of media spectacle.

Numerous publications and blogs by critical scientists, independent journalists, and individuals were created in opposition to the authorities' news releases, in an attempt not only to understand the threats of radionuclides but also to analyze the nature of post–nuclear disaster governance. What follows are just a few examples. Since the wake of the accident, Citizens' Nuclear Information Center (CNIC) has been invaluable for providing those in and out of Japan with the most trustworthy assessments of the reactors' probable damage and its possible consequences. The independent journalist Soeda Takashi has tirelessly investigated the profit-centered negligence of TEPCO and the political irresponsibility of the Japanese government. A blog called Chidaism has aggregated information on food contamination that is more detailed than the data publicized by the Ministry of Health, Labor and Welfare. Methods of mapping radioactive contamination have proliferated, generating all manner of maps, which are then collected and published on the internet.[28] Viewed in ensemble, these maps present a reading of the terrain of our lifeworld (the Earth) that diverges significantly from the geopolitical maps of the Japanese government. We also observe the expression of fury against those behind nuclear proliferation, identified by critics as the "nuclear village," in publications detailing the rapport of their interests and also personal data, including even the addresses of private residences.[29]

People began to learn from the longtime efforts of the physician Hida Shuntaro (1917–2017). An eyewitness to the Hiroshima attack, Hida became the director of the Hibakusha Counseling Center, which sought compensation from the US government and supported casualties' lives-as-struggle.[30] His experience and knowledge concerning internal exposure provided people with indispensable lessons for their practices of court battle as well as health protection.[31] His response to Fukushima was unequivocal: "People in Japan are no longer free from internal exposure."[32] Accordingly, he made a number of clear, simple, and substantial proposals for autonomous actions people should take: make extremely detailed medical records for court battles and be self-motivated in everyday life to strengthen the immune system in order to counter internal exposure. Crucially, he insisted that all children must be evacuated from the highly radioactive zones.

Civic organizations based on the people's will to know the truth began to appear in many cities, providing DIY radiation monitoring and means of sharing information. Soon after the disaster, some of my friends were engaged in the Tokyo Sunaba Project (*sunaba* means sandbox), a loose association of people who went around residential areas in the metropolis to monitor radiation in public parks and exchanged their information. As many as seventy-four radiation-measuring organizations appeared across Japan.[33] Since affordable Geiger counters cannot generally detect radioactive contamination in food and water, people gathered to collectively purchase more sophisticated detectors and established monitoring stations where nearby residents could bring food to be tested for cesium concentrations.[34]

Passions to study science and practice technology—nuclear and medical—permeated commoners. We saw in these developments the germinating of a minor science in the sense of Deleuze and Guattari, which, alongside the Geiger counter used as collectivized prosthetic, became a weapon for survival.[35] As opposed to the royal science that persists in invariant principles, this is a pragmatic science that deals with the shifting variations in chaotic reality. Commoners' technoscientific practices post-Fukushima tackled the most necessary and difficult task of developing ways to live with mutant flows—namely, the heterogenesis of radionuclides. This heterogenesis is precisely what the state-backed royal science mechanically neglects by reducing it to fixed standards, models, or numbers in order to index an imaginary threshold.

The sum total of these practices to confront radionuclides has been referred to as "zero-becquerelism." Coined by anarchist activist and thinker Yabu Shiro, zero-becquerelism declares a dual battle for lives-as-struggle post-Fukushima: to confront the physical threat of radiation technically as well as to abolish the government that imposes this threat politically.[36] The theory collective Hapax has associated zero-becquerelist practices with the ancient philosophy of atomism, in terms of the scandal they cause within a social order based on the logos of the World: "What is at stake in their struggle is to provoke the scandal of the absolute decomposition of social order and to render an anarchic heterogeneity based upon atomism, or the materialism of the invisible."[37] If these practices are scandalous, it is because, by responding to the virtuality of radioactivity, they have begun to disquiet the sense of reality that is constantly produced and reproduced by royal science and capitalist development.

///

Responses to the catastrophic situation were nevertheless uneven among the populace. In the big picture, the nation seemed to split in half; there were those who insisted on continuing the same way of life and those who questioned it, investigated the truth of radiation, and determined to make changes.

As bodies began to mutate explicitly or implicitly according to their susceptibility to radioactivity, divergences emerged between people with differing sensibilities regarding radioactive contamination. Susceptibility was concentrated in the residents of radio-contaminated zones, farmers, fishermen, nuclear workers, sanitation workers, homeless people, and the younger population with their vital genetic activity. Differing sensibilities within families, friends, schools, workplaces, and local communities created fissures over ways of life, including food choices, behaviors, political judgments, and places to live. Generally speaking, the most susceptible (after nuclear workers) were those dealing with raw materials in primary industries, such as farmers and fishermen, and the most intense sensibilities could be observed among those who take charge of the reproduction of life in families and communities: reproductive/care workers. Simply said, those in charge of creating life tended to be affected most dramatically, both materially and immaterially.

In common households, mothers or those who care for everyday needs tended to question the government's reports and to act on their own initiative for the sake of their children and families, while fathers or breadwinners tended to think everything was OK and called their wives paranoid. Sometimes fathers remained at their workplaces/homes in Tokyo or northern Honshu, while mothers and children moved west or to Hokkaido.

After the wake of the catastrophe, it was mothers who spearheaded most of the efforts to protect people from radiation and to protest the government's irresponsibility. As many pointed out, their initiative reflected the gendered role imposed on women in a patriarchal society. While this role was intensified doubly and triply in the reproductive crises wrought by radioactive contamination, it allowed women to create innumerable projects by politicizing their historically nurtured sensibilities, techniques, and knowledges of care. In other words, it was women who, through their everyday engagement in reproduction, responded to the situation most radically, resisting nuclear permeation through both their historically charged labor and their historically nurtured wisdom.[38]

In everyday life, individual mothers and caregivers devised various strategies to address the potential harm from radioactive fallout: avoiding food from affected areas, changing places to shop for food, seeking ways to cook that would reduce contamination, evacuating to safer locales, and so forth. These strategies were often condemned as irrational, emotional, or hysterical by the authorities as well as by other family members. Concomitant with the widely circulating term *fūhyō higai*, they were also labeled *hōsha-nō* (radioactive brain), a pun mocking the fear of radioactivity as a sign that the brain itself has become radio-contaminated.[39] Food safety measures were interpreted less as a form of dedication to family health and more as a lack of rationality, patriotism, and sympathy for the affected areas. Ultimately, no one has problematized the fact that the authorities have tacitly taken advantage of these popular efforts, which conveniently exempt them from their responsibilities to take charge of the well-being of the people.

On top of their individual efforts, many women led collective projects such as radiation-measuring organizations, voluntary evacuees' associations, and evacuee support groups, demanding safety regulations for school lunches and the revocation of loose governmental radiation standards, filing civil lawsuits against TEPCO and the government, organizing street protests, and so on.[40] Spearheaded by women (popularly referred to as "enraged mothers"), people's power began to emerge. This power disseminates the will to live the event—the will to act—actualizing the horizon of a new political ontology that is simultaneously vaster and more minuscule than that of mediatized spectacle and the registered discourses of politics: that is, the arena of life-as-struggle. Some have seen in the rise of this power a new feminist movement against the historically congealed patriarchal society, which, in the form of reproductive struggle, covers all practices of making human life.[41]

One remarkable example from the counterradiation movement for protecting health was initiated by local mothers in Fukushima. In November 2011, they established a radiation-monitoring station called Tarachine in Iwaki City, at the frontline of peoples' lives-as-struggle in and against radiation fallout. In the Japanese poetic tradition, *tarachine* is the pillow word (or figure) for mother. Tarachine's statement of purpose lists seven objectives: (1) to measure radiation in food upon request by local residents, (2) to measure internal radiation upon request, (3) to advocate for residents' safety, (4) to publicize data concerning the state of local radioactive contamination, (5) to train others in radiation measurement techniques, (6) to collaborate with scientists and physicians in the advancement of medical knowledge regarding radioactive contamination and health protection against it, and (7) to contribute to the wide diffusion of information concerning radioactive contamination in collaboration with other monitoring stations. Since its inauguration, Tarachine has been increasingly active with new programs, such as the Oceanographic Research Project, which implements fixed-point sampling and radiation measurement at 1.5 kilometers off the coast of TEPCO's Fukushima Daiichi nuclear facility.[42]

///

However vital the measures of health protection have been in the wake of nuclear disaster, the difficulty and urgency of enacting them tended to raise questions of political priority. These eventually caused splits among activists, according to the differing intensities of their radiosensibilities. On the one hand, there were individuals and groups who were eager to go to Fukushima to support the victims in disaster areas. On the other hand, there were those proponents of zero-becquerelism who argued that going to Fukushima tacitly supports government schemes to bind people to the hazardous land, and who therefore prioritized well-being by encouraging exodus. Within activist milieus, heated debates took place between the two groups. The former was figuratively called Those Who Go North and the latter Those Who Go West, reflecting the opposing orientations vis-à-vis Fukushima from the geographical standpoint of Tokyo. Those Who Go North consisted of independent activists participating in the voluntary activities organized by nongovernmental organizations (NGOs) or by Fukushima Prefecture to help those who had been living in townships destroyed by the tsunami and those who had been relocated to temporary housing. This category also included a small number of labor organizers who sought to support subcontracted nuclear workers at the Fukushima Daiichi plant in improving their working conditions, with the hope of organizing them. That aspiration was motivated by the ultimate prospect of ousting nuclear power and the analysis that such could occur only by the will, technique, and action of nuclear workers.

After the disaster, the realities of the working conditions of subcontracted nuclear workers were illuminated more than ever. Innumerable documents, reports, and memoirs reveal how nuclear power plants function through strict rules of secrecy and strict hierarchical orders, going down from the electric company to as many as eight layers of subcontracting companies and labor brokers (including yakuza organizations in the bottom layers).[43] This hierarchy entails clear divisions. While the formal employees of electric companies monopolize crucial information, do mostly managerial work, and rarely intervene in hazardous sites, the workers hired by lower contractors take care of physical work in highly radioactive environments, without sufficient information, industrial injury insurance, or other safety measures. In this order, the voice of the electric company is nearly absolute. Its main demands are low cost and good reputation, which produce two absurdly terrible conditions. First, the value of life-risking work is reduced significantly stage by stage—with cuts taken by contractors and brokers—and ultimately disfigured in the minuscule wages of irradiated workers, averaging 10,000 yen per day after 80 percent is taken away. Second, the electric company does not want the public to know the reality of nuclear labor, whereby workers are susceptible to constant accident and predestined illnesses such as leukemia and heart disease. Subcontractors, in compliance with the company's demands, try to settle cases of worker injury and illness informally by private settlement, without formal insurance. This hierarchical structure has a fatal flaw: TEPCO managers who rarely visit radioactive sites know very little about the real problems and situations that the underinformed workers face there, and thus accidents continue to take place and crises endure. In the years to come, the never-ending crisis of the Fukushima Daiichi plant will only irradiate more and more underclass workers, foreigners included.

While Those Who Go North got involved with disaster victims and nuclear workers, the priority of Those Who Go West was the protection of everyday reproduction through a broad horizon of practices whose ultimate pole was the politicized support and encouragement of voluntary evacuees, or exodus. Some came to interpret the difference between these tendencies as an embodiment of conflicting class politics, dividing the former as an underclass workers' movement from the latter as a middle-class citizens' movement. While this division indicates some aspect of social reality, as we shall see in chapter 4, such crude class politics fail to grasp that possible milieu wherein various practices interact—the horizon of the lives-as-struggle of planetary inhabitants who are facing the decline of the World of capitalist nation-states. In terms of this new milieu, some came to see the concept of exodus (mass evacuation) as a way to conceive an imaginary synthesis of migrant day laborers (i.e., subcontracted nuclear workers) and evacuating commoners.

In relationship with evacuation, I heard a story around a colloquial maxim, handed down from generation to generation by the inhabitants of coastal areas, about how to confront a tsunami triggered by an earthquake in the seabed. Based on historical experience, the phrase *tsunami tendenko* instructs that when a tsunami hits, everyone must escape each for her own before worrying about others. The idea is that dispersion is necessary for people to meet up again somewhere safer on higher ground.[44] In fact, there have been innumerable instances, including in March 2011, when people failed to escape while looking for loved ones or trying to gather together by communal order. Though its imperative is psychologically and morally difficult to follow, the collective wisdom of tsunami tendenko suggests the necessity of detour by split for more people to be saved in the end.

The revival of this maxim today is a reminder of the national history wherein the periodic catastrophe of earthquake and tsunami have radically transmuted political, social, and economic courses of events. The Great Kanto earthquake of 1923 destroyed the capital Tokyo, which also stimulated the reinforcement of emperor fascism and imperialist expansion into the Asian continent. (For that matter, Tokyo is the epitome of a megalopolis that grew bigger after every major destruction.) Since the Meiji period, eight big tsunamis have hit Japan, especially the Tohoku region. These tsunamis, in interaction with political and economic crises, were primary prompters for the immiseration of peasants: those who lost subsistence and homes flowed into the cities and especially into Tokyo, which thereby amassed surplus populations of underclass and unemployed. It is said that during Japan's war of aggression, the majority of foot soldiers sent to China from Iwate Prefecture were victims of the 1933 Sanriku tsunami.[45]

Some have spoken of tsunami tendenko as a prefiguration of the post-Fukushima exodus, interpreting the act of evacuation as the ultimate prioritization of the avoidance of radiation exposure, which could only be made possible by the will of individuals, determined to protect their well-being at the expense of loyalty and attachment to community. But this line of thinking should not be considered a reinstatement of individualism; rather, it emphasizes the necessity of decomposing old assemblages of relations—families, friends, and communities—in order to confront the catastrophe. The temporary decomposition of existing social relations could act in favor of everyone's well-being, in expectation of an eventual recomposition of new social relations. Those activists who affirmed evacuation politically, then, nurtured the prospect that it could lead to the creation of new territories of autonomy against and outside Tokyo-centered consumerist society—namely, the nation-state of Japan. As such, the maxim tsunami tendenko was shared as a counternarrative to the national conformity promoted by the post-Fukushima regime to keep the majority of the populace in the area and to ensure the continued functioning of local businesses and municipalities.

In such a context, the problematic nature of the government's evacuation policy was highlighted. This policy made a divisive categorization of evacuees according to where they had lived, distinguishing those who were "mandated" to leave from those whose evacuations were "voluntary." The mandated evacuees were from the hazard areas affected by radioactivity of more than twenty millisieverts (20 mSv) per year. The government offered these victims support, but for the others there was much less, or nothing.[46] Objections were voiced over the arbitrariness of this policy and the dubious division between mandated and voluntary. Before the disaster, the safety standard for radioactive cesium had been set at a maximum annual dose of 1 mSv, and it was suddenly raised to 20 mSv.[47] The logic behind this raise was suspicious. The most plausible explanation is that the government needed to normalize the condition of living with much higher radiation exposure. It was also becoming clear that areas of high radioactivity and high instances of thyroid cancer did not overlap with the government's zoning; the distinction between those who needed to evacuate and those who did not was not geographically determinable in any strict sense. The government could not make a formal definition of "voluntary evacuees" and would not count their number.[48] In consequence, all those who decided to evacuate without governmental support have been pushed into an extremely precarious status.

Heated debates on evacuation have continued in varied contexts. The difficulties of life-as-struggle for those who determined to remain have been discussed as well, in numerous reports and films. Meanwhile, evacuation has been increasing slowly and quietly. The Association of Voluntary Evacuees (Jishu hinansha no kai) was organized in October 2015, seeking to unite evacuees of all kinds, in opposition to the government's policy to divide. All in all, underlying the issue of evacuation policy is a deeper conflict of interest: the assailants responsible for the accident—the government and TEPCO—had the power to judge who was entitled to be considered their victim and to determine the quantity and quality of support they would receive.

On May 23, 2011, a group of Fukushima mothers stormed Tokyo and besieged the Ministry of Education, Culture, Sports, Science and Technology to demand that the minister revoke the 20 mSv standard, especially in consideration of the susceptibility of children. Varied groups pressed both local and central governments to take responsible measures for public health, that is, physical examinations for those living in risky areas, careful planning of children's activities in schools, safety inspection of ingredients in school lunches, inspection of food products distributed nationally, and so on.

June 11, 2011, was a big no-nuke day. There were demonstrations and rallies calling for the total abolishment of nuclear power in some 140 locations across the world. Within Tokyo alone, there were four separate actions in Shinjuku, Shiba, Shibuya, and Kunitachi. I participated in the biggest of these, a demonstration in Shinjuku that mobilized seven thousand people. It was organized by a coalition of varied antiauthoritarian groups, including groups who fought together at the Toyako G8 summit in 2008. A majority of the participants were new to antinuke activism and had just begun learning from the experiences of previous antinuke and environmental struggles, as they sought to approach the post-Fukushima situation with their anticapitalist inclinations.

During the demonstration, I observed a transmutation of representation from previous protests. While many participants were singing and dancing as usual, using cheerful, funky, and clownish images to express their anger playfully and festively, there were new elements I had never seen before: grotesque, ghostly, and cursing images in costumes and placards. The colorful images that had played counterpart to the anonymous black (Black Bloc) of the antiglobalization movement were gradually being replaced by the image of a cursing ghost, as clowns turned into Mothers of Wrath, or Shamans. I envisioned that the age of the curse had arrived—no longer simple anger—against a regime that insisted on nuclear power and energy-centered social reproduction, exposing the nation to radiation. A few friends observed in these images a return of the 1970s struggles against the Chisso Corporation in Minamata and other industrial polluters, wherein the ultimate expression of protest was the presence of victims' own mutated and dying bodies, wearing signs imprinted with the character *curse* (呪).[49] That was perhaps the ultimate form of protest witnessed in postwar Japan.

The highlight of the June 11 action took place at the postdemonstration gathering point of Alta Square. In defiance of repeated police warnings, demonstrators refused to leave. Many sang and danced for several hours; some stayed until the next morning. It was reminiscent of scenes observed everywhere throughout 1960s Japan and still in many places around the world today, whenever more than a certain number of people—a critical mass—are involved and the power of the crowd incapacitates police attempts at control (unless by extreme measures). We wondered when the Japanese crowd would be determined enough to stay indefinitely, like those occupying city squares in Greece, Egypt, or Spain at that time. We all felt that the antinuke actions in Japan were inspired by and part of the ongoing global uprisings of the planetary crowd. At that moment at least, people shared the sense that their movement went beyond mere response to the post-Fukushima regime.

In the constituency of this new impetus, however, a blot arose. On one occasion, an event space with a politically nonchalant composition ended up allowing the participation of a racist group, which not only showed up at the demonstration but also demanded to have its representative speak. This group was notorious for denying the existence of comfort women, part of the growing nationalist tendency of historical revisionism denying Japan's aggressions in Asia.[50] A harsh dispute followed and the group's representative did not get to speak at the rally. But the situation made us aware of one of the problems with the single-issue slogan "No Nukes!" *What does "no nukes" mean in the post-Fukushima climate, in terms of politics, economy, culture, and everyday life?* Fascists and nationalists were also antinuke for the sake of the nation's well-being. Neoliberal entrepreneurs proposed alternative energy as a new means of profit making. Even Prime Minister Noda could promote a future denuked society.

Another question troubling antiauthoritarians concerned the limits of demonstrations themselves. Mass demonstration in the city center is always important and should continue. But if demonstration itself is the goal, it would be futile. If that is all that the political imagination can materialize, that would be sad, considering the magnitude of the dystopian situation, affecting all aspects of everyday life and social reproduction. The people had already begun their less mediatized struggles, tackling issues of everyday reproduction. The issue of the subcontracted nuclear workers who were made to sacrifice their lives was not sufficiently addressed in the demonstrations; a few labor organizers who were active in day laborers' communities attempted to organize nuclear workers.[51] Some local communities across the country were waging direct actions and lawsuits against the government to terminate the resumption of nearby reactors.

The antinuke impetus lasted for about two years. The last remarkable action was the disruption of the restarting of reactors 3 and 4 at the Oi Nuclear Power Plant. Between June 30 and July 2, 2012, tent villages were organized with the call "beyond petitions and rallies, it is now necessary to disrupt the restart with our bodies."[52] Local groups, older leftists, and young activists gathered and waged direct actions at the municipal government offices of Kyoto Prefecture, at the headquarters of the Kansai Electric Power Company (KEPCO), and during briefing sessions at Oi town hall. Finally, they occupied and blockaded the gate of the Oi facility for several days. But ultimately the reactors were restarted and remained in operation until they were taken offline in September 2013 for inspections.[53]

///

During my first visit back to Japan after the disaster, my friends and I had numerous conversations from which we developed the following ideas about engagement in the post-Fukushima world. The implication of "antinuclear" in the ongoing Fukushima event is yet indeterminable, as it is expanding to unknown arenas of existential territories that we will have to continue to experience and observe, following the development of our lives-as-struggle. But definitely, these new antinuclear imperatives cannot be summarized by the preventative call for "no more nuclear accidents," though it continues to play an indispensable role. There is an irreversibility to the event. *It has already happened and still continues!* A massive population, including the residents of the Tokyo metropolis, is now exposed to radioactivity, more or less. Exposure to unknown doses is expanding across the world. From here on, no matter what we do—even if we accomplish the important tasks of shutting down nuclear plants and finding alternative energy—we will still have to live with various forms and intensities of radiation from the accumulating waste, whose effects are varied temporally and spatially.

Neither can the implications of antinuclear be limited to the single-issue slogan, though it sustains its crucial position in the entire spectrum of our lives-as-struggle. The conviction we conceived after Fukushima is that nuclear power has never been just a bad choice of energy, something to be replaced by a better source of energy when we all are enlightened. Rather, nuclear power has been assigned a very privileged position in the apparatuses that sustain and expand the World by capitalism and states. Nuclear energy faithfully plays its role in the military–industrial complex that hinges capitalism and the state most solidly, and gives them an upper hand in the power contestations of the World. In order for us to tackle the Fukushima problematic in its full sense, we must approach the complexity of the apparatuses driving endless development/mutation on the Earth, from the singular positions of our lives-as-struggle.

Finally, it has become clear for us that the question of the Fukushima event is not about Japan alone: it involves global power relations. And, while we are well aware that the Fukushima disaster is not the only disastrous or dystopian occasion, still its irreversibility and its magnitude shed an intense light on the World that has begun to collapse on the Earth and force all its vital activities to commit double suicide with it. The name *Fukushima* is an index of the climatic and environmental injustices wrought by the apparatuses of capitalism and state, and of their ultimate plane of operation: the total management of our lifeworld by way of dystopian control. If so, for us Fukushima must be an occasion to connect anticapitalist movements, climatic and environmental justice movements, indigenous movements, and innumerable lives-as-struggle fighting against the control of our everyday life and life forms.

RECAPTURE

Within several years, the event of Fukushima was made less and less visible by the normalization of mutation and transmutation. Today its problematic is treated as one of many, and it no longer commands the media attention it once dominated. Amid the scenery of hyperconsumerist society, the rise of nationalist populism can be felt in the air. Program after program on TV highlight celebrities joyfully tasting delicacies nurtured in localities across Japan, and especially those from Fukushima. While the obsessions with food and tourism are staged, the slow process of radiation is spreading. The joy of eating and traveling— a fatal match for desire and exposure—is turned into the basic apparatus for disaster management. Rituals of hoisting the Japanese flag and singing the national anthem are newly mandatory in many schools, following the demands of the Ministry of Education, Culture, Sports, Science and Technology. Xenophobic groups abuse immigrants on the street (resident ethnic Koreans especially) more graphically than ever. The increasing numbers of those who immigrate for work and education are mistreated by the government, schools, and industries. Enthusiasm for realizing the 2020 Tokyo Olympics is orchestrated on television by Nippon Hōsō Kyōkai (NHK, Japan Broadcasting Corporation), fabricating the appearance of a unified inclination for infrastructure reconstruction. All-nation unity seems to be back in full gear toward a wealthier and stronger country.

The drive of ongoing "recovery" is far from a simple return to the previous status quo. There are active forces in operation to reinforce national conformity and intensify redevelopment, employing the catastrophe as a fulcrum. These are initiated by the imposed presumption that the recovery of what was lost is consensual, and that this recovery should take the form of returning to the original: the strong bond of the nation. In fact, in order for new reconstruction initiatives to move ahead, it is necessary to actively invoke historical repetition, namely, the dramatic return of the apparatuses of capture stratified in collective memory: insular territoriality as a geohistorical receptacle to confine mass corporeality and mind-set, the symbolic emperor system as a spiritual receptacle to unify the nation, the Thanatos drive of patriotism to orient people's desire into national suicide, mass media as a machine of homogenizing discourses, techno-state apparatuses (i.e., nuclear apparatus) to realize the slogan "wealthy nation and strong soldier," and Tokyo as the expansive and contractive movement that absorbs and reorients desire for the capitalist-state mode of development. (These are scrutinized in chapter 2.)

The antinuclear manifestations of the metropolitan crowd dwindled after the Oi Nuclear Power Plant was put back online in July 2012. By the following December, when the Abe administration rose to power, mass protests had congealed into a populist movement (on the progressive/liberal side), as their organizers banned all political expression beyond the main antinuclear slogans and precluded the collective coordination of multiple tactics, in order to create a broad movement of "normal citizens"—a nominalism that effectively assimilates heterogeneous crowd into homogeneous nation.[54] This movement realized a pattern of large mobilizations for strictly legal protests in Tokyo and other main cities. While keeping the same time (Fridays until 8:00 pm) and place (the prime minister's official residence in Tokyo), the protest's theme mutated from antinuclear to anti-Abe, and its mode was reduced from open-ended opposition to electoral campaigning for candidates from progressive political parties. In 2015 this impetus was reorganized into a liberal movement of students, activists, and intellectuals, all more or less associated with the Japan Communist Party or with a new group known as the Students Emergency Action for Liberal Democracy (SEALDS), which insisted on centralizing all issues in the decision-making within parliamentary politics. On the one hand, this movement called for the defense of peace and democracy in the postwar constitution against Abe's reforms, and on the other, it demanded that all participants cooperate with the police, interfering forcibly in the desires of the crowd to expand the realm of street action by mobilizing informal policing units.[55]

Liberal ideologues appeared in the media to promote this populist movement while discrediting the radical movements of the 1960s as failed vanguardism. Though it is true that the Japanese radical left historically internalized the problems of authoritarian vanguardism, the negative effects of this tendency have long been critically scrutinized by antiauthoritarians in the post–New Left movements, from the citizens' movements of the 1970s to feminist and minorities' movements to the antiglobalization movement of the first decade of the twenty-first century. Still, within such antiauthoritarian tendencies, the radical impetus to change society, which was witnessed in Japan in the 1960s, has never really grown as it has elsewhere in the world—except for smaller milieus of autonomous struggles, such as day laborers' ghettoes, homeless camps, neighborhood communities, and small affinities of anticapitalists. All in all, as we shall see in chapter 4, the shift of political ontology from the 1960s to the post-Fukushima climate embodies multidimensional metamorphoses of peoples' lives-as-struggle, far beyond the shift from authoritarian vanguardism to populist parliamentarism that liberal ideologues wanted to emphasize.

For its part, liberal politics has evaded the anticapitalist, globalist, and revolutionary perspectives of previous radicals. Its discourses lack critical consciousness of its own social organization, which is, as one Marxian analysis would have it, "determined by the class interest of the people involved in it, by its relationship to capital, its historical, geographical and psychological conditions."[56] Most crucially, this thought/ movement has turned out to be totally ineffective in confronting the post–nuclear disaster regime from a global perspective, unable to conceive any sense of the problematic interconnectivity between the strategic nature of the postwar constitution (subservient to US global hegemony), its entanglement with nuclear power, and Abe's post–nuclear disaster governance. By reducing the event to the national politics of Abe versus anti-Abe, liberal politics ended up unconditionally glorifying the postwar democracy that invented the Fukushima event in the first place. Liberal populism thus shares an introverted view with nationalist populism.

This introverted view treats the problematic of the Fukushima nuclear disaster, which is essentially planetary, as exclusively Japanese, and attempts to solve it exclusively for the survival of the nation. The last resort of the introverted stance is *national conformity*. After Fukushima, national conformity was revived not only within nationalist and liberal tendencies but also by the critics of nuclear power. For instance, Koide Hiroaki is an important antinuclear nuclear scientist based at Kyoto University (retired in 2015) whose all-front analysis of nuclear power continues to provide an indispensable point of reference.[57] Yet Koide exemplified the revival of national conformity when he suggested that senior citizens eat the risky products from Fukushima in order to preempt the younger and more vulnerable populace from having to eat them and, at the same time, to protect Fukushima's primary industries from declining.[58] Many voices from the left echoed this sentiment that the whole nation should share the burden of radiation in the unavoidable tasks of waste treatment and incineration. In this manner, the blackmailing potency of nuclear catastrophe as an *all or nothing crisis* finds its ideal prey in people's honest sense of belonging: the feeling of debt to the nation must be prioritized to solve a problem of this magnitude, before ousting the regime. Here returns the historically crystallized predisposition wherein people's solidarity is replaced by national conformity, in such a way that difference is glossed over and class politics are nullified.

The national spirit has been held aloft intensively in cultural politics. Neoliberal entrepreneurs and certain intellectuals of an age-old postmodernist bent sought to enterprise national projects for revitalizing the economy and culture of Fukushima. One outstanding example was the Fukushima Kanko Project, instigated in 2013. Through publications and a website, this project promoted a plan to make Fukushima Daiichi a tourist site, claiming that the "tourization" of the disaster site had already begun by concerned visitors and supporters, and that it would be positive to invite more visitors and have them observe the reality of the nuclear accident.[59] Furthermore, in support of the 2020 Tokyo Olympics, the proposal included an "Expo of Revitalization" at the site of J-Village—a soccer stadium near the reactors that had been used for clean-up operations of radioactive waste—and a "Memorial Museum" in Tokyo's Shinagawa Ward for improving disaster education.[60]

In such an initiative, one can see the elaborate revival of the 1960s "village revitalization" (*mura-okoshi*) designed to counter the depopulation of rural areas triggered by the absorption of labor forces into cities by industrialization.[61] Mura-okoshi involved the nationwide promotion of local products (such as food and crafts) and the invention of tourist sites, in collaboration with the media and Japan Railways.[62] In another dimension, the new Fukushima tourization echoes postmodernism, the ideological driver of the bubble economy during the 1980s and early 1990s, which collapsed culture into consumerism, political engagement into economic development, and politics into aesthetics.[63] As such, the tourization of Fukushima was a most untimely revival, from a period when history was considered to have ended and Japan was internationally acclaimed as a futuristic model for business and society—untimely precisely because it was the Fukushima event itself that had dealt the fatal blow to this model of society free from historical contingency and catastrophe. On the other hand, if the Fukushima Kanko Project appeared timely to some, it was only because it represented in a most graphic gesture what the postdisaster regime had dreamed to do. It is clear that for the intellectuals as entrepreneurs, the Fukushima event was merely a little bad luck for their consumerist heaven.

From the opposite vector—from the world to Japan—global apparatuses of capture have begun to intervene in the post–nuclear disaster nation. The ETHOS Project, originally designed and implemented in Belarus following the Chernobyl catastrophe, stands out. This organization receives part of its funding from the European Commission, France, and other members of the nuclear lobby, and its coordinator is Jacques Lochard, the director of a number of French nuclear lobbies and a member of the International Commission on Radiological Protection (ICRP), an international pronuclear organization founded in 1950.[64] The ICRP claims to improve life in contaminated areas. Its objective is to facilitate the return of evacuees into highly radioactive areas by emotionally encouraging residents, including pregnant women and children, to keep living in contaminated areas, through carrying out decontamination and radiation measurements. It is of vital importance to recognize the difference between this objective and those of the radiation measurement practices organized by and for local residents. Critics pointed out that in Belarus, the ETHOS Project was an accomplice in the removal of almost all local radiation-monitoring stations—precisely like that of Tarachine—which constituted a system to protect children from the toxicity of cesium-137.[65] The ETHOS Project is now in Fukushima as a branch of the ICRP, with this melodramatic appeal: "Live in Fukushima after the nuclear disaster—the life here is wonderful. A much better future can be handed down. In Iwaki City, we continue our tiny, tiny efforts to measure, know, think and look for a common language between you and me."[66] Less than concrete scientific, technical, or medical practices, what this project motivates is cultural production. It aims to create a holistic system of domesticated life in the catastrophe, by propagating mishmash discourses of suffering, hope, community, and tradition. This organization is global in terms of not only its structure but also its ultimate goal: to make the planetary populace accustomed to life with radioactivity.

UNCAPTURED

The virtual flows of radioactive nuclides travel beyond Japan's national border, which happens to coincide with an archipelagic territory surrounded by the seas. As a number of dreadful maps show, radioactive pollutants are thus spreading across the Pacific Ocean, toward the Pacific Northwest of the American continent, along with the wind and oceanic currents.[67] Meanwhile, within the land, radioactivity flies and permeates irrespective of the territorial articulations of national politics (administrative divisions) and economy (development maps) that constitute the orders of society, nation, and world. Its traveling and accumulating pattern is an extremely complex and chaotic heterogenesis that slips through the territorial articulations of the human world. As we have seen, those who live the Fukushima event—the radiosensitive and radioactive crowd—have been seeking to grasp this heterogenesis through their acts for survival, such as measurement, mapping, and evacuation. Their difficult efforts are revealing a new horizon of the political, divergent from that of the politics of the World (national and international politics). How can we think of this horizon?

The radioactive flow synchronizes omnipresent and minuscule movements that deterritorialize any territorial articulations, thus pointing to an alien ontology of the planet. These movements are of something that exists everywhere and moves to every direction. In terms of Deleuze and Guattari's geophilosophy, this is the Earth itself, described as that which "carries out a movement of deterritorialization on the spot, by which it goes beyond any territory: it is deterritorializing and deterritorialized." Furthermore, "it merges with the movement of those who leave their territory *en masse.*"[68] Therefore, the technopolitical horizon of the struggles against radiation indicates the ontology—or more precisely, the *becoming*—of the Earth.

Radionuclides thus open fissures in the World, through which the complexity of all movements called the Earth is overflowing. This flowing complexity has always already been there in our unconscious existence but is newly arrived to our political attention by the lives-as-struggle of radiosensitive/active crowds, in and as the battle to detect, measure, map, and avoid radionuclides. In other words, in response to radioactive contamination, the radioactive crowd unwittingly bridges two ontologies, namely, two faces of one and the same reality, which all of us share: the World and the Earth. The ontology of the World embodies the way the expanding and totalizing movement of the capitalist/state mode of development involves our existential territories: individual mind/body, society, and the environment. This is the apparatus (*dispositif*) which has been increasingly devastating rather than hopeful for us. The ontology of the Earth is yet unknown, a new horizon that we are experiencing like aliens who have just arrived on a new planet, thanks to the revelations of people's lives-as-struggle. After all, the ontology of the Earth has been experienced not only via the Fukushima nuclear disaster but through many other forms of catastrophe. And we are still in the process of understanding its full implications.

///

Radioactive fallouts have polluted living environments in the vicinity of Fukushima Daiichi most severely. Immediately after the accident, the task of decontamination surfaced as an absolute necessity for all inhabitants living there, in order to protect their living environments and reproductive resources. Therefore, in the earlier phase of the disaster, it was those who were affected most directly (inhabitants, farmers, and fishermen) who undertook such initiative by and for themselves. However, due to the increasing intervention of the power over of the government and general contractors, alongside overwhelming difficulties, the projects based on the power to / power with of local residents ended up either being absorbed into or replaced by the post–nuclear disaster enterprises.

The decontamination of soil requires the tireless physical labor of shaving off surface soil by shovelfuls, packing it in plastic bags and storing it away. The question was raised as to whether this method was effective at all, given that, after each and every effort of shaving-off, the radionuclides continued to accumulate on the surface. In fact, radionuclides certainly were accumulating in certain areas; nonetheless, the laborious process had to be repeated time and time again in order to prevent the contamination from worsening. Such desperate work was first undertaken under the auspices of both local communities or municipalities and the central government, according to the division of districts. Innumerable residents participated in this work voluntarily, for the sake of protecting their own living environments. The choice of dumpsites also required difficult negotiations among residents, since nobody wanted them nearby.[69] Eventually, general contractors took over more of these projects, employing subcontractors and their part-time workers. Now the accumulation of radioactive soil has become one of the worst embodiments of planetary devastation, as we see in picture after picture of piles of black plastic bags, endlessly accumulating with no place to go.

Farmers have been severely affected by radioactive contamination. All their products—rice, vegetables, and dairy—have been wasted. It was amid a price crisis in agricultural products and the threatening impacts of the Trans-Pacific Partnership created by the World Trade Organization (WTO) that they were first hit by the radioactive hazard. Today their products are monitored at multiple stages, and only those that meet the maximum dose standard (100 becquerels per 100 kilograms) are distributed nationally, while many foreign countries either ban Japanese agricultural imports completely or impose harsher regulations on them.[70] Meanwhile, the National Association of Farmers (Nōmin undo zenkoku rengō kai) has been seeking compensation from TEPCO.[71]

Aside from direct measures against radioactive fallouts—decontamination, measurement, mapping, and evacuation—people have developed many indirect responses to the disaster, or new initiatives inspired by the disaster that, in diverging existential dimensions, conceive a potency to open up the horizon of a new political ontology vis-à-vis the Earth, outside the geopolitics of the nation. In sum, these can be bundled together as projects to create new forms of life, outside the hyper-consumerist society developed in the postwar regime.

As a critical response to the prosperous society that ended up inventing nuclear disaster, many people came to question their own ways of living as being driven by energy-centered development, and began to seek different ways of being. As one epitomic example, a so-called off-grid movement appeared in several places throughout the Tohoku and Kanto regions. In Kanagawa Prefecture, a group called Fujino Denryoku, established by commoners right after the disaster, sought to transform communal life in locality by detaching it from the centralized system of energy supply and reconnecting it with the singularities of place—environment, terrains, and resources—via self-sufficient energy sources created in a decentralized system.[72] Similar networks of communities have appeared both in and out of Japan.[73]

Along with an increasing awareness of health and ecology provoked by the disaster, many forms of permaculture—experimental practices to create symbiotic relations between plants, animals, and the environment—are spreading today more than ever, in both cities and countryside.[74] Some voluntary evacuees have created communities in new places—especially northern Kyushu and Hokkaido—with the adamant will to create new forms of life that are as distant and different as possible from those nurtured in the Tokyo-centered capitalist nation-state. Some of these evacuees have learned farming, hunting, fishing, and other techniques and wisdoms for survival from local people. Some have been experimenting with gift economy within their new communities through systems such as barter. They identify themselves as "generalists" who practice a hundred means of subsistence (*hyakushō*, as traditional farmers used to call themselves), rather than as "specialists" who gain success as professionals in consumerist society. What is crucial among these practices is that they seek to live in the same place but in an essentially different manner (as the Earth) from those who live as the Japanese (in the World), by taking initiative to metamorphose their reality through what radioactivity reveals.

///

Contamination is spreading over the smooth space of water, escaping the striated confinement of Japan's insular territory. Planetary rotation creates an eastward wind from the Asian continent to the Pacific Ocean via the Japanese archipelago, which fatally determines the general orientation of radioactive dissemination. Increasingly, people of the US Pacific Northwest have begun to speak up about the present threats of radionuclides from Fukushima to their environments and fisheries.

On the Fukushima side, when TEPCO announced they would release contaminated water from overflowing tanks into the ocean, it was the Fisheries Cooperative Association that most strongly objected. Due to their inherited affinity with the richness of marine activities, fishermen have been most sensitive to the incalculable effects of this release on the future of the planet. Thus, they made an extraordinary effort to fish, not for selling but for grasping the truth of contamination by measuring their catches. They discovered that the seabed mud along the coast and the organisms therein were affected most severely, and that, via the life chain, the fish that fed on them began to disseminate the pollutants.[75] But gradually, pressured by legal stipulation, it turned out that the fishing industries had no other choice but to distribute their catches (the government's standard was again set at 100 Bq/100 kg, while theirs was 50 Bq/100 kg); in order to get compensation for damages, they had to remain engaged in commercial activities.[76]

Herein exists an epitomic manifestation of the Fukushima problematic: the ocean that is the largest portion of the planetary commons and the source of all vital activities in the entire planetary ecosystem is being irreversibly contaminated by radiation—on top of being irreparably devastated by other contaminants such as trash, noise, oil, and carbon emissions. With the Fukushima event, we have reconfirmed that the priority of the capitalist nation-state is to treat the ocean in terms of territoriality, merely for the sake of fishing rights, naval supremacy, and as a dumpsite. In order to protect national economy and sovereignty, the capitalist nation-state would do anything to the biggest commons of planetary inhabitants, even exhausting and contaminating it to the extent of its biological death—which is precisely what is taking place now.

In Japan, the capture of the national economy and sovereignty is effective enough to silence public discourse on the magnitude of the damage that the country is inflicting on the entire planet. It seems that nobody in Japan has initiated collective discussion on the problematic of national/planetary asymmetry. At present, people in Japan are lamenting their own losses and sufferings, but it could be that in the future, they will feel increasingly guilty about the source of unending harms to all planetary inhabitants that their nuclear state has implanted. While no individual commoners can take responsibility for what their nation-state has done, if anybody should change the regime, it would be them.

This is to say, we are living in an age when planetary interconnectivity can no longer be dealt with by the reductionist and divisive politics of capitalist nation-states (the World). In this sense, one of the most radical lessons of the Fukushima nuclear disaster is that, should we change the course of the World away from its processual annihilation, it would be necessary to decompose capitalist nation-states and to create different existential territories, which would establish transnational associations from neighborhood to neighborhood, community to community, bypassing nation-state to nation-state negotiations while constituting singular relationships with the planetary body—environment, terrain, and resources.

Another remarkable development in people's initiatives after Fukushima is that global exchanges among young activists of anarchist or antiauthoritarian veins have been accelerating more than ever. Those involved with the group Amateur Riot have begun to visit and invite individuals and groups active in various places across East Asia: South Korea, Okinawa, Taiwan, Hong Kong, China, and the Philippines. Resonating with the migration of Those Who Go West from eastern Japan to Kyushu, their itinerary draws extensive lines of flight that trace the territoriality of archipelagic Japan, which, as opposed to the isolated territoriality of insular Japan, connects with the Asian continent at multiple points. With the map of these Asian connections in mind, we begin to see how northern Kyushu is located in proximity to the southern tip of the Korean peninsula via the two islands of Tsushima (Japan) and Jeju (South Korea), or how the southern tip of Kysuhu is connected to the Okinawan Islands and then to Taiwan via a line of islets. These exchanges are creating new cartographies that escape the capture of insular territoriality developed and congealed around the Tokyo metropolis.

CHAPTER 2 / *Catastrophic Nation*

ARCHIPELAGO AND INSULAR

In order to examine the spatial and temporal extension of the Fuku-shima revelation, it is necessary to expand the scope from the event of the Fukushima disaster itself to the power composition of the regime that prepared it, and to analyze how this regime nurtured its internal composition in catastrophic relationships, both with planetary move-ments and with the external world, and especially with the United States, former assailant through atoms for war and present partner through at-oms for peace.

This analysis will continue to employ a geophilosophical or geohis-torical view, thereby to see how the primitive mechanism of a communi-ty's autodefensive consolidation—or the "original state" (*Urstaat*)—is institutionalized into the state form in response to catastrophe, while apparatuses of capture are equipped in order to organize its internal composition by subsuming and reorienting the vital energies and de-sires of heterogeneous crowds.[1] It will further employ the concept of the apparatus (*dispositif*), adopted from a line of thought traced through Michel Foucault, Giorgio Agamben, and the French collective Tiqqun, in order to identify varied mechanisms that, in the sense of Deleuze and Guattari, capture energy and desire and crystallize them into in-stitutional forms.[2] These various apparatuses are integrated into a solid nation-state, which is itself the apparatus of apparatuses.

From the geophilosophical/geohistorical view, Japan's primary ap-paratus is nothing other than the geopolitical creation of insularity—or the insularization of an archipelago—from which various other appara-tuses are bifurcated. In the process of modernization, there have been three major catastrophic encounters with the Other that triggered the nation to congeal, expand, and contract again, transforming first from an archipelago into an insularity and then from an insularity into an empire, and then again from an empire back into an insularity.

1. The Tokugawa Shogunate's policy of *sakoku* (national enclosure) strictly limited trade activities and prohibited both foreigners from entering the territory and Japanese from leaving it. In response to the shocking arrival of the West with Christianity and guns, sakoku was instigated around 1633 and remained in implementation until 1853.[3] This enclosure shaped the introverted nature of nationhood that still persists today. As if discovering an antibody to protect an internal organism from invading viruses, sakoku marked the advent of a primary apparatus of capture: insular territoriality as a receptacle to confine a mass corporeality and mind-set that had previously traversed the open space of the archipelago.

2. The Meiji Restoration in 1868 took place in response to intensifying threats from the West across Asia, which had given rise to a nationalist consciousness based on faith in the unbroken line of the emperor. In 1853 the US Navy steamed four warships into Edo Bay and threatened to attack if Japan did not begin trade with the West. The turmoil that ensued in the process of reopening the country's closed door weakened the Shogunate's rule, already overpowered economically and militarily by a coalition of rebellious domains in the south—Satsuma, Choshu, Saga, and Hizen—which pit emperor nationalism against Tokugawa feudalism. The Meiji government restored the emperor system as an absolute monarchy while it strived to realize the chauvinistic slogan *fukoku kyōhei* (wealthy nation and strong soldiers) as quickly as possible, by introducing Western civilization (modern science, technology, industry, and military), in order to prevent, compete with, and overpower the Western colonizers by whose intervention all other Asian nations had been devastated. The emperor system fostered exceptionalism—of a divine race superior in the world—on the soil of introverted nationality. This layered effect facilitated the delusional expansionism of the following decades. The insular territorialization of the archipelago worked paradoxically to facilitate imperialist expansion into the Asian Pacific regions. While the geographical archipelago, ad-

jacent to the Asian continent at multiple points, allowed quick and massive military operations, the introverted mentality of supremacy made the nation disrespect the real existence of the Asian Other. If any, it is this moment which could be called the origin of Japan.

3. Toward the end of World War II, the Imperial Japanese Army was defeated by the Allied Forces in major battles, and its over-stretched front lines were severed everywhere by local resistance. Inside the country, strategic bombings by the US Army Air Force destroyed the infrastructure of all industrial cities; for just one example, after a single night of bombing on March 10, 1945, Tokyo was left with more than 100,000 deaths, 1 million injuries, and 1 million homeless. On August 15, 1945, Japan surrendered unconditionally, after the nuclear genocide at Hiroshima and Nagasaki and the Soviet Union's intervention in the war. The actual use of the new type of bombs influenced the lingering members of the Imperial Conference to accept the Potsdam Declaration of the Allied Forces. So it was that the US government's *irreversible acts* marked the beginning of a new age, when nuclear power dominates both international politics and civil society—as an ultimatum. In this new age, Japan sought to revive its wealth and strength mainly in the economic sector—with the "peaceful" introduction of nuclear power—under the protection and control of the US military.

So it is that the nation has been affected by various kinds of catastrophe, on top of the encounters with the Other: earthquake, tsunami, fire, bombing, economic crisis, pollution, accident, and so on. As we shall see, the monster that Edo/Tokyo has become today has grown in response to these catastrophes—precisely like its illegitimate child, Godzilla—ever renewed, reinforced, and enlarged through the absorption of tremendous amounts of vital energies and desires and their mobilization for various megaprojects in favor of capitalist-state apparatuses.

Thus, the insular apparatus has nurtured various kinds of apparatuses. Tentatively speaking, those that have to do with the formation of the nation-state are insular territoriality, the emperor system, the writing system that grows by absorbing foreign concepts and words, the Thanatos drive of patriotism to orient people's desire into national suicide, the techno-state apparatuses (including the nuclear apparatus) to realize the slogan "wealthy nation and strong soldiers," mass media (in the postwar consumerist society) as a machine of homogenizing discourses, and, finally, Tokyo as an expansive and concentrative movement that absorbs and reorients people's energy and desire for the capitalist-state mode of development. Through the interaction and mutual reinforcement of these apparatuses, Japan's nation-state form has been renewed through every occasion of major catastrophe.

///

Stretching north-south over the fault lines of four tectonic plates, the Japanese archipelago consists of four main islands and thousands of isles and islets in the sea to the east of the Asian continent. This land-sea configuration is a remnant of the Pliocene Epoch, when the Sea of Japan was a mammoth puddle. The spines of the archipelago's islands are the uplift of volcanic activity—sign of imminent cataclysm—since time immemorial. Geological conditions also create the particular ecosystems providing the rich vegetation, densely connected food chains, and ubiquitous hot springs that are cherished by vital activities. The *fire mountain* was thus an object of awe in prestate tribal societies, pairing with its sibling the *boundless ocean*, which, from time to time, assailed the land by storm and tsunami but also granted the fruits of the sea, as well as routes for planetary exchange. The major wind currents, blowing from the plateaus of Siberia and Mongolia toward the archipelago, facilitated sailing long before recorded history. These same currents are now depositing radioactive nuclides from Fukushima into the Pacific Ocean and pushing them toward the Americas.

Japan is a construct in the process of modernization, and the widely shared assumption that the territory of the nation-state was always inhabited by a homogenous people called the Japanese is but a projection of nationalist historiography. In a work that effectively deconstructs the Japanness of Japanese history, historian Amino Yoshihiko (1928–2004) shows how the eastern and western parts of the country followed different patterns of social, political, economic, and cultural development. While the western part was connected to the southern part of the Korean peninsula, the eastern part interacted more with the northern territories of the Asian continent. The inhabitants of the archipelago—commonly thought of as farmers confined to their insular territory—actually included oceanic peoples who were not only fishing but also actively trading and pirating over the smooth space of water, along pathways from river to sea, among series of islands and isles, and between islands and various parts of the continent.[4]

Seeing a map of Japan with this insight, we can easily trace permanent sailing routes from the northern tip of Hokkaido to the Kamchatka Peninsula, from northern Kyushu to the southern part of the Korean peninsula via Jeju and Tsushima islands, and from the southern tip of Kyushu to the Okinawa Islands via a series of isles and islets. This is the *archipelagic space* forbidden to us living today in the age of the nation-state. But we should also remember the fact that this archipelagic space functioned in two conflictual ways: it originally provided people with free and wide spaces of exchange, but later, during the time of imperialist expansion, it facilitated military access to the north and south ends of the Asian continent.

To be precise, insularity is not only Japanese but a universal condition of national territory, which creates an internal space of conformity in response to external pressure. The insular form of the modern nation-state spread like a virus; in consequence, we have this hellish world consisting of nothing but nation-states. This is because for local communities, becoming a nation-state itself was the only way to survive the encounter with the instigator, Western nation-states; if not, communities had to either hide in remoteness or simply disappear. In this sense, the introverted formation of nationhood is not necessarily an instance of isolation but an active response to a foreign power. In the case of Japan, however, its interiority was exceptionally essentialized—as a pure uniformity—in the national spirit because of its geographical features, wherein naturally given coastal lines were directly utilized as a protective national border: the gift of gods (fire mountain and boundless ocean) whose symbolic personification was the emperor.

It appears to us that this geohistorical condition also gave rise to the variation of ontometaphysical ideas all more or less echoing insularity—repository, museum, place, receptacle, nothingness, and so on—which ended up grounding the shared notion of a pure race as well as the ideology of imperial expansion, and which continue to influence the identification of national character in varied forms and contexts.

Okakura Kakuzo (1862–1913), a Japanese aesthetician who established the basis for the collection of Japanese art at the Boston Museum of Fine Arts, was the earliest introducer of Japanese culture to the West through his writings in English.[5] His view of Japan was based on the belief that "Asia is one," the Pan-Asianist slogan that was circulating across Asia during the time of independence movements against Western colonialism. For Okakura, the "privilege of Japan" was to realize "Asian unity-in-complexity." Thanks to its "insular isolation," Japan became "the real repository of the trust of Asiatic thought and culture."[6] He continues: "Thus Japan is a museum of Asiatic civilization; and yet more than a museum, because the singular genius of the race leads to dwell on all phases of the ideals of the past, in that spirit of living Advaitism which welcomes the new without losing the old."[7] Advaita-veda is an offshoot of the Indian monist philosophy of the Upanishads, with an ontology based on the nondual essence of beings. As such, Okakura's nationalism addressed itself less to an internally nurtured essence than to Japan's role as a rich receptacle absorbing heterogeneous Asiatic civilizations thanks to its geographical location, which allowed it throughout history to receive migrating peoples and cultures from the continent.

A little later, Nishida Kitaro (1870–1945), the founder of the Kyoto School, created a philosophy elaborating an ontology around the productivity of nothingness as a kind of rich and active receptacle by developing a series of conceptual frameworks such as the logic of "place," "predicate," "nothing," or the "self-identity of absolute contradictions." As he posits: "The world of reality must be one qua many. It must be the world wherein individual things define each other. This is why I say that the world of reality is self-identity of absolute contradictions."[8] Considered a singular source of inspiration by some, interpreted as an identification of Japanese essence by others, Nishida's philosophy influenced various veins of thought in different disciplines. For instance, inspired by Nishida's ontology, the linguistics of Tokieda Motoki (1900–1967) pointed out a particular grammatical feature of the Japanese language whereby asignifying markers (called *ji*, or particles) encase signifying words (*shi*, nouns and adjectives) and suggested that, thanks to this predicate-led structure, the Japanese language could function as a productive receptacle for subjectivation by intuitive action.[9]

During the time of Japan's expansionism from 1930 to 1945, this line of thought was politically appropriated in the ideology of emperor worship as well as that of the Great East Asia Co-Prosperity Sphere, the propagandistic concept that the empire of Japan designed and promulgated for the populations of the Asian countries it occupied. Declaring the intention to create a self-sufficient "bloc of Asian nations led by the Japanese and free of Western powers," the emphasis of this propaganda was precisely

"Asia is one," namely, Pan-Asian ideals of freedom and independence from Western colonial oppression.[10] It advertised Japan as a common vessel—not as a self-centered ruler—"creating multilateral relations in the Asian community" united in opposition to Western imperialism.

In the postwar period, the representation of Japan as empty receptacle has continuously been amplified in the cultural context. Japan provided the ideal place for Roland Barthes to discover his semiotic paradise, the land of the empty sign wherein everything is a symbol, not for something concrete but for another symbol, or else for emptiness.[11] In the rise of postmodernism debates, Japan was paid special attention to as a kind of ahistorical model, one that mixes everything from everywhere and from all ages, free from any contextual strains, and propagates erotic mutants, as a creative receptacle.[12]

In a sense, it was true that the cultural and intellectual scene of hyperconsumerist society was unprecedentedly growing in the Tokyo metropolis, where flows of crowds from across Japan and East Asia streamed in for work, study, or tourism. Along with its political, economic, academic, and cultural centrality, the source of attraction to the metropolis has been its flow of information and commodities, endlessly introduced from everywhere into the insular enclave, which, after the failure of expansion, was internally densified like a black hole. The Tokyo metropolis has always been the mediator between the empty receptacle and its outside. Meanwhile, the bursting bubble of the 1990s and the series of crises that followed shook the ontometaphysical function of the representation of Japan as an ahistorical receptacle. Then it was the Fukushima catastrophe that gave it a fatal blow by running fissures in the receptacle.

NUCLEAR DOUBLE BIND

Hiroshima and Nagasaki were bombed sequentially on August 6 and August 9, 1945. The actual use of nuclear weapons marked the advent of a new epoch. It created the precedent that every human being now dreads for its possible recurrence, intensification, or diffusion. It changed not only the mode of warfare and international power relations but also the view of the world shared among people in many nations. It changed the existential horizon of the human world in an irreversible manner.

The destructive capacity of the bombs was unprecedented: the estimated death toll by explosion alone was 140,000 in Hiroshima and

70,000 in Nagasaki. It came to be known that the explosion would exert unending aftereffects on vital activities by radiation. The surviving
victims suffered from irremediable radiation illnesses such as leukemia
and keloid. Furthermore, their children and grandchildren continue to
suffer from hereditary effects caused by genetic mutation.

These genocidal attacks seem to have been motivated more by experimental purposes than by strategic considerations; different fission
substances were tried in Hiroshima (uranium) and Nagasaki (plutonium). A number of critiques have questioned whether this atrocious
experimentation would have ever targeted Western nations, if even such
enemies as Germany and Italy were not too close, if it were not only an
enemy in the territory of the Asian Other at the far end of the Pacific
Ocean that could be subjected to such atrocity. Beginning from these
bombings, Japan became an elaborate island laboratory for US global
strategy.

The new type of bomb transformed the spatiotemporality of warfare. The age of the nuclear arms race led by the United States arrived,
wherein the logistics of speed and movement were more determinant
than those of holding and expanding territories; this tendency was further consolidated along with the development of projectiles. In accordance, the territoriality of the American empire came to consist of a
network of points (islands and small bases) rather than the expanse of
a plane (land over continents) that previous empires occupied. In this
new paradigm, the Japanese archipelago became particularly vital for
the United States to settle into for confrontation against its enemies on
the Asian continent.

The American empire took hegemony over much of the territory
in the Pacific and in Southeast Asia that the former Japanese empire had
claimed. From its front line of military bases across the Japanese archipelago, the United States and its capitalist allies began to collide with
the national liberation forces backed by the socialist bloc in consolidation. The end of the Asia-Pacific War and the beginning of the new wars
in East Asia occurred one after another without much pause. In the view
of World History, these were equal to the closure of the open space of
the Pacific Ocean by nuclear warfare, which was second to the fifteenth-
century closure of the open space of the Atlantic Ocean by triangular
trade. There was no more substantially large open space remaining on
the planet, and yet the expansion of the World by capitalist nation-states
persisted with increasing participants in power contestation.

It has been three-quarters of a century since the Hiroshima and Nagasaki genocide. The two cities are fully reconstructed, with memorial museums and monuments where many visitors learn and commemorate their tragic histories. Annual ceremonies attract the sympathetic attention of people across the world. Notwithstanding all this, the events can hardly be deemed over. Suffering continues among victims' descendants. The nuclear arms race never ceases. The cathartic process of mourning has never reached a conclusion. Especially after the Fukushima disaster, many of us feel that we have not settled accounts with the magnitude and complexity of nuclear things.

In the society of postwar Japan, a counternarrative to the tragic memories of World War II—including Hiroshima and Nagasaki especially—was emblematized in two terms: peace and democracy. Through publicly shared perception, the majority of Japanese people embraced these ideals as symbols for their new society, a society that would never repeat the mistake of letting a fascist, militarist, and totalitarian regime lead the nation to war. But despite their significance, these ideals were quickly captured by US/Japan nuclear promoters as a catchphrase for development, construing the peaceful use of nuclear energy for the future of the democratic society. The lesser-spoken fact about both *peace* and *democracy* is that they were originally introduced to the defeated nation during the postwar occupation as the main clauses of its new constitution, all part of the US strategy to pacify and rule the devastated nation. Following US directives, the postwar Japanese government adopted peace and democracy as a political frame to recapture heterogeneous crowds within the insular territory, especially crucial at that moment right after the collapse of the doomed empire, when those crowds could potentially develop impetuses for rebellion. Before people in Japan were able to find a way to realize the ideals of peace and democracy according to their own desire and necessity, they were employed preemptively by the nation-states of the United States and Japan to facilitate governance and development. This is why, among the general public, peace remained a mere prayer, while democracy meant nothing but parliamentary politics—excepting the rise of anti–US base struggles, anti–Vietnam War movements during the 1960s, and antiauthoritarian or horizontalist organizing among autonomous groups thereafter. Thus, with the symbols of peace and democracy, the insular territory came to be double-bound by the two faces of nuclear power—weapon and energy—until the Fukushima catastrophe tore it apart.

///

The catastrophic defeat of World War II prepared the formation of the postwar regime, which professed to create a democratic, peaceful, economically thriving, and middle-class-centered society. These goals indicated a significant reorientation away from the previous regime. However, the new society sustained vexing remnants of its historically accumulated strata, embodied as they were by mutated apparatuses of capture.

The insular apparatus continues to confine the national territory, now doubly territorialized by the political, economic, and military interests of the United States. The emperor apparatus lost its sovereign power but so much so that it began to exert a softer and more permeating power—the capture of bodies and minds of the nation—by circulating itself into everyday reproduction through mass media. Tacitly inheriting the will to "wealthy nation and strong soldiers," the techno-political apparatus—epitomized by nuclear technology—continues to play a role as it captures inhabitants in a double bind between the memory of genocide and the dreamy future of technological advancement. The mass media and consumerist apparatuses have flourished dramatically along with high economic growth. And it turned out that Tokyo, once bombed down to ashes, could make a miraculous recovery while connecting all other apparatuses through its expansive and concentrative impetuses.

National conformity is assured now under the control and protection of US global strategy, wherein no political or economic decisions can be made without regard for US interests. Now, for the nation, the world primarily means America. The intellectual historian Harry Harootunian speaks of American occupation policies in terms of "the cruel, mad, but 'masterful physiologist' Dr. Moreau in his island laboratory but on a scale never imagined in H. G. Wells's novel." As he explains: "Occupation authorities envisaged Japan as a vast social and political laboratory, dedicated to 'experiments' that would lead to changing and altering the deepest behavioral and institutional patterns of society."[13] It was this experimentation that gave America the prototype for its subsequent interventions in the extra-Western world, though none has ever gone quite so smoothly as it did in the insular laboratory.

The first thing that the General Headquarters (GHQ) of the Occupation Army did after its arrival in 1945 was to instigate total information control with the Press Code, which outlawed any expression that was critical toward the Occupation Army or might provoke resentment against Allied countries. Crucially, there was no freedom of reporting or exchanging information on the treatment of atomic-bomb sickness; this policy was responsible for countless misdiagnoses. Not to mention that no information on the bombing was allowed in the media. This information control was only lifted in 1952 by the Treaty of San Francisco.

In the postoccupation period, testing of the consequences of the experimental bombings was conducted on the bodies of their casualties. The Atomic Bomb Casualty Commission (ABCC) was founded in 1944 under the auspices of the US Atomic Energy Commission. Considering the post–Hiroshima and Nagasaki situation as a "unique opportunity to systematically investigate radiation effects on the human body," the ABCC began to investigate the hereditary effects of radiation and radiation's effects on children. From 1948 to 1953, the bodies of more than seventy-five thousand casualties were tested in Hiroshima and Nagasaki.[14] Suspicions against this project quickly surfaced among the victims and the general public in Japan because it was conducted by an institution of the assailant country—an institution made for the perfection of nuclear weapons. The victims were treated as guinea pigs and not as patients entitled to treatment for their ongoing sufferings. After all, the organization was erected purely for scientific research, not as a provider of medical care. In 1975 the ABCC and a branch of the Ministry of Health and Welfare of Japan established the Radiation Effects Research Foundation (RERF) in Hiroshima and Nagasaki, funded by both American and Japanese governments in order to succeed the mission of the ABCC. The RERF revealed its incapacity while facing the Fukushima disaster because of its inherited attitude of paying attention only to the effects of external radiation. In 2017—seventy-two years after Hiroshima and Nagasaki—the organization finally made a public apology on the nature of the investigations that its predecessor conducted after the war.[15]

Throughout the occupation, GHQ instigated a number of experiments for democratic reform, including the decomposition of *zaibatsu* (mammoth business conglomerates), the democratization of labor policy (Trade Union Act / Labor Standards Act), the liberalization of education, land reform (decentralization of land ownership), and the release of political prisoners incarcerated during the war (communists and socialists). In the big picture, these reforms sought to eliminate Japan's war potential and to turn it into a democratic capitalist nation. This process nevertheless involved a hind side: to make the archipelago a front-line of military bases for confronting the new Cold War enemy on the Asian continent. The Sea of Japan thus became the forefront of all US interventions over air and water.

The new constitution came into force in 1947. It was allegedly drafted by the Japanese government in 1946, but under the threatening pressure of the Supreme Commander for the Allied Powers (SCAP), General Douglas A. MacArthur, including his demand to make it look like the will of the Japanese.[16] The constitution included two distinctive sections that have confined Japan's political horizon in insularity up until this day: the symbolic emperor system (Article 1) and the peace clause (Article 9). Both of these were designed by SCAP in negotiation with the remnants of Imperial Japan—*never by the will of the people.*

Emperor Hirohito (1901–89), along with other first-class war criminals, was exempted from trial and persecution and kept on the throne as symbol rather than sovereignty. Both Japanese and American rulers believed this to be necessary in order to prevent the national body from decomposing and heterogeneous crowds from rising up. For the people, the transition from defeat to the new constitution was the missed moment for taking initiative to determine their future by their own subjectivation—rather than by their submission.

The emperor and his family members—the Imperial Household—declared against deity and began to appear in public to perform their living roles. In the age of mass media, they appeared as the incarnation of mercy, love, humility, and diligence, sharing joy and sorrow with the nation. Thereby the Imperial Household became an apparatus in and of itself, to effectively capture the mind-set of the insular nation. On the one hand, it models the behavior of good citizens in a democratic nation-state, while on the other, it acts as a spiritual guardian of identity, sustaining the historical construction of a superior race.

Under the protection and control of the United States, the Japanese government came to focus on economic growth in order to sustain and reinforce its national might, via a transference of its organic desire for expansion from war to industry. Within the island laboratory, economic growth turned out to be the most effective means of governance. Through the fluctuating situations of the Korean and Vietnam wars, Japanese industries enjoyed opportunities for timely profit making by the wars' special demands, during the period of recovery from Japan's

66   Chapter Two

own war. Meanwhile the Self-Defense Forces, whose role was originally restricted to the passive protection of the territory, have been gradually extended and are now approaching a normal military. The constitutional clause of "abandonment of war" has been subtly amended by the nationalist sector in the government. For the people, however, this clause continues to play a crucial role, freeing them from military draft and any engagement in war. They have been so accustomed to it that they have come to feel as if it symbolized their own will to world peace. Or rather, understandably, they have developed the will to protect it as their stronghold against the return of another militaristic regime.

In parliamentary politics, too, the marks of US interests remain inscribed, as the US persists in holding tight to its most ideal client state in the world. This gives the ruling power (the Liberal Democratic Party) its ambivalent nature: unable to move out from under US protection and control and constantly attending to its moods, the ruling power nevertheless seeks to strengthen its sovereignty and to make the nation-state wealthier and stronger by reforming the constitution step by step. Meanwhile, the role of progressive and liberal parties (communist, socialist, social democratic, etc.) is confined, more or less, to protecting the peace constitution with its ideal of a *one-nation pacifism* that could be realized only in an insular nation. The contradictions between serving American expansionism and keeping a peaceful enclave have always been passed on to people in the vicinity of US military bases, including those in Okinawa, Jeju Island, and the Korean peninsula, living in the presence of arms as well as environmental destruction by the military–industrial complex.

///

Postwar political and social arrangements came to be entrapped by nuclear power with its Janus-faced function: weapon and energy. Amid the formation of these arrangements with the slogans of peace and democracy, nuclear energy was introduced by a collaborative scheming among Japanese and American industrialists, scientists, and governments into the civilian life that had just experienced atomic genocide.

The antinuclear feeling was consistently strong after Hiroshima and Nagasaki, but it was meticulously twisted by industrial ambition and tragically split by political ideologies. The campaign to promote atomic power began as early as 1946. Propagating discourses and images aimed at turning the dystopian memory of the bomb into a utopian dream of the future, it circulated cunning logics of persuasion: with the creation of the absolute weapon there will be no more war, thanks to its deterrence; the peaceful use of nuclear power makes the bright future of humanity; the peaceful use of nuclear power must begin in Hiroshima, the victim of the nuclear weapon. Hiroshima mayor Hamai Shinzo (serving 1947–55 and 1959–67) said that a nuclear plant in the first atom-bombed city in the world would serve as a tribute to the deceased victims; he was sure that his citizens would welcome it.[17]

In 1953 the United States instigated the "Atoms for Peace" policy, advocated by the Dwight D. Eisenhower administration in order to quell global antagonism against nuclear weapons and US foreign intervention. Technically, its aim was to maintain US nuclear dominance after the loss of its monopoly by placing the international transfer of enriched uranium and other nuclear materials under the control of an international organization (the International Commission on Radiological Protection [ICRP]) subject to US control. Japanese men in power, who had long dreamed of Japan's own nuclear development, responded enthusiastically behind closed doors.[18] Thus, bombastic campaigns were orchestrated for the US/Japan joint conspiracy to promote nuclear power to the mediatized masses by disseminating images of an ideal energy of the future, including pronuclear animations produced by Walt Disney.[19] Central Intelligence Agency (CIA) agents operating within the Liberal Democratic Party and major media outlets such as Yomiuri Shimbun and Nippon Television Network Corporation led the campaigns to manipulate the popular mind-set by taking advantage of the social atmosphere amid economic growth and the advent of mass media.[20] The tactical goal was to shift the public dread of nuclear bombs and anger at the United States to the dream of an almighty energy source and aspiration for a middle-class heaven—from the dystopian to the utopian sublime of the nuclear. This was how the ideals of peace and democracy were mutated by the nuclear Janus head.

Another objective of introducing the "peaceful" use of nuclear energy was the suppression of a massive surge in the antinuclear movement that arose after the Lucky Dragon Incident of March 1954, wherein a Japanese tuna fishing boat—not to mention countless Marshall Islanders— was exposed to nuclear fallout from the US Castle Bravo thermonuclear device test on Bikini Atoll.[21] This surge contained two corresponding oppositional currents: anti-imperialism (against the United States) and anti–nuclear weapon. Its first wave was initiated by a group of women in Tokyo's Suginami Ward who organized a signature campaign that quickly spread nationwide, collecting more than thirty million signatures. The surge of the anti–nuclear weapon movement grew so intense as to force the general resignation of the Eisaku Satō administration, which played proxy to the United States and its expansionism. In 1955 in Hiroshima, the Japan Council Against Atomic and Hydrogen Bombs (Gensuikyo) was established, backed by a coalition of progressive, liberal political parties and labor unions.[22] This created a prototype for the large-scale antinuclear movement that seeks to influence public opinion, parliamentary politics, and international organizations through rallies, conferences, petitions, signature collecting, and public education.

Soon after the anti-US/Japan Security Treaty uprising in 1960, however, Gensuikyo faced a crisis and finally split along politico-ideological lines, as it was forced to confront a new situation: what position the anti–nuclear weapon movement should take toward nuclear weapons testing by socialist countries. The Soviet Union's 1961 announcement that it would resume nuclear testing shocked the movement and resulted in severe internal discord. Those Gensuikyo members associated with the Japan Communist Party held that the movement should not protest the Soviet Union, asserting that its nuclear arms were necessary to deter the United States from unleashing nuclear war—and, therefore, that they were necessary for peace. Meanwhile, Sohyo (General Council of Trade Unions of Japan)—in alliance with the Japan Socialist Party, along with most other groups—opposed the imposition of this ideological line and insisted that nuclear bomb testing by any country should be opposed.

In 1965 Sohyo left Gensuikyo and established Gensuikin (Japan Congress against A- and H-Bombs), a new antinuclear and antiwar movement. In addition to opposing nuclear testing by any nation, Gensuikin gradually expanded its problematization of nuclear power to include the destructive effects of radiation on the environment and vital activities, affected by the escalating environmental destruction and pollution occurring due to high economic growth. In the early 1970s, local inhabitants' struggles against the construction of nuclear plants took place across the country, increasing the need for networks of antinuclear (both weapon and energy) and antidevelopment struggles. In response, Gensuikin sought to take on this role.

Meanwhile, there appeared divergences among the positions of intellectuals vis-à-vis nuclear power and its dual function. During the 1960s, the campaigns for the peaceful use of nuclear energy were dramatically successful, and nuclear optimism permeated the insular nation. A number of progressive and liberal scholars and novelists—including celebrated novelist Oe Kenzaburo and prominent physicist and Marxist Taketani Mitsuo (1911–2000)—promoted the positive prospects of nuclear energy. Taketani insisted on a policy of restarting nuclear research, on the condition that it follow the three basic principles of autonomy, democracy, and public disclosure and that it be limited to peaceful purposes. He argued that "nuclear power is now a fact of life" and that "if we do not pay close attention to its peaceful use, we will fall behind the rest of the world."[23] Oe was adamant in opposing nuclear weapons, no matter whether they were developed by capitalists or socialists. But he fostered a naive hope in nuclear energy, as "it embodies the new life of humans." Kurihara Sadako (1913–2005), a poet and survivor of the Hiroshima bomb, radically criticized his position: "While Mr. Oe sees mass extinction in Hiroshima and Nagasaki, he cannot see the nuclear workers whose deaths by radiation exposure are always denied by the disclaimer made under the pressure of nuclear enterprises, that the causality is unclear." As Kurihara stressed, such nuclear optimism ended up facilitating the schemes of nuclear promoters, for whom "curing the nuclear allergy of the Japanese people" was necessary in order to push forward with nuclear development.[24]

The reintroduction of nuclear power was thus realized. Today there are fifty-four nuclear power plants in fourteen locations across the archipelago as well as an unknown number of nuclear warheads (on US military bases). However, one should not forget that since the 1970s, the inhabitants of *at least twenty-seven* regions have successfully ousted nuclear installments through their unyielding opposition.[25] Under the shadow of mediatized protests in big cities, the achievements of these local struggles have not been much acknowledged. Thus, we should also stress that nuclear plants have been built in *only* fourteen locations, despite the intense efforts of pronuclear conspirators in the governments of both the United States and Japan.

Muto Ichiyo, a longtime political activist and theorist since the early antinuclear and antiwar movements, articulates three elements or desires that implanted and sustain nuclear power in Japan: the "peaceful use of atomic energy" as an integral part of the US hegemonic strategy, in particular, as a psychological warfare strategy administered to counter the influence of the anti–nuclear weapon movement in the 1950s; the ambitions of postwar Japanese conservative political forces to make and possess nuclear weapons and accordingly change the pacifist constitution; and the adoration of, and cravings for, scientific and technological progress, coupled with a modernization ideology, that were shared by a large number of scientists and intellectuals who espoused progressive social trends.[26] From a geohistorical standpoint, the context that allowed these three elements to converge was the insularized territory of postwar Japan. In other words, it was only within the island laboratory of Japan that the experimentation of US global strategy was able to achieve such miraculous success—by mobilizing both the local collaborators' will to "wealthy nation and strong soldiers" and the progressivists' hope for the advancement of science and technology for the nation. The lesson here is that the third element, scientific and technological progress, can never take place in and of itself as a machinic process but always develops in tandem with the will to "wealthy nation and strong soldiers," or with the capitalist-state mode of development.

In Japan, the progressive techno-state apparatus was nurtured during the early phase of modernization between the late Edo period and the Meiji Restoration, and it has been operating continuously since then. The science historian and 1960s student movement organizer Yamamoto Yoshitaka describes this progression well:

> In the late Edo Period, Japan was enlightened by Western science and technology. Beginning from the Meiji Era, the new government began to absorb them, which supported the nation's modernization and economic growth. Modernization was progressed by collaboration among central authorities, industrial society, and the military and imperial universities, all sharing the goals of economic development and technoscientific progress. The postwar reconstruction was a continuation of this impetus.
>
> The will to "wealthy nation and strong soldiers" in the Meiji Era was succeeded by "construction of an advanced defense state" advocated by the total mobilization regime during the war, and then inherited by "high economic growth for international competition" in the postwar period.
>
> This ideology constructed by the government/industry/military/ academia collaboration was the progressivism tacitly backed by a jin-

goistic nationalism. This was emphatically characterized by a fanatic faith in technoscientific development. From the Meiji Era to today, the nation has consistently been faithful to this proposition: it is new scientific discoveries and technological renovations that trigger the increase of production and economic growth, thus the improvement of people's living condition, and ultimately the realization of social development and civilizational progress.[27]

This explanation speaks to the fact that in Japan's modern history, what really persists untouched throughout regime changes has been the faith in technoscientific progress shared by both the nationalists and the liberalists, by both the right and the left. And it is the Tokyo metropolis that provides this faith with limitless sources of inspiration by introducing them from abroad, and also the most effective stage of operation by way of assembling all other apparatuses that constitute the insular nationhood.

TOKYO APPARATUS, TOKYO MACHINE

One of the most significant effects of the Fukushima catastrophe was the cancellation of an expectation that the majority of the populace had tacitly shared: that Tokyo will live forever. After Fukushima, many began to sense the beginning of the end of Tokyo. The matter was not a question of when, but the awareness that at a point in the future, the end of the metropolis will come by the slow permeation of radionuclides. This turn of events was a bolt out of the blue for those who had witnessed Tokyo's unilateral expansion since they were born, and whose life activities had been totally based on it. This shift made us perceive the universal truth—that the material end of a civilization is a predetermined course of events—in the concrete context of nuclear disaster.

In the early 1960s, when I was still in infancy, my mother and I migrated to the Tokyo metropolis from Okayama City, located in southwestern Honshu. This was before the Shinkansen, but it was already the time of high-speed economic growth and the unprecedented transformations of urban space and transportation systems. In a new living environment, I was shocked by its monstrous scale and velocity of activities; I was intimidated by the atmosphere of pride that excluded a country boy like me who did not speak the Tokyo dialect, that is, standard Japanese.

I was perplexed by the multiplicity of urban features, as I realized that Tokyo actually consisted of a number of internalized towns (satellite cities)—Ueno, Asakusa, Ikebukuro, Shinjuku, Shibuya, and others— all comprising heterogeneous zones from messy slums to historic sites to neat residences to clean business blocks, all of which embody visible traces of their different origins, their various historicities and regionalities. This was telling of the fact that the majority of Tokyoites were originally migrants, or their descendants.

Finally, I came to be fascinated by the impetus of development, rushing toward the unknown with the endless introduction of the new, such as big spectacles, futuristic buildings, transportation systems, and electric appliances. Even such common households as ours began to be equipped with TV sets and refrigerators, if not air conditioners and cars. Walt Disney animations and Hollywood movies were shown on seventy-millimeter-wide screens. For the 1964 Tokyo Olympics, the mega streamline of the Yoyogi National Gymnasium was under construction. Tokyo dwellers were intoxicated by the fact that an international sports event of this magnitude was happening soon in their city. In elementary schools, kids were studying English, expecting they would soon communicate with foreign visitors.

Meanwhile, the city space was increasingly polluted by exhaust and congested by overpopulation; traffic jams and overcrowded commuter trains became part of the everyday landscape. On the street, the tensions of class division stood out. I began to notice differences among passersby: white collar (office worker), blue collar (engineer or factory worker), and no collar (informal worker). The harshest division seemed to derive from these workers' origins: middle to upper classes came from Tokyo while the underclass came from the countryside. Crude parents used this categorization to teach their children about success and failure in life. The last category included dramatically increasing numbers of migrants from the countryside, moving to do the low-paid jobs that Tokyoites would rather avoid, mostly in the service, sanitation, and construction industries.

During the agricultural off-season, needy peasants migrated to Tokyo in order to find temporary and informal jobs in construction, dock work, or road repair (and later, in the nuclear industry). Junior high school graduates from the countryside—called "golden eggs"—were sent to Tokyo in groups to be recruited for live-in jobs in small factories, restaurants, newspaper delivery, and so forth. Tokyo was desperately in want of innocent, cheap, and disposable labor power for its unprecedented expansion during the high economic growth.

Seasonal workers were either assembled in groups to live in the dormitories of construction sites or they went individually to the day laborers' ghetto called Sanya, to find a bed in a flophouse during their temporary stay. This particular ghetto was notorious among middle- to upper-class Tokyoites as a no-go zone because of its poverty, messiness, crime, and, most of all, its periodic riots that challenged the order of civil society.

My childhood happened to overlap with the decade of the 1960s. These were schizophrenic years, when the capitalist-state mode of development achieved dramatic upsurge, while intensifying oppositions against it were permeating the archipelago. Tokyo provided the youth with conflicting impetuses: miraculous development, intense street fighting, and information on everything from everywhere, including ongoing revolutions and rising countercultures. In many senses, I believe I was really educated by Tokyo rather than by any academic institution. Many friends and I developed an ambivalent feeling about the city. We loved and hated Tokyo. In a sense, we had been entrapped by it. But now Tokyo's binding force is waning. Fukushima crushed it.

What is Tokyo? Tokyo is material and immaterial. It is space and force, a particular place and an expansive movement at the same time. After all, its substance is nothing but the desire and energy of people. In an abstract and machinic term, it is an assembly of energo-signaletic flows: labor, information, and capital. In other words, Tokyo's body is substantiated by aspirations and struggles for happiness. Tokyo is a space wherein people's power is concentrated more than anywhere else. And this is the very power that the state necessitates for realizing its projects of governance, development, and expansion. Herein another, official function of Tokyo intervenes, that is, to serve the state's projects in two ways: facilitating them by regulating flows of labor, information, and capital as well as by emblematizing them as the capital city.

Historically, the city has always grown larger by absorbing the currents of migrants kicked out of their homes by catastrophe: natural disaster, economic crisis, or primitive accumulation. Tokyo is always fed by catastrophe. There is a twist or duplicity in Tokyo's growth. What destroys the subsistence of locals are often infrastructural developments and financial operations that are part of Tokyo's expansion; in turn, Tokyo absorbs those who lose their subsistence and become migrants by the attraction of well-paid work, rich culture, or central authority.

The migrants who flowed into Tokyo from various places in Japan and East Asia created their settlements or ghettos in downtown areas, which housed chaotic aggregations of the so-called industrial reserve army. These areas were marginalized by municipal zoning, to be clearly detached from well-ordered residential areas. These marked places historically provided capital with the cheapest and most disposable labor power for large-scale developments, as they provided the state with foot soldiers for its wars of aggression. In this sense, Tokyo has consistently been the biggest laboratory for the Japanese capitalist nation-state to experiment with the best means to realize "wealthy nation and strong soldiers."

Thus Tokyo always assumes two functions, in two existential dimensions at the same time. On the one hand, it is a machine of desire that works as a gigantic converter, shifting orientations and quantities of energo-signaletic flows. On the other hand, it is an apparatus that captures energo-signaletic flows by entrapping them in territorialized zones. Tokyo is deterritorializing and reterritorializing at once.

///

Tokyo is located in the rich and vast Kanto Plain spanning seventeen thousand square kilometers; it is a humongous urban space by Tokyo Bay where several rivers stream into the Pacific Ocean. The city that was called Edo was built around the old fortress of a local lord—Ota Dokan (1432–86)—to become the capital of the regime of the Tokugawa Shogunate, which centralized control over the feudal domains by requiring the lords to live in Edo every other year. When in 1867 the feudal rule of the Shogunate was replaced by absolute monarchy, Edo became Tokyo (meaning "eastern capital") and the emperor was relocated from the older capital of Kyoto. Ever since, Tokyo has been considered the center of politics, culture, science, and all other disciplines that embody progress and authority, while the Kansai area, including Osaka and Kyoto, has continued to represent "good old Japan." It is not too much of an exaggeration to say that Tokyo as an apparatus produced the national subjectivity of modern Japan. While Osaka sustained Asiatic heterogeneity in its mass corporeality, more and more Tokyo became the center of homogeneous nationhood.

With both the Imperial Palace and the central government, Tokyo gradually developed the self-consciousness of being the nation's center. The language used in the residential area of its upper class—the Yamanote dialect—was designated the national language, which was authenticated by grammartization and propagated through textbooks and later through the media network of NHK, all the while marginalizing innumerable colloquial speaking machines (dialects). At the same time, the majority of the main academic institutions were established in Tokyo. From the metropolis, lines of transportation began to stretch outward. Capital investment was increasingly concentrated there. Waves of migration from the countryside streamed in. The capital city became the door to global politics and economy. The development of Tokyo began to determine the course of the nation vis-à-vis global power contestations. Thus the exceptionalist consciousness of Tokyo was implanted in the minds of both metropolitan and countryside inhabitants.

Tokyo, however, was never a well-planned, ordered urban space. Visitors are shocked to find that much of residential Tokyo actually resembles the low-rise, high-density habitats normally associated with cities in the Global South. Beside the futuristic visage of skyscraper Tokyo, densely populated villages lie along rambling roads and alleys, haphazardly connecting the main avenues and boulevards where mom-and-pop stores sell soap and sandals; innumerable small restaurants and bars provide street food such as oden, yakitori, okonomiyaki, and ramen; and private homes double and triple. Once you get lost in the labyrinths of these downtown residential areas, it is impossible to find the address you are looking for without asking a local for help. As already mentioned, inside the metropolitan area, there are a number of satellite cities (towns) with varied atmospheres embodying the origins of residents, all interconnected in haphazard ways.

Tokyo covers only 3.5 percent of the entire territory of Japan, but it accommodates more than one-fourth of its population. Two-thirds of the nation's total capital is concentrated there. In this sense, Tokyo is a movement not only of expansion but also of condensation. It is an apparatus to gulp the desiring machines of the archipelago, at the same time as it expands its apparatuses to the external regions. Its movements have a history of becoming dramatically quick and pronounced, especially when triggered by catastrophic events. The metropolis has always fed itself with disasters for its enlargement, reconstruction, and condensation.

In the Edo period (1603–1868), there was a vogue phrase, "fire and brawl are flowers of Edo," which speaks to the intriguing fact that seeing catastrophe as festivity was popular among Edo dwellers. In fact, Edo was known for its frequent incident of fire at various scales. It is said that one of the biggest troubles that triggered the collapse of the Shogunate government was the Great Ansei earthquake of 1855, which caused some seven thousand to ten thousand deaths and destroyed fourteen thousand buildings.

In the age of Tokyo, the Great Kanto earthquake of 1923 destroyed a large area that included the metropolis, causing one hundred thousand deaths and innumerable missing persons. During this seismic calamity came social atrocity: vigilantes captured and massacred thousands of resident ethnic Koreans and Chinese, as well as socialists, labor organizers, and anarchists.[28] Rumors spread that Koreans and Chinese would riot in Tokyo, in reverberation with the uprisings in their homelands. Police and military played a leading role; some neighborhood organizations of civilians were also involved in the massacre.[29]

Due to the devastation of Tokyo, large sums of bank notes turned default. Relief loans from the Bank of Japan could not prevent a recession. Then in 1929 the Great Depression hit, badly affecting the agricultural sector, especially in the Tohoku region. These synergetic effects accelerated the reorganization of the social body into a totalitarian machine, ready for the war of aggression. What followed thereafter were two big catastrophes: the Tokyo bombings during World War II and the Tohoku earthquake and tsunami in 2011.

Tokyo thus inscribes the traces of catastrophe. Speaking of the urban space, catastrophic events result in a substantially congealed unevenness between well-invested, redeveloped zones and unplanned, piecemeal, and irregular zones. The former roughly correspond to the central area and the "upper town" (*yamanote*), that is, to the government, financial, and wealthy residential zones, while the latter exist "downtown" (*shita-machi*) and in the peripheries, that is, in industrial zones, poorer neighborhoods, and ghettos such as Sanya.

But in microdimension, unevenness spreads more or less everywhere across the metropolitan area, like a macular pattern, due to both recurring catastrophe and the absence of any thorough and clear zoning. After calamities, in poor and middle-class areas, it has been mostly inhabitants themselves who have rebuilt homes and neighborhoods, without much government support. As Kon Wajiro (1888–1972), pioneer of a branch of urban sociology called modernology (*kogengaku*), observed in the wake of the Great Kanto earthquake: "The shacks that appear amid the burned-down city initiate reconstruction from the disaster: these are the *perpetual organs* of the Metropolis."[30] Omnipresently internalizing these self-generated organs, the growth of Tokyo can never be fully controlled. In a larger scheme, we also detect the unplanned growth of a number of satellite townships in peripheries, forming the constellation of the metropolis. This aspect of Tokyo—its self-generation, its becoming—I would attribute not to its apparatus but to *Tokyo machines*. If so, the Tokyo metropolis consists of two ontological strata: machine and apparatus.

The immaterial traces of catastrophe are seen in collective memory. In a nation whose history inscribes the memories of catastrophe—periodic earthquakes, the total defeat of an all-front war, the nuclear attacks at Hiroshima and Nagasaki, and so forth—apocalyptic representations obsessively appear as collective imaginaries in films, comics, anime, and literature, as if people are expecting the return of such rupture. The dystopian images in these works seem to be more or less taken from Tokyo experiences: for example, the gap between spectacular high-tech city and chaotic slum, or biosocial mutation after apocalyptic rupture, not to mention class wars generating the movement of collective corporeality, toward either condensation or dispersion.

In 1980 Shiba Ryotaro (1923–96), the prolific, popular, and conservative novelist known for his innumerable epics of Japanese historical figures, saw the root of crises in contemporary Japan in the lack of policy and reckless commodification of the land.

> Since 1955, pathological symptoms have begun to appear in the land of Japan. But they have appeared simultaneously with other malignant symptoms affecting all aspects of society, including individual morality. We were thus captured by their particular appearances and kept busy tackling them, mostly unaware of the fact that the root cause of all these issues existed in the absurdity and ambiguity of land tenure.
>
> Unbelievable as it may be, the entirety of land in Japan has not yet been registered as title deeds. It is well-known that more than 70 percent of the territory is occupied by mountains and forests, most of which have not been surveyed. Even the records used in government offices are based upon measurements taken by eye, these having existed since the Edo period or even before.

The most extensive land survey was the one conducted by Toyo-tomi Hideyoshi (1537–98) during the 1590s, which was his most am-bitious project. It is marvelously large and accurate even by today's standards. However, the object of survey was limited to agricultural lands, which were only about 20 percent of the territory, leaving mountains and forests alone, as they were untaxable.

The Meiji Restoration came, but even in the time of such transfor-mation, mountains and forests were left out, and no new land policy was instigated. Thereafter during the land reform instituted by the US occupation army after the defeat (1945), it was only the owner-ship of farming land that was evened out. Even today, mapping is still based on that established by Hideyoshi's survey in the late sixteenth century.

Heated capital investment began around the mid-1950s, more as uncontrolled competition among companies than as a precisely planned project. This situation was never critically scrutinized even after the problematic phase arose, that is, the rise of property value—especially that of land acquired for factory sites—which itself was considered as the achievement of the executives, rather than the suc-cess of their industrial investments per se. . . . Such stimulation radi-cally changed the economic mind-set of the Japanese, resulting in the atmosphere where the entire population came to behave like real estate brokers.[31]

In other words, the desire of the nation was concentrated on the land as property, captured as it was by the real estate apparatus. Shiba's view was based on his faith in "good capitalism" realized by "healthy produc-tion" and the state's fair taxation of land. In other words, he believed in the national ownership of land in order to realize a production-based capitalism; he did not see the primitive process of capital's accumulation that severs land and people time and again, in different critical phases. Nonetheless, Shiba makes an interesting discovery about the missing link in land surveys: mountains and forests. Indeed, these ended up be-ing the very target of ungoverned investment and development across the archipelago during postwar economic reconstruction. Thus in Ja-pan, the main commodity that determines the value of all commodities has become land.

In postwar Japan, there were two major policies for colossal rede-velopments: one that provoked the Tokyo-ization of Japan and another that focused on the Japanization of Tokyo. The former was the "Re-modeling of the Japanese Archipelago" plan by Prime Minister Tanaka Kakuei in 1972. The objective was to diffuse a flow of humans and money from big cities to the countryside by way of facilitating the re-distribution of industries and national networks of transportation and information. This project was responsible for initiating the transforma-tion of the landscape toward its homogenization, on the one hand, and the maximal provocation of tourist desire, on the other—which still sustains Japan's intraterritorial commodification.[32] The latter was the "Fourth Comprehensive National Development Plan" by another prime minister, Nakasone Yasuhiro, in 1987. This was a two-pronged plan: its basic slogan was "formation of multipolar, disperse territory," but at the same time, it defined Tokyo as one of the core cities of the world, with its superior function in the distribution of information and the develop-ment of global economy. In consequence, the plan came to promote the massive concentration of capital for the development of the Tokyo Bay area. This development initiated an increase in Tokyo's population, or rather its "one point concentration," during the 1990s. Certainly, along with capital concentration and population increase came the massive privatization of state institutions and the dramatic increase of informal workers roaming the streets of Tokyo.

Since then, the Tokyo apparatus has been continuously reinforced. A combination bridge/tunnel called the Tokyo Bay Aqua-Line connects two major industrial zones that used to be separated by Tokyo Bay (Ka-wasaki in Kanagawa Prefecture and Kisarazu in Chiba Prefecture). To-kyo Skytree, the tallest structure in Japan, hosts broadcasting, a restau-rant, and an observation tower, and it is located in the quintessential downtown area, where Edo/Tokyo commoners used to live in their per-petual organs. The Tokyo Gaikan Expressway, an underground high-way network now being planned, will vertically connect with the exist-ing highways that function as veins for the Tokyo metropolis.

In October 2012, the devastating situation after Fukushima notwith-standing, the annual meetings of the International Monetary Fund (IMF) and the World Bank took place in Tokyo. In fact, they were re-located from the originally designated city, Cairo. All in all, it was the struggle of people in Egypt that ousted the global finance manipula-tors. Meanwhile, Japan is one of the main economic forces promoting global financial operations. One of the schemes in moving the meeting to Tokyo was to fog up the severity of present devastation by staging praise for the nonexistent success of recovery from disaster.[33] Blindfold-ing themselves to the deadly situation, the IMF and World Bank became worldwide promoters of the most outrageous and impossible project to reconstruct the radioactive zones for the benefit of US-Japan business interests, a project rooted at bottom in the desperate need to sustain the metropolitan functions of Tokyo and its neighboring areas in the Kanto Plain as long as they could hold. From Cairo to Tokyo, they shifted their priorities from oppressing the Egyptian revolution to reorganizing in-vestment in the reconstruction of post–nuclear disaster land and the management of a population living under radiation. Global capitalism has chosen radiation over revolution as its premise.

The first IMF–World Bank meeting in Japan took place in Tokyo in 1964, the same year as the first Tokyo Olympics. Its aim was to inter-nationally promote Japan and its miraculous reconstruction just nine years after its total devastation by war.[34] In 2012 the idea was to show the world Japan's strong recovery following the Fukushima disaster. Both times, global finance rhetoric emphasized successful recovery and the underlying economic and technological power of the nation. Omitted completely were the real sufferings and struggles of the people. "Recov-ery" in the proper sense is questionable in both cases: there is no recov-ery in sight from endless nuclear devastation and, without the Japanese government's acknowledgment of its war crimes and full compensation for its victims, the wounds from World War II have never healed. Lurk-ing behind this rhetoric is a desperate need for reconstruction for the sake of financial order and the profit making of global enterprises. It is this automatic mechanism for reconstructing the Tokyo apparatus that is ultimately responsible for letting the multitude be exposed to radiation.

Meanwhile, the Tokyo apparatus itself also seeks to sustain its func-tions. As we have seen, it endeavors to tie the people of Fukushima to irradiated land and to condition them to continue their "normal lives" as if nothing had happened. Yet simple sustenance is not its only aim, and its post-Fukushima endeavors serve a second purpose: reconstruc-tion for the 2020 Tokyo Olympics. This is a new kind of atrocity, already underway in the guise of constructing the national spectacle. It is this Tokyo that is the apparatus.

In order to think of the contemporary Olympics in terms of spectacle, let us turn to Guy Debord, especially to his third and final categorization of spectacle from 1988—the *integrated spectacle*.[35] This embodies the elements of both of his earlier categories: the *concentrated spectacle* epitomized in totalitarian society, whose order word is "obey!," and the *diffuse spectacle* operating in the society of the commodity economy, whose order word is "buy!" On the surface, the integrated spectacle looks like the diffuse spectacle that captures our desires in commodity form. But in this case, the commodity form is based on the *occulted state* where power is actually concentrated, while becoming more and more opaque. In the society of the integrated spectacle, very much like capitalist society today, the two order words "buy!" and "obey!" are interchangeable.[36] In this manner, as a concentrated form of the integrated spectacle, the contemporary Olympics have been realized by maximally coupling the strategy of spectacle that seduces the desire of the masses with the logistics of the state that exercise coercive development.

In another register, according to Deleuze and Guattari's distinction between city and state, the Olympics seem to be an ideal method for the state as *intraconsistency* to capture the city as *transconsistency* into its concentrated orders, and to combine commodification and nationalization.[37] In other words, they are the most effective means to congeal desiring machines operative in the city into the state apparatus. This is precisely the reterritorializing function of the Tokyo apparatus vis-à-vis the deterritorializing force of the Tokyo machine. When that happens, the transconsistency of the city, expansive beyond national borders, is subordinated to the confinement of state policy. The Olympics, like war and nuclear power, are a most effective logistics to unify state power and capitalist commodity economy.

When Tokyo was chosen to host the 2020 Olympics, there were not many in or outside Japan who were not dumbfounded—dumbfounded, that is, by the fact that international society had approved this unprecedented match between radiation contamination and the international festival of sports. Though it was easy to predict that Prime Minister Abe would lie about the possibility of controlling the crippled reactors, it was a decisive lesson to learn that the International Olympic Committee (IOC), an organization supposedly representing international society, would normalize the situation of humans being more or less exposed to radiation. Nonetheless, even that might have been known to us; on a deeper level, there was a sense of *déjà connu*.

This has to do with what nuclear disaster means to global capitalism and the state. The fixed capital called a nuclear reactor breaks down, becomes uncontrollable, and releases a decommodified energy source called nuclear fission, which then spreads across the planet following an invisible complexity of atmospheric movement as well as social circulation. This situation must be an unmanageable predicament for both capital's self-reproduction and the state's social management. Unpredictable loss is expected in both infrastructure and labor power. The future of demography is also critical. The only course is to adopt all possible temporary measures and to hide the catastrophic reality as much as possible. The priority in any event is to protect the social production of northeastern Honshu and Tokyo, at least until the critical situation can be reoriented toward redevelopment and placed in the circulation of commodity production.

The principle of this operation does not involve subjective judgment. What drives it is the apparatus of intertwined mechanisms for capturing heterogeneous desires and pursuing indefatigable interests. Its priority is not the liquidation of disaster or the protection of people's health but continued self-reproduction and expansion, and finally, sustained real estate value. As we have already seen, the Japanese government instigates new policies for supporting capital's strategies of reproduction in the post-Fukushima catastrophe so that they can be realized as smoothly as possible. In this precise sense, protecting and supporting the metropolitan functions of Tokyo is the crux. And it is the 2020 Tokyo Olympics that provide the best possible instance for that objective. By orienting the desires of the masses toward the construction of a megaspectacle that would inspire and reunite the national spirit, it becomes possible to offset the unsolvable and unconcealable nuclear disaster and radiation contamination—that is, by the logistics of reconstructing metropolitan infrastructure and function, recapturing information networks and media, and reinforcing the security system.

For the local residents of host cities, inscribed in Olympic experience has always been the separation of people from land in the process of the reconstruction of infrastructure, such as new building facilities as well as transportation and information networks, the reinforcement of security, and the destruction of means of subsistence. The journal of communist theory *Endnotes* points out: "The initial separation of people from the land, once achieved, is never enough. It has to be perpetually repeated in order for capital and 'free' labor to meet in the market time after time. On the one hand, capital requires, already present in the labor market, a mass of people lacking direct access to means of production, looking to exchange work for wages. On the other hand, it requires, already present in the commodity market, a mass of people who have already acquired wages, looking to exchange their money for goods."[38] For every host city, the Olympics have provided a most effective opportunity to realize the original process of accumulation on bigger and bigger scales, at faster and faster speeds, and in denser and denser concentration, except that in its case the process must always leave, to those who are severed from land and subsistence, at least the desire to buy.

Looking at the Olympics historically, each one embodied elements of either the concentrated spectacle (as in Berlin 1936) or the diffuse spectacle (as in Los Angeles 1984), but today, as evident especially in Athens 2004, the tendency has been inclining toward the integrated spectacle.[39] After hosting a transient event of such magnitude, there is no outcome other than economic collapse. Furthermore, what we observed in Rio de Janeiro in its redevelopment for the 2014 World Cup as well as the 2016 Olympics was the violent removal of people living in favelas, by both the rise in land prices and the physical intervention of security forces.

In Tokyo, as early as 2013, homeless people living in parks in central Tokyo already began to face eviction for the construction of a new stadium. The residents of a municipally owned apartment complex (Tsuyugaoka) and the inhabitants of Meiji Park lost their homes.[40] Meanwhile, the majority of people in Japan predict and fear the end of the era of retirement money and bonuses. Along with the effects of the Fukushima disaster and the primitive accumulation accompanying the redevelopment for the 2020 Olympics, the policies of the current Abe administration make the people—and especially Tokyo residents—realize that they are nothing but disposable machines; fixated on raising employment rates (largely by introducing work sharing), Abenomics turns the entire working populace into day laborers. Many people expect to be exhausted by overwork at an early age. As it repeats, the process of primitive accumulation becomes larger, faster, and denser, and labor conditions are affected accordingly. This is precisely the situation confronted by the desiring machines captured by the Tokyo apparatus, waiting for the 2020 Olympics.

Olympic redevelopments are moving ahead toward fully realizing the integrated spectacle. On TV and in media reports, the Olympics are eulogized and blessed by words of praise and admiration that would inspire and provoke national spirit, in order to swallow and recycle the interminable nuclear disaster and expanding radiation contamination. But we stand still at this juncture, in confrontation with this decisive fact: radiation contamination can never be recycled, and it can never be spectacularized. Nuclear fission is a pure event and an *absolute anti-spectacle*. Ironically, it is here where the moment to confront the 2020 Tokyo Olympics could exist.

As we have begun to realize, the struggle against nuclear capitalism and state under radiation contamination—the extreme case of "slow violence"—must comprise a network of multiple fronts involving varied spatiotemporal horizons, whose arrangement is yet to be clarified. The 2020 anti-Olympics is the first big manifestation of such struggle. It is important to note that the inhabitants of Yoyogi Park, whose dwelling has been threatened imminently, have taken the lead to organize No Olympics 2020 (Hangorin no kai), a national and international coalition, including anti-Olympic movements from Rio de Janeiro (2016) and Paris (2024).[41]

At the core of coordinated action, there must exist strategies, tactics, logistics, and techniques vis-à-vis the Tokyo apparatus. This apparatus has long served the state of Japan in its project of coagulating the Far Eastern archipelago, where heterogeneous Asia has always existed, into an insular nation for a homogeneous race called the Japanese, by pushing a series of logistics for the self-reproduction and expansion of capital/state conglomeration. After Fukushima, the Tokyo apparatus began to reveal the forms of its operation to capture and entangle the land and our desires into its mechanism. Therefore, undoing those forms of operation should be the general orientation in the struggle to confront the Olympics—that is, deterritorializing the Tokyo apparatus and decomposing it into various machines of desire.

At the moment there are two strategic domains that stand out: one of information and one of cartography. First, it is necessary to circulate the minute realities of radiation contamination in the Tokyo metropolis, through every possible form of information, throughout the world. Based on our existential dread of radiation, we must develop an information war against the apparatus of the spectacle. At the same time, it is necessary to undo the ocular machines implanted in all of us, which make us passively consume the spectacle in living rooms during the sports event. The objective of the information war should be to create a global countercurrent to the spectacularization and tourization of the 2020 Tokyo Olympics.

Meanwhile, slowly, gradually, and steadily, the second strategic possibility has emerged—that is, a cartography of the new alliances of evacuees (Those Who Go West)—from Nagoya as the frontline, through the Kansai and Chugoku regions, to Fukuoka as the base. With this new impetus, new alliances are expanding to connect cities in East Asia such as Seoul, Naha, Taipei, and Hong Kong. De-Tokyo-ization of the archipelago could be substantialized by way of this movement, driven by desires to develop life forms outside the Tokyo apparatus.

We have been too much attached to our love/hate relationship with Tokyo, for too long a time—throughout the three hundred years of the Edo period, since the Meiji Restoration, from the Great Kanto earthquake to the Pacific War to the postwar regime—but we can say that the binding force of Tokyo is waning now, after the Fukushima disaster. What remains instead are skeletal frames of infrastructure and bare mechanisms of interests that sustain them. Now it is high time to begin our project to deterritorialize the Tokyo apparatus, by reactivating the archipelagic machine in counter to the insular apparatus. It is imperative to nurture techniques for forgetting Tokyo and for living outside the territoriality of its apparatus, in both material and immaterial senses. Whether we reside in Tokyo or not, we should be able to develop de-Tokyo-ization. This would become a substantial part of the antinuke, anticapitalist, antispectacle, and antiapparatus struggles of the planet.

A HYPOTHESIS: NUCLEAR POWER IS IMMORTALIZING CAPITALISM

Why is it easier to imagine the end of the world than the end of capitalism? This question was circulated among a few prominent Marxist theorists some years ago.[1] The question of capitalism has always been essential in imagining totality, the totalizing entity called the world—today more so than ever. This act of imagining is now far from wishful dreaming about unknown places. Rather, it is forced upon us by an invisible and uncontrollable interconnectivity and our anguishing sense that, through overwhelmingly complex trajectories, we are affected by *and* affecting forces and events in unknown places. This interconnectivity is the embodiment of the way the World is organized by the operative logic of capitalism: axiomatic equivalent value together with the monopolization of violence by the state. This can be considered the driving force of World History. This drive was once spoken of as the making of one world where more locals and localities on the planet would be acquainted for building unity; now it is mostly seen as the creation of intensifying fissures and frictions everywhere within a totalizing entity whose oneness is incessantly pushed away. Or rather, it is that the oneness we are experiencing is only the presumed collapse of the planetary ecosystem: the Apocalypse.

We have reached a tipping point where it is hardly possible for us to think of making a better world within such totalization, since it is becoming synonymous with all the crises besieging our existential territories. World History seems to have failed in achieving a synthetic unity with the planetary environment by its dialectical logic, and instead it forces us to share all its messes. Thus, the said question illuminates the ontology of messy entanglements in the World expanding continually over the planetary body. This problematic of the present in World History can be approached from the problematic of atomic power, with this hypothesis: it is nuclear production that is playing a key role in indefinitely postponing the end of capitalism, both ontometaphysically and technopolitically, as the knottiest apparatus of capture.

In post–nuclear disaster Japan, the commodity economy dogged by collapsing reactors is facing an unprecedented crisis, with its labor power (or variable capital) exposed to radiation, waiting for illness and death, and its nuclear plants (or constant capital) uncontrollably releasing radioactive particles in an irreparable process of collapse. In other words, dead labor is ravaging living labor with its most revered and dreaded commodity: nuclear fission, or split atoms of uranium. Once unleashed, these become an anticommodity, or 無主物 (mushubutsu, masterless object), in the term circulated in post-Fukushima Japan. Assuming that the situation must be a disastrous crisis for the economy, still we also know that capitalism is in principle a movement that ceaselessly creates new occasions for greater investment by actively involving disaster, contamination, immiseration, war, and everything that disrupts the previous cycle of its reproduction in order to articulate a new one. During this process, a number of desperate recompositions take place, involving renewals of both knowledge and power. When a bigger crisis attacks and the deficit gets larger, capitalism is prone to play an even bigger game—thus inviting endless crises, risks, hazards, calamities, and uprisings.

As we have seen in previous chapters, post–nuclear disaster socialization is accelerated by the will to reconstruct and driven by the consequent nationalization of radiation. What kind of mechanism is behind all this? We would say capitalism, but here it is necessary to speak of a specific capitalism: namely, the post–nuclear disaster capitalism that still relies on and even further develops nuclear operation with the reopening of off-lined nuclear plants as well as with futile yet profitable experiments of endless aftercare (decommissioning of plants and waste management). To survive, the capitalist economy must create a mechanism to commodify the masterless object. In an alternate view, however, it would be more accurate to say that by creating the endless necessity of aftercare, nuclear industry guarantees capitalism its zombie life of permanent stop-gap operation. It is in precisely this apocalyptic sense that nuclear industry is a matrix of all the major trends of capitalist development.

With the question of why it is hard to imagine the end of capitalism resonates a lingering question: Why is it hard to abolish nuclear power? With these overlapping questions in mind, I examine the main attributes of the capitalism that is outliving the end of the world: *apocalyptic capitalism*.

A BRIEF OVERVIEW OF ATOMIC WORLD HISTORY

Nuclear power is essentially Janus faced: military and civilian. It offers to the state a dystopian dream of sublime weaponry and to capitalism a utopian dream for sublime energy, creating the strongest bond between capitalist economy and state sovereignty. This bond has played a fatal role in the becoming of the contemporary world. Since the industrial revolution, this fatal bond has been solidified particularly through the shift in primary energy source from animals/firewood to coal to oil/nuclear. What is crucial to note in this transition is that it has led to a new arrangement of infrastructure for the totalization of the World, and furthermore, that none of these energy sources have been abolished completely by being replaced: all are placed in major or minor position according to demand and used in ensemble. There seems to be an irreversibility to World History, wherein no technological invention disappears once it has been put into use somewhere in the strata of infrastructural arrangements. All in all, the World has been totalizing itself around the production and distribution of these energy sources. Environmentalist projects to discover and utilize more economical and safer sources of energy are truly crucial but have not been successful enough to counter the major trend. Most of these efforts have not yet discovered a way to synchronize with other transformative projects, that is, to create autonomous territories of life-as-struggle and to decompose the capital/state conglomeration.

Energy has always been the central concern for capitalism, for it is the key commodity that affects the values of commodities in all other industrial sectors; thus, it has been given privileged support by the state as protector of national economy and enforcer of national sovereignty. However, it is important to note that throughout human history, the original energy—the creator of value—is always human labor, reproduced by communal relations and the natural environment created by solar energy, prior to capital's production. Being the original energy means being ontologically distinct from other energy commodities. Herein exists the precedence of human labor in the making of the world, whose status, however, is buried by the exploitive mechanisms of capitalism. As the philosopher George Caffentzis points out, in the history of capital's reproduction and expansion, the "microstruggles" of workers to refuse work in various forms—their lives-as-struggle—always come first and instigate capital's crisis and thus its drive to discover new sources of energy and to invent machines in order to create new modes and relations of production. This is the process of class struggle, or capital's crisis and recomposition. Its history has been developing in tandem with scientific revolutions, that is, from the Newtonian theory of the solar system to Carnot's laws of thermodynamics to Mayer's law of the conservation of energy to Taylorist labor management to Teller's proposal for new production systems based on the energo-informatization of society.[2] This last is the infamous nuclear scientist/politician Edward Teller, the alleged model for Dr. Strangelove.[3]

As Timothy Mitchell's *Carbon Democracy* details, the age of coal inaugurated modern labor movements. The remarkable achievements of general strikes in many industrial sectors were largely thanks to the geographical concentration of mining, production, and transportation netted around coal. While the age of coal is considered to be the age of modern democracy in the West, with its geographical expansion (imperialism) continuing from colonialism, the age of oil embodies the limit of the production and circulation of the previous age as well as the limit of democracy.[4] The latter announces dystopian transformations within the modern paradigm: the end of the welfare state; dispersion/expansion of production points and circulation networks; the invention of spatio-temporality and culture based on the automobile; the emergence of an economy whose main commodities are information, service, and energy; and a spatial limit to the colonization/expansion of capitalist commodification, which is increasingly reoriented from macro- to microdimensions, that is, from megascale developments to genetic information copywriting.

It was into this paradigm of oil that atomic energy was inserted. Though at first just an offshoot of the accelerating information-energy-dominant tendency of capital's reproduction/expansion, it came to play a pivotal role in capitalism's survival as ultimate stronghold. Initiated as a military technology and concretized in the Manhattan Project—which technically terminated the Pacific War—nuclear fission was quickly readapted to energy production in an effort to merge two separate sectors (weaponry and energy, military and civilian) into one process of production/circulation via plutonium generation.[5]

After World War II, the United States became the dominant power in the Pacific—at the end limit of the westward expansion of the colonial West from Europe—and in this process, a new, mobile, and flexible geopolitics was introduced. The network empire connected by island territories replaced the conventional empire based on the permanent occupation of continental territory. This was made possible by the superior mobility of land, marine, and air forces equipped with nuclear warheads.[6] In this context, we cannot ignore the role of the information network in creating the cybernetic space of control.[7] After all, these networks realized a militarization of space that has come to control our everyday lives in an invisible yet substantive manner.

In international politics during the past few decades, we have observed an emphatic pattern to US intervention: claiming the threat of developing nuclear technology to produce "weapons of mass destruction," the United States moves into oil-rich countries to establish its business monopolization, or, indeed, into any other territory insistent on discord with America. This pattern speaks to the secondary yet pivotal role of atomic power in the petroleum-dominant economy, wherein military might consistently lurks behind economic expansion as economy and military fuse into one strategic tool for global hegemony. In other words, what the historian Gabrielle Hecht calls "nuclear exceptionalism" is at work in international power relations, determining who is and is not entitled to enjoy the supreme power of rule. Exceptional status is conferred based on accessibility to the nexus of nuclear production.[8] The international politics centered on the United Nations (UN), the International Atomic Energy Agency (IAEA), and other organizations is indeed the platform for negotiations among pro–atomic energy/weaponry states.[9] These powers employ all their economic, scientific, political, and military capacities to achieve and monopolize the *sublime power* of destruction and energy. While nuclear states and nuclear capitals are always in competition and sometimes in virtual or real war among themselves, they all form one entity—what I call the "global nuclear regime"—that is exponentially turning the Earth into a radioactive planet.

Nuclear production appeared in a recent stage of World History on the strata of power relations from the past: colonialism, imperialism, postcolonial contestation, Cold War relations, and today's global capitalist regime. Here we see a synchronic power dynamic, the stratified temporalities in which everything that has once taken place in the past is summoned from historical strata, thrown into new arrangement, and made to play new roles without ever being sublated properly. For instance, within global power relations around nuclear exceptionalism there exist *combined and uneven* arrangements, whereby different roles are distributed to different territories in the nexus of nuclear production, involving uranium mining, global trade, concentration of capital, state intervention, international politics, scientific research, energy production and distribution, weaponry production and distribution, military intervention, plant decommissioning, waste reprocessing, and waste shipping and storing. The countries that achieved independence relatively recently—such as Canada, Australia, Niger, Namibia, and Kazakhstan—took over uranium mines from their former colonial rulers and continued to play the role of servitude, that is, by transferring the surplus value of their massive, cheap, and irradiated labor power to the catastrophic machineries of electric power companies in cutting-edge nuclear states such as the United States, France, Israel, and Japan. In other words, companies in leading capitalist countries—namely, the successors of former colonizers—tend to absorb surplus value from the labor of the former colonies as well as that of other industrial sectors across the planet.

In this manner, apocalyptic capitalism operating behind the global nuclear regime is producing combined and uneven hells in which people suffer differently according to their historical and geopolitical positions—in innumerable mining sites in Africa, Canada, Australia, and elsewhere, in nuclear bomb-testing sites, in war zones bombed by depleted uranium warheads, and amid radioactive pollution from power plants, factories, and dumpsites across the globe. Therefore, lives-as-struggle across the planet are confronting the same power, differently yet simultaneously. The possibility of planetary rebellion against this capitalism exists in how struggles can reverberate and coordinate among themselves, by sharing agonies, perceptions, aspirations, and techniques, in order to walk different paths but strike the same enemy— the global nuclear regime—at the same time.

Now it should be clear why it is hard to abolish nuclear power entirely. Beyond the matter of finding a better source of energy, the real difficulty lies in the fact that the global nuclear regime insists on the worst source of energy for the power contestation of the World. However, it is not that the global nuclear regime is run by a conference of executives or representatives of individual nuclear capitals and states, presenting and discussing their ideas about how to accumulate more capital by immiserating the labor power of the world and contaminating the environment on the planet. It is less *run* than *driven by*—and furthermore, less *by* than *as*—the power contestations within it. This is the real and virtual condition for the regime's ongoing global war. If the global nuclear regime is considered as a power, it is an acephalic one. It cannot stop itself. It does not think, feel, speak, or respond. It is nobody: it does not have a body! Therefore, it continues to operate as an automaton, despite all our crises and without listening and responding to our desperate protests.

Seen from the viewpoint of atomic world history, Fukushima 3/11 is not a single, exceptional case. Yet it is the worst of all the disasters that atomic energy has ever caused. It is a revelation for us all, showing us the real existence of the nuclear regime that feeds itself by distributing the nexus of nuclear production globally, a regime that not only persisted in this production after the worst disaster but utilized the catastrophic situation in order to maintain its rule. Furthermore, it reveals the consequence of the expansion of a technopolitics based on nuclear production over the planetary body: more radioactive contamination and more potential nuclear accidents will be shared by all planetary lives. In different terms, Fukushima announces the advent of an age when the commodification of everything by capitalism has reached the point where the *general equivalence* of value is increasingly approaching the proximity of the *general catastrophe* of living.

HOW DOES NUCLEAR ENERGY TECHNICALLY MERGE CAPITALISM AND THE STATE?

It was not humanity that created the atomic bomb, put it into actual use for genocide, and inflicted radioactive contamination over the planetary environment. But specific players of World History have been individually engaged in these projects in sequence. It is imperative to identify who they are. The fact that the event of nuclear fission was employed to make weapons and then energy appears to have been inevitable, ever since it was first artificially generated in the laboratory by cutting-edge scientists. But it should not be ignored that this employment took place through historical contingencies at specific historical conjunctures. During the recomposition of global capitalism, the European empire was declining while the American empire was rising, with transferences of tremendous power and knowledge from the former to the latter. It was the combined drive of excessive fear, rage, and fantasy generated through that process that prompted the employment of nuclear fission. Utopian and dystopian dreams—both nurtured at the end limit of the conquest of new worlds by the West—have haunted American politics ever since. Thereafter, the nuclear attacks of Hiroshima and Nagasaki marked a violent closing of the open and heterogeneous space of planetary exchange over the Pacific Ocean.

As we have already seen, the atomic players in postwar Japan were those who persisted in their will to "wealthy nation and strong soldiers" in the new regime. They shared a fanatic propensity for power within the apparatuses of capture and sought to control society by creating a syndicate of influential individuals and groups across the public (bureaucrats) and private sectors (industrialists and media), led by the faith in developing infrastructures that would transform everything for the empowerment of the nation, using cutting-edge science and technology. The nuclear ambition was an implant of the dream capitalism of America on the Japanese fanatics for power and progress, except that the Japanese territory of dreaming was now conditioned to be confined to the insular. Dream politics in postwar Japan thus inherited the apparatus of the apocalypse that is most cutting-edge and invincible but with essential perils and deficiencies, glossed over by the dreamlike discourses and images that make it look ideal.

Despite its discourses and images, atomic energy is not in the least economical, clean, or safe. It is one of the most absurd projects that industrial societies have ever undertaken. What it does is just boil water and make steam, but for this it is devised to involve excessive labor and machines; it includes extensive sectors such as mining, transportation, research, trade, and security, which all cause deadly hazards in different ways. This is a most concentrated and dreadful form of capture. It is a new form of "megamachine," as conceptualized by Lewis Mumford, which creates, regulates, and controls the entire social body and space by overcoding the land and populace, in installing an insanely mega-lomaniac project.[10] It is an invisible pyramid for the present age, constructed on a planetary scale.

It is a false notion that atomic energy is low-cost. In fact, the expenditure for its production of electricity is much higher than that of both hydraulic and thermal power, if we take into account all the costs for preparation and cleanup: uranium mining, refinement, enrichment, processing, and transportation as well as the governmental installment of infrastructure (land acquisition and facility construction). Furthermore, it produces excess. Due to mechanical inflexibility, atomic energy production cannot be stopped during the period of operation, and in consequence it generates excessive energy. In order to consume this excess, a mechanism called pumped-storage hydroelectricity is required, wherein two water pools are prepared. During the nightly period of repose, water is pumped up from one pool to the other to expend the excess energy. During the day, water is poured from one pool to the other to generate energy for the production of electricity. Each of these operations loses 30 percent of the energy. This cost is added to our electricity bills.

It is another untruth that atomic energy does not produce carbon dioxide. This should be rephrased time and again: nuclear fission itself does not produce carbon dioxide. But before electricity can be generated, all the above-mentioned stages of uranium processing and transportation must take place. Each of these requires fossil fuels and produces large amounts of carbon dioxide.

It is a sheer lie that nuclear power is not causing global warming. It is said that in an average nuclear plant, three million kilowatts of heat are produced daily inside the reactor, only one-third of which is transformed into electricity, while two-thirds is released into the ocean (when the plant is located on the sea, as in most cases). Indeed, seawater near nuclear plants is always approximately seven degrees Celsius warmer. This devastates oceanic ecology and further escalates global warming.[11]

How can such absurdity be legitimized? The secret lies in the way the state—the coconspirator—takes special care of this industry. First and foremost, the siting of nuclear plants is based on the geopolitics of modern nation-states. The location of a power plant is supposed to be chosen to meet three conditions: it must be located in a nonresidential area, its surroundings must be underpopulated, and it must be far away from densely populated zones. Namely, it must be remote from metropolises and industries, in consideration of the possibility of accident. This determination of location is based on the historically strategized uneven development between metropolis and countryside: in the case of Japan, for example, between Tokyo and the northeastern region of Honshu where Fukushima is located. The countryside has long been made to service Tokyo, not only with agricultural and marine products but also by offering electricity as its lifeline and disposable labor power (industrial reserve army) for its construction, as well as for nuclear industry. So here is the accident; and the reason why it is so difficult for the people living in highly radioactive zones to evacuate and live in safer places is due to the hierarchical relations among territories of interests, between local industries, sustenance of Tokyo, and the global economy.

Second, the operation of nuclear plants is made possible by various financial tricks, such as state subsidy and insurance limitation. Even when the production of atomic energy is privately funded, the state protects investors with special legislation that limits insurance costs in case of accident and disaster. On top of that, laws have been coined for the benefit of atomic energy production. For instance, Japan's Atomic Energy Damage Compensation Law (1961) states that in case of accident caused by unexpected large natural disaster or social upheaval, the electric company is exempt from responsibility.[12] That is, it is tax money and electricity bills that would have to pay off a large portion of postdisaster liquidation and compensation (all costs in excess of 120 billion yen). In normal conditions, while the government pays hardware costs such as land acquisition, facility construction and decommissioning, and waste reprocessing and storing, the power companies absorb most of the profit by playing a managerial role in running facilities and distributing electricity.

Third, the electric power companies that operate nuclear plants exert a dominant power of influence over society by their invisible network and monopoly status. Japan's so-called nuclear village consists of those in the government, academia, media, and industry who are making a profit by running nuclear plants. The nuclear village attracted attention especially after the disaster because it is this network of players that continues to lead and support the government's pronuclear policy.[13] While the term *village* implies a quasi-secret society connected by common interests and personal acquaintances, these connections are made practically by the donations of electric companies to politicians, bureaucrats, scholars, media personas, and industrialists. In return, the members of this village are willing to make policies, investments, reports, and discourses for the sake of eternalizing nuclear operations in society.

For a long time, electric power companies in Japan enjoyed the status of monopoly capital, and they still do so technically. Tokyo Electric Power Company (TEPCO) and Kansai Electric Power Company (KEPCO) are the most powerful two among Japan's ten regional companies.[14] Residents of the Tokyo area have no choice but to buy electricity from TEPCO, while those in the Osaka area buy from KEPCO. No matter how high the price, people have to buy it. Protected by this monopoly status and secured by the Electric Utility Industry Law, companies can draw profits from electric bills determined in such a way that the so-called comprehensive costs—including depreciation, business expenses, tax, and business returns—turn into profit. In other words, the profit rate of an electric company is determined by the rate base (fixed assets) plus the business returns rate. This means that the electric company can add a certain percentage of its fixed assets onto its profit rate. In order to increase its rate base, there is nothing better than constructing more nuclear power plants.

When the liberalization of electric power became a worldly current around the turn of the twenty-first century, Japan's electric power companies confronted a situation in which they had to go along with the market principle in deciding their electric fees. Japanese businesses had long been troubled by the most expensive electric bills in the world, set by the ten electric power companies, and subsequently with liberalization, some began to equip their own power stations. Thus, retail electricity sales began vying for the business of large-lot electricity users. But a backlash came, due to the dominant interests of nuclear technology providers and contractors, that is, such transnational enterprises as Mitsubishi, Hitachi, and Toshiba, whose interests are tightly intertwined with those of the ten electric power companies. Together, the mammoth nuclear-related industries already constituted a three trillion yen industry, with apparatuses stretching across the nation and the world, effectively unstoppable. The Electricity Business Act of 2016 again attempted to liberalize the retail of electric power. In consequence, many venture companies appeared to produce and sell their energy (sometimes eco-oriented). And yet the quasi-monopoly status of the ten persists; they still own the transmission lines, and new electric suppliers still have to sell their products back to them in order to compete in the market—thus the difficulty in developing regional autonomy of electric supply.

Now let us consider the complexity of global nuclear operations, a complexity that imposes extra fetters on our existence as well as on our aspirations to make a better world. This complexity consists of the overlapping attributes of nuclear power that emerge from its Janus face of weapon and energy: (1) the sublimity of the destructive power of the nuclear, which paralyzes our thoughts and actions; (2) the global extension of its production and operation that solidifies the fatal bond between capitalism and the state as it exploits and victimizes us in varied manners, from homes to workplaces to disaster/war zones; (3) the highly specialized nature of its knowledge and technology that rejects access to commoners; (4) the hierarchical system and secretive culture built around it that are responsible for social exclusion, control, and oppression; (5) the capacity of its endurance by the coercive logic of absolute negativity—*if not, then the end for all*; (6) the blurred boundary between determinability and indeterminability in the monstrous effects (or the virtuality of effects) of radiation on genetic activities, which evades the logic of causation and consequence certified in medical, legal, and political institutions; and (7) its overidentification with the necessary development of national economy and security, to reign supreme over energy requirements for capitalist development against life and ecology, to build deterrence by more weapons, and to develop more enterprises for dealing with existing facilities and accumulating wastes.

Some of these core aspects have been elucidated by several pioneering thinkers after World War II. The philosopher Günther Anders (1902–92) tackled the unprecedented threat of nuclear weapons after the experiences of Hiroshima and Nagasaki. He pointed out that the total annihilation that could be triggered by a trivial incident or insane passion is real now, but at the same time blocks out our power to think and imagine the sublimity of the possible. He called this unthinkability "apocalyptic blindness" (*Apokalypseblindheit*), which is embedded systematically within the technoindustrial society that created nuclear fission artificially.[15]

Austrian writer and journalist Robert Jungk (1913–94) pioneered, along with Anders, the early international antinuclear movement. Jungk's seminal book *The Nuclear State* (1979) premised that, in terms of the deadly effects of nuclear fission on body and environment, "there is no fundamental difference between atoms for peace and atoms for war."[16] In terms of nuclear labor, he pointed out the mechanism of incapacitation confronted by workers striking at a nuclear fuel-processing facility in La Hague, France, in September 1976, wherein the privatized, secretive, and hierarchical company organization was able to orchestrate severe internal fissures within the union and, most crucially, the moral pressure on workers to maintain public safety undermined their will to persist in their refusal to work.[17] Nuclear operations involve the risk of accidents endangering many lives, which nullifies the problematic of resistance and coerces workers to be "saviors" or even "martyrs"—as we observe today at Fukushima Daiichi. In the social milieu, Jungk warned us that the civilian control and security culture concomitant with nuclear production not only exclude commoners institutionally and technically from highly specialized secretive operations, but also spread authoritarian systems across the nation-state and the world.

Consider as well the American historian, sociologist, and philosopher Lewis Mumford (1895–1990) and his historical-machinic theorization of nuclear apparatuses. His concept of the megamachine, later adopted by Deleuze and Guattari, was in fact a retrospective observation—from today's assemblage to ancient arrangement, such as that materialized in the pyramids—of the project of megaconstruction/development that centralized an entire social system by absolutist order.[18] He considered the nuclear apparatuses to epitomize the modern megamachine: on the one hand, associating the fateful commanding power of the US president under the exigencies of war (such as that actually carried out by Harry S. Truman in 1945 and that now wielded by the accursed Donald Trump) with the power of ancient despots, and on the other hand, illuminating the global stretch of the military–industrial complex, which "commands whole regiments of diversified units, with superhuman power and superhuman mechanical reliability, and not least with lightning speed."[19] After all, it is *for* and *by* the nuclear megamachine that we are made to serve, while being victimized in multiple dimensions—as laborers offering its blood (from uranium mines, transportation, processing facilities, power plants), commoners whose land is expropriated by power plants, payers of tax and electricity bills, casualties of war, and victims of radiation exposure. In the nuclear megamachine, the division between labor and casualty/victim is indefinitely blurred.

More recently, the philosopher Brian Massumi conceptualized the new operative logic of world domination (backed by nuclear exceptionalism) initiated by the George W. Bush administration after September 11, 2001, in terms of "preemption"—in distinction from "deterrence," based on the preventative logic of the Cold War.[20] The fall of the Soviet Union made the paradigm of deterrence a thing of the past. Its necessary condition of balancing polarity no longer obtains. The age of asymmetrical warfare has come. After 9/11, anomaly is everywhere. While preemption shares many characteristics with deterrence, the process of preemption is qualitatively different; its "epistemology is unabashedly one of uncertainty" because "the threat has not only not yet fully formed . . . it has not yet even emerged."[21] The logic of preemption is to rush headlong into producing the very catastrophe that exists only—if at all—in a state of indeterminate potentiality.

Massumi points out that, in the logic of preemption, the ultimate reason Iran must be attacked is because it might well put a "choke hold" on the Strait of Hormuz in order to block oil deliveries to the West and thereby endanger the economy. This is telling of the privileged role that nuclear power plays in the petroleum-dominant economy. Nuclear power, after all, is not simply an energy source, replaceable with coal, oil, hydraulic, or wind power: its alternate face provides the preemptive power for achieving *prototerritorial* control over the world—with the will and potency to attack anytime and anywhere—in order to protect and expand the interests of oil industries.[22]

With the above-mentioned concept of nuclear exceptionalism, Hecht provides a global spatiotemporal mapping of power contestations within the global nuclear regime.[23] Even after the fateful tension of the Cold War has ended, accessibility to nuclear production is still determinant in guaranteeing the upper hand in global power conflicts—now in terms of prototerritorial rule and possibly the space war. Within nation-states, expertise of nuclear technology is privileged in government, industry, academia, and media, from which commoners like us are unequivocally blindfolded. From our existential standpoint, being threatened and victimized by the actual and virtual wars among the players—whose technopolitical details are veiled—is itself equal to being ruled ontometaphysically by the global nuclear regime.

Antinuclear movements also share a sense of exceptionalism in confronting the magnitude of nuclear threats, which compel them to persist in single-issue organizing around the priority of saving humanity.

Nuclear exceptionalism thus plays a dual role: it is a material means of dominating global trade and violence technopolitically and a way of governing the planetary populace by incapacitating their thinking and confining their engagement ontometaphysically.

Nuclear proliferation continues as if the supreme accident in Fukushima were merely an interruption of minor significance. This is precisely because, according to Caffentzis, "the current crisis has demonstrated that the capitalist system *qua* machine is operating in a way analogous to a nuclear reactor: it offers no guarantees of preventing failure in the process of reproducing society nor does it provide any insurance in case of failure. . . . So now we have a default theory that claims that 'there is no alternative' to the system, but which fully recognizes that it cannot guarantee an end to crisis any longer."[24]

Caffentzis takes up the concept of nuclear exceptionalism and gives critical and analytical dimensions to it. He suggests an antinomy to undo its haunting ideation: "(1) to see the nuclear power industry as a purely capitalist enterprise, organized to make money; (2) to see the capitalist economy as more and more appearing to be modeled on a nuclear reactor. In other words, the nuclear power industry is becoming just *One* (industry) among *Many* and, at the same time, it is the *One* the *Many* are becoming."[25] Following the Three Mile Island accident in the late seventies, Midnight Notes Collective had already elucidated the specific status of the nuclear industry vis-à-vis capitalism in general:

> The nuclear industry represents a synthesis of all major trends of capitalist development. All aspects of the general perspective of capital are concentrated in this industry: high capital intensity (less workers and more electricity production), extreme discipline and command over the labor force, combination of state and private capital (in research, financing, supervision), internationality, computerization, and extension of the planning horizon far into the future (nuclear waste). The nuclear industry is able to occupy all free spaces geographically (reactors are independent of local resources), politically (all police state measures can be justified by radioactive dangers), and in time (even if we "win," we will have to deal with the nuclear waste; our "utopias" are infested for thousands of years).[26]

Along this line of analysis, the nuclear industry is seen as the generic being to capitalist development. Today, capitalism assimilates itself into nuclear capital because the survival of capitalism in permanent crisis relies, at least on one level, on the interminability of the nuclear industry continuing to reproduce itself by expanding a task that it can never fulfill. In other words, radio-infected capitalism elongates its vampire life through a dystopian scheme of moneymaking: while endlessly experimenting with utopian technology that might or might not treat the radioactive wastes it endlessly accumulates, it continuously supplies the well-guaranteed demands of governments for power and those of related worldwide enterprises for money.[27]

Thus, while nuclear capital is not exceptional, being just one sector of capitalist development, the extremity of the nuclear industry involves the complexity of existential capture. The extremely high "organic composition" of this industry as compared to others, for instance, relates to several of its overlapping attributes. It is one of the energy industries—namely, a key industry—whose commodity price influences the commodity prices of all other industries. The price of its product (electricity) is much greater than its value (or the labor involved at the electric company) in a degree incomparable to other industries, namely because of the enormous subsidies that it gets from the state for security, research, compensation, and siting as well as tax and insurance exemptions—but incomparable too because of the absurdity of developing excessively elaborate and dangerous machines just to boil water. Thereby nuclear production sucks up the surplus value produced by cheaper, harder, and massive labor at the bottom (i.e., subcontracted nuclear workers at the plant) and in the peripheries (i.e., uranium mines) of its stretch, in an extremely high ratio.

Beginning with Hiroshima and Nagasaki, the production of nuclear weapons accelerated during the Cold War. Incessant nuclear weapons testing created victims of radioactive exposure on the islands and deserts of the invisible fringes of the world.[28] More recently, the effects of depleted uranium weapons have been observed among the residents of war zones. Uranium mining (e.g., in the aboriginal areas of Australia and the Navajo reservations of North America) has been linked to radiation-related illnesses. In nuclear power plants across the world, workers are made to work under severely hierarchical and strictly secretive conditions; those who are subcontracted at the bottom are exposed to high radiation without proper security and information, as their vital energy is sucked up by the extremity of nuclear accumulation. The siting of nuclear power plants illustrates uneven development: the areas that are far from the center and whose products are weak in the market are targeted and subjected to the high risk of accidents and pollution in exchange for flowing remuneration to local communities, which instantaneously destroys their subsistence, culture, social relations, and environment.

The stretch of nuclear tentacles may or may not cause an instantaneous, total annihilation of the world, but it does substantially intensify combined and uneven effects on the planetary populace, the motivation of which is unequivocally moneymaking. In this light, the production of nuclear power is seen as the most guaranteed, complex, and deadly means to make money. Thanks to its capacity to produce weaponry and energy in one and the same process of nuclear fission, nuclear capital enjoys all manner of legal and financial privileges as well as political protections, while its proliferation has resulted only in devastation. Yet it survives and expands. Indeed, it cannot stop itself. It shows an end limit of what the power of the axiomatic sequence of moneymaking—M-C-M'—can absorb from the body and land in toto (the Earth) while imposing the extremity of destructivism through capitalist accumulation over its entire productive and reproductive organization (the World).

THE MASTERLESS OBJECT (無主物)

Radiation emitted through nuclear fission is the source of nuclear energy. As we all know now, its leakage is an inevitable consequence of that energy production. It happens sooner or later at some point in time, because the half-lives of certain radionuclides outlive the endurance of any built structures. The facilities wane. Operators make human mistakes. Mechanical accidents take place. Earthquakes or hurricanes hit. That is, radioactive contamination is inevitable, more or less, in our environment. Radionuclides unleashed from the encasement permeate the environment in a way we can hardly control or predict; this permeation embodies what we call *chaos*. As we have seen, the acts of radioactive/radiosensitive crowds to deal with radionuclides are opening a new ontological dimension. Hypothetically, I think of this as a shifting ontology from the World to the Earth, but there are unknown elements involved in the shift. It is necessary to approach it in various registers.

///

The Japanese term *mushubutsu* (無主物) is translated into English as either "masterless object" or "ownerless object" and corresponds to *res nullius* (nobody's property) in Roman law. It refers to anything—land, plants, animals, slaves (or labor power), fire, and so on—that is *not yet* or *no longer* the object of any specific subject in the legal sense.

In post–nuclear disaster Japan, this term captured public attention when TEPCO made a shameless yet candid statement at a hearing against it in November 2011, saying that radioactivity is originally a masterless object that does not belong to TEPCO, and that therefore the company is not responsible for cleaning up the radioactive nuclides unleashed from its crippled nuclear reactors. Executives from TEPCO argued that removing these nuclides from the property of the plaintiff, Sunfield Nihonmatsu Golf Course, would be an unheard-of challenge and would cost an astronomical sum, as the nuclides could no longer be separated from the land.[29]

In using the concept of mushubutsu, TEPCO implies that its ownership of the energy commodity—split atoms of uranium—is limited to instances in which atomic energy is confined within constant capital (nuclear reactors) and when these are running smoothly and accruing profit. However, once that encasement is torn apart, the unleashed radioactivity is no longer under its technical mastery and corporate ownership. Simply put, TEPCO claims that once atomic energy misbehaves, the company is no longer obligated or even able to take care of it.

The treatment of this special commodity by TEPCO has thus begun to mirror the ways in which the company has always treated another original and special commodity—namely, its variable capital (human nuclear labor), which is disowned once one develops radiation-related diseases and begins to malfunction. This follows the modus operandi of capitalism, which is to extract resources from society and the environment (in the form of capital) and impose back on them the wastes created. Such is the formula of all industrial pollution. But in the instance of Fukushima and all other radioactive leaks, the consequences are catastrophic, as this particular waste cannot be recycled by any known procedure, and its nano activity will ceaselessly continue to attack and genetically mutate all life forms in the surrounding environment, for years to come.

Nuclear contaminants behave like a group of disowned workers roaming around society and posing threat to its stability. These unleashed objects need to be reowned by the company and remastered by the state in a new way. Otherwise, the situation will lead to an unknown sociobiological mutation—an ontological anarchy!

The self-exemption from responsibility by TEPCO was alarming but anticipated; it is not a surprise that the company would sacrifice anything to its corporate interests. At the time of the 2011 hearing, the desperate entreaty of TEPCO executives for permission to abandon the crippled reactors and evacuate their workers from the area was still vivid in collective memory. This request came during a critical phase when the exploding reactors could have set Armageddon into motion and made most parts of Japan and indeed the world unlivable. Japanese prime minister Kan Naoto rejected TEPCO's request and issued an executive order demanding that the company remain onsite to continue tackling the devastating conditions. As the world knows, TEPCO is still doing this.

In the years after the disaster, we have learned the following truths about atomic energy: (1) it is fundamentally impossible to manage radioactivity; (2) despite this, the Japanese government, electric companies, and nuclear industries—the nuclear village—insist on restarting offline nuclear reactors and seek to expand foreign markets to sell the nation's nuclear technology; (3) other nuclear states, consisting of the world's great powers—the global nuclear regime—give these actions their tacit approval for their own benefit; (4) meanwhile, unrecyclable radioactive waste is accumulating without proper sealing for protection; (5) no political protests or activist movements in Japan or the world can stop the global threat of the nuclear sublime and yet, all the while, people continue to struggle endlessly to protect their lives against the effects of nuclear radiation.

Thus, we are coerced to cohabitate with the unleashed radionuclides, namely, the masterless object. In a strange inversion, the concept of the masterless object shares ontological characteristics with that of the commons. The principle of autonomous communities, "the commons," puts forth the idea that all natural resources, human labor, intelligence, and technology be put to communal use, *not yet* or *no longer* being commodified and privatized. The commons originates in the environment in a broad sense, when the resources there are not yet or no longer owned or mastered by particular humans. This is the state in which the world as an assembly of human communities would be becoming itself in a proper arrangement, not only within itself, but also together with planet Earth.

There are many dimensions of commoning, the original form of which is the sharing of solar energy. The Sun offers its free and universal gift of endless energy, which it creates in nuclear fusion of its solar activity, to its daughter, the planetary body and her inhabitants. But in this scenario, the daughter can sustain herself only by keeping a proper distance from her dreadful father. From the vantage point of the planet and its inhabitants, the Sun can be figured as the primary commons.

Prometheus, who in Greek mythology stole fire from Olympus and gave it to mankind, and who then suffered Zeus's eternal punishment, is nowadays spoken of as an allegory for humanity having discovered radioactivity. Similarly, the nuclear reactor is often figured as a "small sun." In these allegories, the history of nuclear power—beginning with the generation of radioactivity in the laboratory, to its use for producing the nuclear bomb (in the Manhattan Project), and then to the diversion of this military technology to energy production for civilian use—represents humanity's desecration of the Sun. The eternal punishment inflicted on humanity for this act is the unprecedented threat of nuclear things against all living beings.

The series of modern nuclear catastrophes, including Hiroshima and Nagasaki in 1945, Lucky Dragon 5 (Daigo Fukuryū Maru) in 1954, Three Mile Island in 1979, Chernobyl in 1986, and Fukushima in 2011, has proven that, for the masses, the use of atomic energy—whether through nuclear warfare, inevitable reactor accidents, or the uncontrollable accumulation of unrecyclable waste—ends up having the same effects on living bodies: namely, internal and/or external radiation exposure. Even when it is used intentionally, either as weapon or energy source, nuclear power belongs to the genetic category of the accident, wherein the half-lives of nuclear decay span an astronomical length of time (twenty-four thousand years)—which, in the case of energy production, can be artificially encased only temporarily, as it waits for the wearing away or breaking down of the encasement sooner or later, at some point in the future.

Be that as it may, can we consider nuclear development an act of "humanity"? Furthermore, can we see the catastrophic consequences it exerts as the "punishment" of humanity by a transcendent entity? As we have seen, the answer is doubly No!

It is imperative to account for the effects of nuclear spillage in light of the political ontology of commons. The principle of commoning prioritizes the willingness and capacity of a community to recycle negative commons—that is, to also treat wastes as commons. In other words, a community must declare itself responsible for taking care of the leftovers of its life processes. Commoning is not only a set of principles for communally organizing access to wealth (natural or social) but also a set of principles for reintegrating wastes, toxins, and hazardous byproducts of production and consumption into the regenerative cycles of distinct ecosystems upon which communities depend.[30] It has proven impossible to do this with radioactive wastes, which remain dispersed in our immediate living environment for an unknowable length of time, and which can never be assimilated into an ecosystem's metabolic cycles. Radioactive wastes are thus the ultimate form of negative commons or the *antiworld*, which is displaced from a proper and safe distance—a distance of many millions of miles, which keeps the Earth daughter safe from her Sun father—and now produced within the Earth's own planetary atmosphere.

As a historical fact, nuclear wastes as negative commons have never been generated by a community of people who have adopted commoning. They have instead been created by the specific form of industrial capitalist development backed by technoscientific progressivism that appeared in the twentieth century during the process of America establishing its global hegemony in the Pacific War, then during the Cold War and the concomitant formation of the global nuclear regime. Nuclear projects were created and developed by this specific power apparatus (or the military–industrial complex) and not by humankind in general. Despite this, the potential effects of nuclear governance are imposed on the entirety of humanity and all living organisms. This conjuncture has prompted many thinkers to speak emphatically of nuclear threat as a concern for all of humanity, especially after the bombing of Hiroshima and Nagasaki in 1945, the event that defined antinuclear discourse in the postwar period; thus antinuclear discourse came to stress the big picture of all-or-nothing crisis.

In post-Fukushima Japan, despite early expectations and hopes, the collusion of nuclear capitalism and the nuclear state has endured up until today, through nine years of wide-ranging disaster. Many of us expected a big change to come. But it did not. Or it has not so far. Beginning in December 2011, the state and Fukushima Prefecture set forth a line of policy progressing from radioactive decontamination to the return of evacuated residents to the reconstruction of the region. Since the onset, the publicized goals of the state and industry have grown more and more distant from the actual situation concerning radioactive contamination in which many commoners are living and struggling. Decontamination creates endless piles of radioactive soil and debris simply packed in plastic bags; every attempt to seal the collapsed reactors has been futile and the dumping of polluted water into the ocean continues. Indeed, statements made by the government and corporations today sound increasingly like sheer fantasy. In accordance with this false narrative, state propaganda campaigns have fabricated the image of a "safe Fukushima" by canceling the evacuation order, rearranging evacuation zones, raising the number at which radiation levels are considered safe so that areas can be deemed decontaminated, dismissing consumers' vocalization of fear as "inciting rumors," and so forth.

Meanwhile, Fukushima and its vicinity have become a big laboratory for testing the endurance of individuals and communities to radioactive contamination. In Miharu and Minamisoma, Fukushima, the Center for Environmental Creation (Kankyo Sōzō Senta) is being established using 19 billion yen from the budget allocated to the revitalization of Fukushima, an initiative that is being comanaged by Fukushima Prefecture, the Japan Atomic Energy Agency, and the National Institute for Environmental Studies.[31] The International Atomic Energy Agency (or Atoms for Peace) will soon relocate one of its offices to Fukushima to conduct research on radioactive decontamination and waste treatment as well as to educate people on how to live with radioactivity.[32]

In this way, the post–nuclear disaster state seeks to absorb the devastating effects of nuclear spillage and to rearticulate them as positive modes for empowerment by means of governance, seeking to make profit from nuclear waste (the masterless object) and recapturing and mobilizing disaster victims, including evacuees (the human form of the masterless object), both for the so-called reconstruction of Fukushima. In collaboration with the pronuclear powers of the World, the Japanese state seems determined to make northern Honshu (and, eventually, the entirety of Japan) a test site for a new type of commercial enterprise in the form of radioactive waste treatment—including the doomed attempts to start the actual operation of Rokkasho Reprocessing Plant in Aomori Prefecture.

It is essential to stress that the primary byproduct of nuclear reactor activity is plutonium, which is used for producing nuclear weapons.[33] The countries that produce the most nuclear energy for civil use as fuel—including, in order of number of reactors, the United States, France, China, and Russia—are overwhelmingly armed with nuclear weapons as well, with the exception of Japan.[34] That is, Japan tacitly reserves the capacity and authority to be armed with nuclear weapons, or at least to take part in nuclear weapons deals in world politics. The escalating rearmament policy of the present Shinzō Abe administration can be seen, then, as Japan's attempt at reentry into the competition among nuclear states for planetary governance.

///

World History has moved through different and distinct phases by means of migration, trade, cultural interchange, infrastructural and technoindustrial development, and war—all of these in interaction with intraplanetary movements over territories small and large, regional and transcontinental. The driving force behind each phase has always been the impetus of commerce and governance toward totalization/expansion. As more or less blood is spilled in atrocities, different totalities emerge from distinct governmental motivations, producing different "world pictures."[35]

The dominant world picture today is an extension or end limit of the imperialist West's colonial expansion and the subsequent formation of global capitalism, with two closings of oceanic space—triangular trade over the Atlantic and the US intervention over the Pacific—which coalesced into the current cartographic configuration of both sovereign states and transnational alliances. The space of the World has been thus closed by the violent acts of the West's expansion, and yet more expansion continues, for example, by China's expansionism epitomized by the Belt and Road Initiative. All the while, the scars on the planetary body are getting larger and deeper.

At the same time, threats against humanity are no longer limited to the nuclear. The effects of industrial development, such as global warming, are increasingly imposed upon us. The philosopher Timothy Morton describes both omnipresent and totalizing threats as hyperobjects: "things that are massively distributed in time and space relative to humans," that are nevertheless becoming increasingly close to humans, such as "a black hole, the biosphere, or the Solar System"; "the sum total of all the nuclear materials on Earth, or just the plutonium, or the uranium"; and human products whose effects are very long lasting such as Styrofoam or plastic bags or the sum of all the whirring machinery of capitalism.[36] These objects derange the order of our spatiotemporal senses that used to give us the stability of world order. The revelation of hyperobjects is *epochal* in the sense that they destine our bodies, minds, societies, and the environment. Certainly, recent debates and discourses on the Anthropocene epitomize efforts to grasp the effects of humankind on the planet.

In such lines of thinking, the World (an assembly of human societies) and the Earth (a material system that [un]grounds the World) are colliding and together appear as a masterless object, a mushubutsu—whose effects are increasingly uncontrollable—as dreadful chaos for us, without any transcendental entity that could possibly master it.

Thus, the logic of totality—of humanity, the World, or the planet being on the verge of ultimate catastrophe or apocalypse—captures our *real perception* on one level. However, on another level, this logic fails to convey the multiplicity of existential sufferings felt by the masses, which are unevenly distributed and engender myriad forms of struggle for survival. This multiplicity can be approached only through the singular experiences of people's lives-as-struggle. We seem to be lost in the vast and complex realm between totality and singularity. It is necessary for us to find a way to coordinate between the macro or totalizing projections and at the same time the micro or empirical investigations, for further empowerment of our lives-as-struggle toward planetary revolution.

///

What is radiation, after all? Is it really an object? As the concept of masterless object (無主物), uttered by TEPCO for self-exemption, revealed unwittingly, radiation is less an object than a mode of existence or event, wherein split atoms of uranium are merging with the environment in nano dimension, following the complexity of planetary flows. It appears as chaos to our perception, that is, as a messy situation wherein our mind cannot make connection with the overcomplex reality in which our body is substantially thrown. It is radiation that makes our reality that is already chaotic *deadly so*. After Fukushima, the chaotic permeation of radioactive contamination in small doses has become an irreversible process, with which more or less people must live. One will still have to see the extensiveness of what we must do and the potency of what we can do to outlive its effects. In this sense, the Fukushima nuclear disaster is far from over; it has just begun.

Radiation is deadly and invincible for all vital activities. But it should not be considered transcendent or treated as mere enemy. Instead it must be dealt with through full passion, care, and rigor, both technopolitically and ontometaphysically, for us to live happy lives in the catastrophe. In other words, radiation must be treated differently from the post–nuclear disaster governance that politically and economically forces us to share it. Therefore, our lives-as-struggle in and against the catastrophe would necessitate two different yet interconnected fronts: one against radiation and another against the nuclear capitalist nation-state.

As exemplified in the efforts of radioactive and radiosensitive crowds, the struggle against radiation is the struggle to protect ourselves from chaos or heterogenesis. According to Deleuze and Guattari, art, science, and philosophy are all seeking to deal with chaos by projecting different operative planes: "They open the firmament and plunge into chaos."[37] Their acts attempt to find a way to deal with chaos on specific planes of operation—by grasping it as varieties (for sensitivity in art), variables (for recognition in science), and variations (for conceptualization in philosophy). While the efforts of radioactive/sensitive crowds are in the midst of expansion and transformation—and thus, undefinable at the moment—it is certain that they are increasingly involving all possible arts, techniques, wisdoms, and ways of thinking. The point is that "the struggle against chaos does not take place without an affinity with the enemy, because another struggle develops and takes on more importance—the struggle against opinion, which claims to protect us from chaos itself."[38] This is precisely the distinction between the two fronts of struggle against chaos and against the nuclear capitalist nation-state. Furthermore, it is crucial for the former to develop in such a way as to empower the latter. Herein the victory of post-Fukushima lives-as-struggle is at stake.

The concept of mushubutsu thus reveals the most crucial arena of political conflicts in the post-Fukushima world, being fought between people's lives-as-struggle to confront the event headlong and the strategy of pronuclear governance to absorb it into the capitalist process of accumulation. To repeat, the real enemy is not radiation but the power that imposes the process of radioactive profitmaking and governance on us, as a way of mastering us.

What this arena of conflict embodies is the breach of World History, along which ontological shifts—including one from the World to flows—are taking place, as the decomposition of the metaphysical principles that hold the logos of the World together and the rise of planetary becoming, which appears to us as chaos at the moment. Along with these shifts, people are fighting against the power of pronuclear governance and the global nuclear regime; however, the modes of their struggles are varied, according to their singular positions in the combined and uneven tentacles of this power. It is the heterogeneity of lives-as-struggle and the reverberation among them which, though effaced by the dominant world picture, contain unrealized potentialities to create other worlds, thanks to their ways of preserving and creating different social relations as well as different relations with the planetary body. In this manner, the concept 無主物 ironically reveals to us the ontological horizon of the antiworld from which many worlds can be created. This is the horizon of our lives-as-struggle: anarchy in the apocalypse.

CHAPTER 4

/ *Climate Change of the Struggle*

Compare the climates of Japan's popular struggles of the 1960s and those of the post-Fukushima present. Why these times? They are moments when many lived a radical change in crisis and unrest, while some sought to grasp an aspiration for a better world. In other words, these are times when the social process was severed and an opening for the unknown emerged—the times of uprising. But there is a profound discontinuity between them, embodied in the different perceptions on the status of the world shared among the fighters of each time. The difference is seen in the stark contrast in conviction about revolution, namely, the idea of changing the world full-heartedly: between the naive faith of the 1960s and the inexorable quandary of today.

According to documents, testimonies, and analyses, as well as my own infantile to juvenile memory, during the 1960s hope for the World itself—the arena of international politics based on the global order among nation-states—was tacitly sustained in the sense that its totalization would continue to be the main battleground upon which struggles could bring something better, or even the liberation of all of humanity. This perception of totality still internalized a space for the unknown that was shared in the social atmosphere.

After all, Japan's '68 took place at the peak of economic growth in the postwar regime. Though the entanglement of everyday life in the apparatuses of totalization was already felt as a threat—especially through the surfacing issues of industrial pollution—this was experienced far less clearly, widely, and fatally than it would be in following decades. The perspective of struggles for revolution was held firmly on the course of World History. Meanwhile, the Fukushima age is perceived by many as the beginning of the end of the postwar regime or even the nation-state itself—that is, the World as the assembly of nation-states. Today, we are suffocated by our sense of the world in enclosure, wherein over-developments by totalization never discontinue. We *know* our lives are unwittingly connected with the driving forces for endless development that we cannot stop. The difference in the perceptions of the 1960s and those of today thus speaks to a shift in political ontology that we planetary beings have been going through.

The difference in the mode of actions also makes a stark contrast. Those of '68 were militant and spectacular, while those in the post-Fukushima present have been modest, legalist, or invisible. As we have seen, liberal ideologues praise the latter as a real citizen's or nation's movement by discrediting the former, while revolutionaries are deeply disappointed by the self-limitation of the latter and revisit 1960s struggles in order to rediscover a revolutionary moment in the present. This project, it should be clear, follows the revolutionary aspiration, but it also acknowledges the perceptions and perspectives of the 1960s as embodiments of the politics of the World in tendential decline. In another dimension, Japanese struggles too were part of the so-called global revolution of '68. This makes us see Japan's 1960s both as an end of world politics and a beginning for planetary politics; meanwhile, the times in between—the 1970s and thereafter—are considered a process toward the climate of post-Fukushima struggles.

This shift might be described as one from Politics with a capital *P* to the politics of everyday life: from macro- to micropolitics, citizens' and nation's movements to residents' and migrants' (inhabitants') movements, internationalism to transterritorial association. Such a shift entails the expansion of political engagement from particular campaigns to all aspects of life, and, at the same time, the singularization of practices in relation to localities and translocalities: the planetary body.

This shift does not indicate a total collapse or disappearance of world politics. Philosophically, it is a shift from the dialectic synthesis of human society and nature to the immanence of planetary complexity. It is not a choice—either/or—but a transition that is less subtraction than addition, less exclusion than coexistence.[1] In other words, from the breach in the Politics of World History, a politics of planetary flows has been emerging, accompanied by both negative and positive impacts: the irreversible mutation of the planetary environment and the reverberation of planetary uprisings. The new dimension of planetary politics affects territorial struggles *climatically*, along with the complexity of planetary movements, that is, that which is revealed by the permeation of radionuclides—chaos.

The global uprisings that began in '68 seem to involve a dynamic more complex than propagation from one place to another: that is, synchronic reverberation among places. This dynamic consists of mutual reverberations along multiple flows of memes over electric signals (via media) and through vital energy (via personal and local connections), all originating in lives-as-struggle in singular places on Earth, rather than under the unilateral command of an international organization located in a revolutionary capital.

To approach this awe-inspiring phenomenon, the concept of the "eros effect" coined by George Katsiaficas is a primary reference. This is both the name of the phenomenon and a means of perceiving it. Katsiaficas developed this conceptualization from his association with Herbert Marcuse, and especially from the latter's *Eros and Civilization* (1955). But in order to fully grasp the implications of the phenomenon, one should insert another philosophical lineage: that of Gilles Deleuze and Félix Guattari. That particular frame of reference can help clarify the status of the eros effect, especially in this age when life, confronted by all-out war on multiple fronts, must be interpreted extensively in its multiple dimensions.

In an interview, Katsiaficas confirms the importance of this lineage in terms of its "focus on micro-dynamic . . . [that] came out of the New Left's desire to change everyday life," while at the same time insisting on his hold of dialectics.[2] The philosophies of Marcuse/Katsiaficas and Deleuze/Guattari belong respectively to the different and even conflicting ontologies of dialectics and immanence, but they nonetheless share the strategy of matching Marx and Freud. Ultimately, that approach allows each tradition to grasp human liberation beyond Politics, or outside the governance of the ordered territorialities of the World.

In anticipation of '68, *Eros and Civilization* set the tone for contemporary uprisings characterized by the conflict of the life principle against both alienated labor and the superego, which together underwrite family, society, and civilization itself. What is important in the Marcuse–Katsiaficas lineage is that it puts primary emphasis on the transindividual or collective dimensions of instinct, emotion, and the unconscious as potentially revolutionary forces. This was a watershed of eroto-politics between the expression of individual interiority and the creation of collective engagements, against the background of a growing consumerist/media society.

For their part, Deleuze and Guattari wrote *Anti-Oedipus* shortly after the experience of '68. Targeting the Freudian tendency to confine the libido within the family triangle (mommy, daddy, and me)—and, in this way, to reproduce the capitalist social relations it could otherwise have contributed to unsettling—this was a revelation of the apparatuses of capture whose operational core is the production of the individual blindfolded to the field of social production. Thus, they sought to affirm the creative and subversive power of desire that is transindividual or social in essence. Following their insight, eros can be seen from the microscopic view of the "desiring machine" to detect phases within which affect (the power of body/mind) produces a spectrum of collective emotions and actions of varying intensities. To be clear, however, neither eros nor desire is free from capture. Both can succumb to the morality and reterritorialization of capitalism and nationalism, as we have seen in the example of the insular laboratory. Indeed, they can even be made into their weapon.[3] That is, the eroto-politics of desire is less a principle of liberation in and of itself than it is a new battleground where lives-as-struggle can reverberate and enhance each other on a planetary dimension, or else degenerate into death squads for mutual annihilation within an enclosed territory (as we shall see soon in Japan's intrasectarian violence of the 1970s).

Katsiaficas explained the dynamic of mutually enhancing, life-affirming assemblages of uprisings in the following way: "It's not simply a chain reaction, not just that A causes B which causes C. Events erupt simultaneously at multiple points and mutually amplify each other. They produce feedback loops with multiple iterations. To put it in terms of a mathematical analysis, we could say that diffusion and the circulation of struggles describe the process of movement development geometrically, while the eros effect describes these same developments in terms of calculus."[4] The complex circuit of mutual amplification—or the self-organizing process—is conceptualized here in correspondence to geometry and calculus, both of which play different roles for the eros effect: territorial mapping and climatological forecast/action. One would be a cartographer who maps struggles and uprisings as they develop and spread spatially and temporally by multilateral attractions. Another would be a weather forecaster who tries to anticipate how the atmosphere of struggle might create unexpected turbulences across multiple territories simultaneously—and then acts on it. Here the turbulence of planetary reverberation may be seen as the self-organization of multiple uprisings that is triggered by the simultaneous sensing of threshold internal to singular lives-as-struggle.

Of necessity, such *climatology* pays attention to planetary conditions in toto: beginning from geology, topography, and climate; and then, human traffic in migration, transportation, and communication; movement of capital; production of infrastructure, apparatuses, institutions, and machines; and creation of ideals. The objective of such attentiveness is to grasp the germination of revolutionary assemblages. What it anticipates is not the advancement of humanity toward the World Spirit as an assembly of national spirits but the mutual attraction (eros) of the lives-as-struggle of those who inhabit the Earth: thus, the age of the climatic politics of the Earth overlapping that of the geoterritorial Politics of the World.

JAPAN'S '68

What is considered to be the first global revolution took place in response to the peak of the World's totalization. The reverberating series of uprisings called '68 realized an unprecedented synchronicity, involving not only concentrated exchange among people from varied locations and social milieus but also shared experiences of insurrection. This was the origin of global image sharing among militants fighting against riot police. Those from Japan were marked with helmets of various colors and designs indicating faction. Their variety looked magnificent when they acted in solidarity, but their difference turned into a sign of terror when intrasectarian violence escalated.

In microscopic view, Japan's '68 was felt not just as an event of that particular year but as a series of events that took place before and after. It had previous lives as well as afterlives. In terms of causality, the eros effect within Japan emerged with several attributes, which some might associate with those of postmodernity: that is, the global connectivity of cities and information networks, the cultural logic of heterogeneity, the society of spectacle, and the relative weakening of patriarchal hierarchy. Certainly, the advent of mass-media society had a lot to do with it. However, the primary attractor for turbulence was the friction and unevenness of the capitalist/state mode of development over the planetary body. The hot wind of struggles had long blown from countryside peripheries or inner-city ghettos; beginning in the mid-1950s, it gradually became visible in the metropolis. In urban space, then, feedback loops were created toward multiple orientations, which made the erotic interactions of varied struggles possible.

In 1954, less than ten years after the Hiroshima/Nagasaki nuclear attacks, a Japanese tuna fishing boat (Lucky Dragon Five) with twenty-three crew members—along with innumerable Marshall Islanders—was exposed to nuclear fallout from the US thermonuclear device test at Bikini Atoll. At the height of the Cold War, the strategy of nuclear deterrence had reached an intolerable level for the people of Japan as well. This triggered a large mobilization against nuclear weapons and US military hegemony. As we have seen, this was Japan's first nation-wide popular movement led by women.

During this time, the common enemy faced by the people of East Asia was recognized to be US imperialism and all its proxy governments throughout the region. The first Asian-African Conference at Bandung in 1955 did much to advance this understanding. Revolutionary winds from China, the Korean peninsula, and Indo-China were circulating a guerrilla war against the incomparably rich and well-equipped forces of the US regular army, and transferring eros to student, labor, and other oppositional movements in Japan. Internally, another current was streaming from northern Kyushu, where throughout the 1950s and early 1960s the Miike miners had been on strike against restructuring and layoffs.[5]

In March and April 1960, there was a wave of uprisings across Korea initiated by high school and university students against the vice presidential election, which had been manipulated by the pro-US ruling power. June of that same year saw postwar Japan's first mass insurgency, in resistance to the US-Japan Security Treaty (Ampo) destined to align the country with US security interests for the following decade. Students, workers, and commoners broke into the National Diet Building—the very symbol of Japan's postwar constitution—and stayed there until the treaty automatically went into effect on June 19.[6] Although the Korean and Japanese uprisings did not have a visible connection, their reverberating co-implication could be seen through people's affinity and their identification of a common enemy—the US military. It is also important to note that there were approximately 650,000 resident Koreans in Japan at that time, due to Japan's coercive pre–World War II labor migration policies and the flood of exiles from the Korean War.

There were four factors that co-facilitated Japan's '68: the development of the New Left, the nature of the student associations, labor militancy, and new national and transinternational connections between urban and rural struggles. We shall see the way these factors interacted to create the eros effect of Japan's '68.

At its sixth national conference in 1955, the Japan Communist Party (JCP) abandoned armed revolution and began to shift toward parliamentarism. The Hungarian Revolution of 1956 influenced anti-Stalinist revolutionary movements to grow across the world. In Japan, the Trotskyist League was organized in 1957, and in 1958 the original New Left sect (Bund, or the Communist League) was established by a group of student members of the JCP who felt the need to create a new revolutionary movement outside the party. Thereafter, Japan's New Left began to radicalize, moving toward mass mobilization as it passed through innumerable divergences, convergences, and intrasectarian conflicts that pitted political ideologies, organizational forms, and natures of militancy against one another. These included Leninism, Trotskyism, Maoism, Left Communism, anarchism, and nonsectarian radicalism.

The leading force of the anti-Ampo uprising in 1960 was Zen-gaku-ren (National Federation of Student Self-Government Associations), which was under the hegemony of Bund, after JCP students lost its grip. In itself, Zen-gaku-ren was not a political organization. It was a national assembly of student associations from different universities and played the role of receptacle for different groups to construct their bases, both financially (with budgets for student activities) and spatially (on university campuses). Nevertheless, after the 1960s Ampo uprising, this assembly was gradually divided and became fixed by the domination of a few main groups; it thus lost its earlier impetus for mass mobilization. Then, in 1968, another form of student network was established: Zen-kyo-to (All-Campus Joint Struggle Committee), which consciously created more flexible, inclusive, radical, and anarchic connections between university and high school struggles across the nation. Around 1968 and 1969, this new form culminated in a wave of university and high school occupations that swept the country from Hokkaido to Kyushu.

The social status of university students changed drastically from the early to the late 1960s. At the time of the 1960s anti-Ampo uprising, leading student activists were the future elites of the nation: upcoming bureaucrats, scientists, lawyers, corporate executives, and so on. Their social status influenced the tendency of the movement toward a national movement against US imperialism. Thereafter, the massification of university education advanced, which made the majority of students middle or lower-middle class. Thus, late 1960s students considered themselves petit bourgeoisie, suspended between the bourgeoisie and the proletariat. This was for them a source of distress in terms of identifying their position in the revolutionary politic. The tendency of their movement was no longer national but antinational, anti-imperialist, anti-Stalinist, international revolution.

Outside educational institutions, there were four indispensable milieus of convergence: mass culture, urban space, local struggles, and internationalism. By the mid-1960s, American civil rights, black liberation, and anti–Vietnam War and student movements had begun to send signals and energy, which mixed with jazz, blues, rock, and the hippie lifestyle. These new political cultures dominated the everyday landscape of big cities for the youth.

One of the busiest commercial centers in Tokyo, Shinjuku, contributed significantly to the spectacular aspect of Japan's '68. Redeveloped as a black market after the bombing of Tokyo, Shinjuku consists of a chaotic and heterotopic mishmash—shopping areas, working-class entertainment, the sex industry, gay and transvestite areas, tiny bars, and progressive culture—which offered a common space for both militant street fights and progressive street performance. It was an asylum for revolutionaries.[7] Every Saturday night, crowds occupied a square in Shinjuku Station for guerrilla folk concerts; street performances by avant-garde theaters and artist groups interacted with passersby with their defamiliarization effects; bars, cafés, and clubs provided niche crowds (hippies, radicals, sexual and ethnic minorities) with their gathering places; and the riots were the critical point of all these events.[8]

The so-called Shinjuku Riot took place on International Anti-War Day (October 21) in 1968. A crowd of more than twenty thousand—coordinated by three New Left sects—broke into the mammoth Shinjuku Station and disrupted a freight train carrying jet engine fuel for the US military.[9] The action was provoked by the explosion of the same freight car in August 1967. On October 21, 1969, the action was repeated. Importantly, during the years '67, '68, and '69, the National Railway Workers Union (NRU) and the National Railway Motive Power Union (NRMU)—the biggest public workers' unions at that time—continued their struggles against rationalization. They instigated more than ten strikes as well as many wildcat strikes. It is said that some sectors of the unions acted in sync with the riots.

Local struggles provided a meeting place for urban militants and rural people to confront their common enemy. They created new maps of interconnection between different lives and struggles. Most notably, the farmers in Sanrizuka, Chiba Prefecture, self-organized and resisted the construction of a new international airport—Narita—between 1966 and 1978. Many individuals and groups joined in the farming community, sharing everyday life and struggle with the farmers. (Today, some speak of this struggle in relation to La zad in France or No tav in Italy.)

Another major source of eros effect turbulence has long been Okinawa. Ever since the Ryukyu Kingdom was colonized by the southern domain of Satsuma in the early seventeenth century, Okinawa has always been placed in a marginal position to be sacrificed by Japan's interest. In the Battle of Okinawa in 1945, the only battle that took place inside the territory of Imperial Japan, the Japanese state forced Okinawans to sacrifice their lives in a no-win confrontation against US Marine Corps and Army forces. Thereafter Okinawa was under US occupation, and Okinawans fought against the presence of US military bases as well as the pro-US policies of Japan's postwar regime.

In 1970 a riot erupted in the US base town of Koza, in response to a car accident caused by a US soldier. The crowd attacked and burned military vehicles and facilities. In 1972 Okinawa was "reverted" to Japan; however, the US bases remained. Its geopolitical status has continued to raise issues concerning the territorial claims of the Japanese state as well as the military strategy of the US network empire. As a result, the island territory has been an important point of convergence for activists and movements across Japan, East Asia, and the world.

Internationalism in the period leading up to Japan's '68 developed around the anti–Vietnam War movement and in solidarity with Third World revolutions. While professing itself a "peaceful nation," Japan was economically flourishing by producing various weapons for the US military and its wars in Korea and Vietnam. After 1965, when the US Armed Forces began bombing in Vietnam, anti–Vietnam War movements spread through Japan. In their early stage, most actions were limited to protest at the National Diet against the Japanese government, based on the legalist line of changing parliamentary politics toward antiwar. Then, there appeared a militant antiwar movement led by workers. The

Direct Action Committee against the Vietnam War called for the disruption of weapons production (trench mortars and tank cannons) in certain factories. Slogans from its 1966 flyers included "Crush the US/Japan security regime by workers' direct action!" and "Don't go to the National Diet; disrupt the factories and the merchants of death!"[10]

A popular movement called Be-hei-ren (Citizens' Alliance for Peace in Vietnam) succeeded in mobilizing the general public for antiwar protests and functioned as a gateway for young activists to become involved in revolutionary movements. It also instigated a clandestine operation called the Japan Technical Committee to Aid Anti-War GIs (JATEC), which helped US military deserters migrate to Finland and Canada via Siberia. The express purpose of this operation was to decompose the US military stationed across the Japanese archipelago.

Meanwhile, a number of small groups had begun to establish clandestine connections with revolutions taking place around the world. Most famous among these, the Japan Red Army dramatically appeared in the anti-imperialist guerrilla war—that is, with hijacks of airplanes and occupations of embassies—in solidarity with the Popular Front for the Liberation of Palestine (PFLP) during the 1970s.[11]

The student movement of the late 1960s was largely inspired by the Cultural Revolution in China. Instead of identifying itself with the new regime ruled by the Gang of Four, it gravitated toward a new form of *everyday revolution* in the city, questioning and opposing hierarchies in family, school, society, and nation, and seeking the reeducation of students by *decentralization*. Around that time, one of the main problems of student activism concerned the social status and class identity of students, who were beginning to question the role of education in reproducing class divisions and hierarchy. The slogan "decompose the university" expressed one of the main objectives of the Zen-kyo-to occupations, which was to transform educational institutions into revolutionary bases. These occupations blocked classes, examinations, and all evaluation systems while encouraging self-motivated discussions, seminars, cultural activities, and communal living.

During the later phase of the student movement, when university struggles and street protests had fallen into decline following the last large coordinated action against the renewal of the US-Japan Security Treaty (Ampo) in June 1970, "decompose the university" metamorphosed into "decompose the self." Practically speaking, this involved destroying one's status as a student to become part of the lower stratum of society—the underclass of workers, peasants, and indigenous peoples. Such decomposition was considered a revolutionary education for militants, who either moved to day laborers' ghettos (*yoseba*) to live and work, or to the countryside (especially Okinawa), where they became farmers. In those spaces, they destroyed their privileged social status and sought to build communes as armed revolutionary bases.[12]

After the birth of the New Left, in the 1960s, conflicts began to take place between the JCP and the New Left as well as among a few New Left sects. Skirmishes came to be part of the everyday landscape, during rallies and demonstrations, on campuses and elsewhere. But after 1970's Ampo, the strife intensified to a level at which the goal was total elimination.[13] This came to be called internal violence (*uchigeba*).[14] Every possible means to discredit and exhaust the opponent was employed: wiretapping, threats of all kinds, information manipulation, distribution of fake publications, and so on. At the peak of uchigeba, group leaders were targeted for torture and assassination. All the main activists of these sects went underground while many others nurtured chronic phobias of going out in public.

All this was the consequence of a few radical groups seeking to occupy the leading position of "true revolutionary party" inside an insular realm. Each claimed to be the vanguard of conscious communists that could conceive the coming society, and for that purpose motivated coalitions with other groups only as a means to decompose and absorb them. What epitomized uchigeba was this organizational principle— based upon the theological faith in telos—which belittled the existence of others.

It is nevertheless surprising that during the 1970s, while three main sects concentrated so much of their energy on uchigeba, turning a large portion of their dedicated members into underground armies, they were still able to sustain their mobilization power for oppositional militant actions against the state, some of which were undoubtedly significant. Were these distinctive phases of power—militancy for opposing the state and violence against each other—essentially different or connected in certain dimensions? Could they be separated so the latter was deterred or abolished? All in all, why was so much power consumed and so many lives wasted (more than a hundred deaths and a thousand serious injuries)? Without tackling these questions, we in Japan cannot approach the problematic of "militancy," in distinction from militarism. While preachy pacifism replaced the militarism of uchigeba, militancy for the empowerment of antiauthoritarian struggles has not yet been nurtured.[15]

Due to the brutality of uchigeba violence during the decades that followed, the legacy of Japan's '68 is often cast as a story about the perils of authoritarian vanguardism, dogmatism, hierarchical structure, and sexism. The phase of "psychic Thermidor" (in the sense of Marcuse or Katsiaficas) or "microfascism" (in the sense of Deleuze and Guattari) — a form of capturing desiring machines by the Thanatos drive — alienated commoners and youth from the '68 legacy of mass insurgencies and aspirations for changing the world.[16] As a result, activists of subsequent generations came to focus more on coalition building and on issues such as minorities' struggles, the environment, and the creation of community. The molecular revolution in this sense was as important in Japan as it was in the broader global context. In Japan, however, the memory of terror endures, resulting in a culture of fear and legalism that is suppressing the desire for militancy and creativity in popular movements.

INHABITANTS' STRUGGLES

During the global uprisings of the 1960s, changing the World as totality was the main trend of revolutionary movements. The imagery of totality was sustained, more or less, within the proxy wars staged in the Cold War structure. Today, as nobody is able to stop totalization, we are bound by the same impetus of World History but in an inverse manner: it is no longer an objective to orient ourselves toward totalization but rather an uncontrollable drive. In other words, the totalization of the World by capitalism appears for us to be the only ontological horizon, so that the material limit it faces is experienced in an increasingly devastating and desperate manner. What is revealed therein is the material limit that the philosophy of the World has come to confront.

This philosophy was nurtured in Europe, along with its colonial expansion and via the Enlightenment, for instance, as Immanuel Kant's idea of cosmopolitan society, which eventually led to the establishment of the United Nations (UN) and influenced today's thoughts on universal human rights and communicative reason. Meanwhile, it was given a formal system or logic by Georg W. F. Hegel in the synthesis of the World Spirit (*Geist*), which was materialistically inverted by Marx as the global subjectivation of workers (Proletariat) and sustained throughout the 1960s uprisings as the main index. Since then, the philosophy of the

World has expanded in varied forms, oscillating between capitalist realism and utopian projection.[17]

As a tacit premise, the view of the World's totality secured the purity and infinity of earthly nature in its margins or in its tacit ground, whereby an optimism for the future was allowed. Humanist progressivism was able to survive. Its image of time was sustained in the linear trajectory of an arrow rather than in complexity. But after the 1960s, the situation has gradually changed. Nobody can ignore the irreversible mutations of the planetary environment, and so the assumption of expansive totality has been replaced by the recognition of its material limit. The Capitalocene is the crucial response from the philosophy of the World to the epochal proposition of the Anthropocene.[18]

From the beginning of the 1970s, a shift has begun to affect the main stage of political and social movements—from a macropolitics focused on changing Politics with a capital *P* to a micropolitics that reconstitutes politics within the arena of existential struggles, such as environmental protection, anti-industrial development, women's liberation, and minorities' autonomy. The crux is that the power of heterogeneous subjectivities—beyond the industrial worker, or the proletariat—has come to the front stage from the invisible peripheries of the world, that is, from inhabitants' lives-as-struggle, which conceptually and materially exceeds the classical notion of class struggle.

Theoretically, the contribution of revolutionary feminists has been crucial in terms of shedding light on the multidimensionality of class oppression and class struggle, and has long provided an indispensable point of reference. For instance, beginning with the Wages for Housework movement in 1972, the work of Silvia Federici makes a seminal shift from production to reproduction, thereby opening a view to grasp the broad horizon of *life qua struggle*—at the site of reproduction (the kitchen, the bedroom, the home) prior to the site of production (the factory).[19] Herein the workerist inversion—workers' struggle comes before capital's crisis/recomposition—is given another, bigger dimension of engagement: that of political ontology for anticapitalist struggle toward a noncapitalist world. From this view, capitalist accumulation is made possible, both historically and presently, through the separation of body and land and the simultaneous creation of waged labor, based on the devaluation of reproduction in toto along with the sexual division of labor.

This shifting stance makes us realize a material truth: Who is making this world? Who has the power (*puissance*) of sustaining—and changing—the world? Those who have the real power to make this world are those who are devalued and made invisible. Thereafter, the paradox is evident: having the power to make the world and being devalued by the world constitute revolutionary subjectivity. To say it differently, what is at stake here is the *ontological asymmetricity* between reproductive *life=struggle* as host and the expansive World driven by the capitalist-state mode of development as parasite.

This asymmetricity is embodied by the lives-as-struggle of the planetary populace, emerging from the breach of World History. The rise of heterogeneous subjectivities—minorities, indigenous, precariat, and all the nameless—has begun to draw a new cartography of planetary becoming, consisting of the lives-as-struggle of the nameless that had been dropped from the map of the World. This new cartography also embodies the shift from authoritarian revolutionary movement (Marxism-Leninism) to antiauthoritarian struggle, which since the turn of the century has created transversal connections among autonomous territories of indigenous and groups of minorities and anarchists across the Global South and Global North.

The rising power of planetary inhabitants was nevertheless dogged by an irreversible degeneration of the planetary environment. Thus, the spatiotemporality of the apocalypse has been unleashed. This is not in the sense of eschatology or the end of the world as a singular event. Nor is it dystopia as opposed to utopia. It is a radical shift in the arrangement of material and immaterial powers. That is, the physical and corporeal contents of the battlefield between power and popular struggle have begun to be affected by the material limit of the expansive World and the tendency of its shrinking. This delimitation manifests itself in the over-enlargement of the negative commons—the masterless object—that all planetary inhabitants are forced to share. Neither the capitalist nation-state nor we ourselves can rely on the unitary order of the infinitely expanding World: be it the UN, the International, or Empire. Now infinity has to be found within internal nature—immanence. The present and future battleground is oriented by the shift from the process of the World's infinite development to the process of its infinite ending—entropy. In the infinite process of ending, the multitude of nation-states will have to reconstruct governance and development through a maniacal *programming of stages* (as in the Apocalypse of John) while calculating the material limit of the natural resources of the Earth. Meanwhile, popular struggles are tacitly creating space and time, or other worlds, outside World History, while rediscovering nature as active creativity (natura naturans) dropped from or uncaptured by the expansive World—within the catastrophe.

///

Roughly articulated, the times in Japan after '68 have gone through bubble economy and burst bubble governance toward the Fukushima catastrophe. The global simultaneity that had expressed itself as eros effect in the struggles of the late 1960s—perhaps even up to the oil crisis of 1973—was gradually lost; this losing process stood out at the moment when the 1975 Strike for Recovering the Right to Strike (Suto-ken-suto) failed to achieve its goal. In postwar Japan, all public workers—with the exception of police officers, firefighters, and corrections officers—had gained the right to strike in 1947 with the Labor Standards Act (Rōdō kijunhō). But this was rescinded by new legislation in 1948, mainly under pressure from General Douglas MacArthur of the Occupation Army. The 1975 strike, led by Sohyo (General Council of Trade Unions of Japan), was fought for eight days. In retaliation, the administration of Kokutetsu (Japanese National Railways) sued the participating unions, including NRU and NRMU, claiming a business loss of 202 billion yen. This major defeat for the unions was the beginning of a strange lag of temporality from the rest of the world that characterized 1980s Japan.

This was the beginning of a syndrome provoked by a series of government policies that reflected the lingering threat that the ruling class felt from the uprisings of the 1960s. In the summer of 1975, Prime Minister Miki Takeo proposed a social policy called "Outline for the Nation's Life-Planning" (Shogai sekkei keikaku kōsō), consisting of four goals: home ownership, lifelong education, social security, and guaranteed retirement benefits for life. Miki announced this policy right before the 1975 strike began with its slogan "Win back the right to strike!" Thus governance sought to nullify the subjectivity of the working class and to manage the body and mind of the entire populace by imposing a homogeneous ideal of life.

Economically speaking, Japan was the quickest of all industrialized nations to recover from the oil shock of 1973, which was perhaps another factor in its falling out of sync with the sense of global reality. This was due to its early, "brave" determination to restructure. And later, what contributed to the 1980s economic boom was the increase of marginal labor—part-time and informal jobs—for students, wives, and increasing ranks of migrant and minority workers. Capital and the state claimed that the economic success was thanks to superior technology and a unique management system rooted in national tradition. But restructuring and informalized labor had already played their crucial roles. At that time, informalized workers did not appear to be so troubled as today; rather, their work was seen as appealing in the sense of pioneering a new lifestyle, especially in the booming service industries.

The bubble economy was a moment dominated by a new current of conservatism called neoliberalism. As any number of analyses of the post-Fordist transformation of social space in the West have shown, in the simplest analysis, in Japan, too, social and public domains were decomposed by the bare principles of market economy; this undermined the welfare system that used to support the disenfranchised. The results were a harsher bifurcation of class and the transformation of urban space and culture in general: public institutions were replaced by multipurpose commercial spaces, while mass media, led by TV and advertising agencies, took over discursive hegemony. Japan also exemplified a conclusive phase of the shift from a society of discipline to one of control.[20] But because of the conditions of Japan's peculiar bubble, the effects of neoliberal policies were not immediately perceived in the social atmosphere.

The real subsumption of the entire social milieu occurred under the influence of the integration of enterprises into conglomerates (*keiretsu*) that absorbed affiliated subcontractors into a kind of cartel. The advent of these monsters accelerated the decomposition of critical labor movements. The unions of state-owned companies—such as NRU and NRMU—were finally dissolved as the companies were privatized and absorbed into organizations subordinated to keiretsu. All political and social problems were addressed on the level of the market economy. Meanwhile, the state expanded the focus of its policy from economic and industrial domains to the entire lifeworld of the people.

After corporate hegemony over the social milieu was established, leading corporations and elite universities joined hands, and the privatization of education became a major trend. Education began to approach entertainment; some large universities moved out of central Tokyo and reestablished themselves in the suburbs, making the educational environment more and more detached from urban space, and more and more fictional. This turned the Quartier Latin phenomena of '68 into nostalgia.

At the same time, critical social science discourses were replaced with cultural analyses influenced by a depoliticized version of semiotics. In consequence, even the emperor system came to be dealt with mythologically, treated as a mysterious and fanciful kingdom that had survived since ancient times. This made the nation forget its modern historicity, wherein the emperor system was fully responsible for a number of wars of aggression and continues to assume ambiguous yet substantial power over.

There was no happy ending. Toward the 1990s, the darker features of the boom were gradually exposed. Everything that used to look positive revealed its negative function. First and foremost, enterprises quickly responded to the recession by discarding so-called Japanese-style management, which was allegedly based on the uniquely intimate relationality (*aidagara*) of Japan's household (*ie*) type society.[21] The core employment secured by permanent contract diminished to a bare minimum. Companies began to throw workers out on the streets, telling them to be responsible for their own lives. Thus masses of homeless people began to roam the city to find public spaces where they could spend the night.

The year 1995 was known for its disasters: the Great Hanshin earthquake, the sarin gas attack in the Tokyo subway by the Aum cult, and the accident at the Monju Nuclear Power Plant. Even Japan's postwar specialty—technoindustry—had become a source of trouble. Also in 1995 was the rape of an elementary school girl by three US soldiers in Okinawa, which rekindled the anti–US base movement and created one of the most powerful currents of feminism ever seen in Japan.[22] At the same time, at the initiative of youth sensitive to catastrophe, more and more volunteer activities and mutual aid communities appeared. Finally, as if in anticipation of the coming antiglobalization movement, antiauthoritarian Marxists and anarchists began to seek connections with foreign activism. Thus 1995 marked a radical shift in the entire social climate.

In 1999 the 145th National Diet announced the government's new policy of intensifying control over the nation. A number of bills were passed: legislation concerning the national flag and anthem (*kokki kokka hō*) that sought to reestablish a tight national body (*kokutai*); legislation concerning national security (*shuhen jitai hō*) that legalized the war mobilization of every local government; legislation concerning residents' registration (*jumin kihon daicho hō*) that intensified control over the populace; and three bills aimed against organized crime, including legislation allowing wiretapping (*tochō hō*), that threatened civil liberties.

All in all, the seeds of today's crises were disseminated during the 1980s; only at the time, dressed in the robe of economic euphoria and technocultural exceptionalism, could they have appeared to be positive signs for the future.

///

Certain territories of life-as-struggle have arisen that bridge the global '68 and today. As already evident, the antinuclear movement in its conventional framework cannot fully confront post–nuclear disaster problematics. Instead, the emergence of four territories, in their singular formations, shed light on new horizons of struggle post-Fukushima: inhabitants' movement defending living environments, migrant or fluid underclass workers' struggle, mutual aid community building, and theoretical and cultural production tackling infrastructural power. These are interconnected either actually or virtually, and together prefigure the associations and frictions—the complexities—of post-Fukushima struggles. While confronting catastrophic mutations of the lifeworld in post-1960s situations, they materialized differential phases or positive bifurcations of catastrophe, in their creation of new forms of life and new modes of thought and practice. It is imperative for us to follow their formations, should we want to grasp both the difficulties and the possibilities of post-Fukushima life-as-struggle.

Defending Living Environment

The environmental scientist Ui Jun (1932–2006) is known for his engagements as a political activist and educator on the hazardous effects of industrial development, including Minamata mercury poisoning and US military base constructions in Okinawa, among others. His classic *Kōgai genron* (Principles of environmental pollution) provides geopolitical, economic, and social analyses from the standpoint of inhabitants' movements against industrial pollution. His concept of "inhabitants' movement" (*jumin undō*)—in distinction from "citizens' movement" (*shimin undō*)—speaks to the difficulties or the complexity that struggles against environmental pollution must face in order to create their politics, through which nevertheless they conceive a new political ontology.

Ui articulates three contexts that contribute to these difficulties. He begins with the largest: the geopolitical conditions that make permeating pollution invisible within the country of Japan. This first context consists of five factors:

1. Being surrounded by seas: all waste can be dumped into the ocean without public attention.
2. With the tides of the surrounding seas, pollutants are carried away from the land.
3. Large quantities of rainfall wash pollutants away.
4. Frequent winds make pollutants disappear faster.
5. Having no land borders and no transnational rivers frees the state from immediate international disputes over responsibility for pollution.[23]

These conditions created the incomparably reckless and irresponsible behaviors of both industry and government vis-à-vis the effects of industrial developments. Thus Japan was the first country in modern history where waterborne pollution—for example, Ashio mineral poisoning, Toyama cadmium poisoning, and Minamata mercury poisoning—killed many nationals. Furthermore, it is vital to note that even after Fukushima, the government has been habitually relying on these conditions— dumping radio-contaminated water into the ocean—despite the fact that today the effects are being experienced and spoken about globally.

The second context is the limit to victims' perception of pollution and the limited indices of their victimization. In other words, the most serious existential problem of pollution is that though it affects the entirety of vital activities in localities and individual existence (body and mind), its victims can perceive it only via its limited indices (symptoms) by their corporeal senses; and they can achieve legal recognition and political justice only via these limited indices. Thus, it is always too late to prevent pollution, and the legislative authority can never take initiative to protect the natural environment from it.

The third context is the policy called "municipal mergers and dissolutions" (shichōson gappei), which since the Meiji Restoration has been repeatedly instigated throughout different phases and in different forms. Its overall effect is the disappearance of towns and villages by the absorption of localities into the national governance, which weakens or destroys self-government.

Finally, our lives are increasingly entangled in the apparatuses of development, by which we are the consumers of the products whose production is the root cause of pollution. It is increasingly hard to distinguish between victim and assailant in both political and ethical senses. Therefore, as Ui stresses, both macro and micro approaches are necessary for antipollution struggle. That is, it is necessary to create autonomous (inconspicuous) projects to support victims' health and sustain their living conditions while opposing pollution in formal (spectacular) political process.

By the late 1960s, struggles against the so-called four big environmental pollutions came to reveal—along with the Sanrizuka farmers' struggle—the nature of Japan's modernization and industrial development, which facilitated the decomposition of farming and fishing communities along with the devastation of their living environments.[24] These tendencies were accelerated further by the gradual shift from fast economic growth to slow economic growth: in other words, as the initiative of development shifted from heavy and chemical industries to the administrative power that manages public investment and energy industries that are semipublic private industries (i.e., TEPCO). In another register, the political and economic restructuring that realized the shift of main energy source from coal to oil triggered new kinds of pollution and accident.[25] Simply said, these shifts resulted in an unprecedented permeation of developments/pollutions that was unimaginable in the previous state of concentration.

By 1973, there were more than ten thousand movements against industrial pollution in Japan.[26] The climate of struggle was changing from the 1960s militant and spectacular political engagements toward the less visible and more enduring struggles of local inhabitants, who were not always politically left. Here we should also situate the local struggles that successfully blocked nuclear developments, beginning in the early 1970s. To be precise, there have been fifty communities that stopped the construction of nuclear power plants; sixty communities, if we include reprocessing plants; and eighty communities, including radioactive waste storage facilities. Here we would not name all the communities, but they are located in the grids of all the electric power companies from Hokkaido to Kyushu, except for the territory of TEPCO (evidencing the concentration of power in Tokyo-centered businesses). Many of these struggles continued for a long time; some have not yet ended, in consequence not only of the long-term project of nuclear installment itself but also vis-à-vis the endurance of community life. The tactics they employ have included strengthening solidarities in the community, collectively buying up targeted land, influencing municipal and central government by organizing the popular vote, sending antinuclear candidates to the city council, and direct actions (i.e., blockading coastal measurement by boats, in the case of fishing communities). The success of these communities' struggles is based upon their nature: that a community solidly shares that which is to be defended and nurtured further, in subsistence, social relations, and culture. In other words, when the struggle is directly tied to the life of community, people do not easily give up their autonomy.[27]

The political scientist Nakata Norihito elaborates inhabitants' movements conceptually, beginning from a simple definition: "people who inhabit a land defend their local living."[28] This conceptualization connects various existing struggles, from antipollution to antidevelopment to anti–military base, whose constituencies are no longer limited to nationals and citizens but include minorities, indigenous, and refugees— the planetary crowd. In the case of Japan, Nakata continues, inhabitants' movements distinguished themselves from the leftist movements that were often backed by progressive political parties (communist, socialist, and democratic socialist) and their associated labor unions. The essence of an inhabitants' movement is in life-as-struggle, and not in political ideology—though it is rarely free from that in practice. Somewhere in their development, these struggles are inexorably implicated in political movements as well as formal political processes—that is, consultation with local politicians, petitioning government and corporations, making court cases. At the same time, certainly inhabitants' struggles can tend toward militant opposition, too. In inhabitants' movements across the planet—from Minamata, Sanrizuka, and Okinawa to La ZAD, Bure, Chiapas, Standing Rock, Rojava, and so on—we observe all strategies and tactics that can possibly be employed, based on inhabitants' own bodies and minds, communal relations, shared resources and techniques, and living environments.

The radicalism of an inhabitants' movement is that it is the struggle of a form of life, which internalizes ineradicable heterogeneity, creates singular rapport with the land, and sustains perspectives much longer than the temporality of a particular political campaign, for such struggle always involves multiple generations. These attributes embody the *ontological asymmetricity* of inhabitants' lives-as-struggle to the power of the capitalist-state mode of development. That is, inhabitants' struggles against developmental power are not those of bipolar opposition (A versus B) but instead of host against parasite or receptacle against filler—as seen historically in the guerrilla warfare waged by a sea of people against the regular army of the state. Therefore, inhabitants' struggle is, on one level, beyond victory and defeat in an immediate sense. For that matter, every inhabitants' movement is doomed to lose at some point in time to the overwhelming force of totalizing development; none of them are able to abolish the root cause of their problems—apocalyptic capitalism itself. But their victories exist in different dimensions: the lives in agony of inhabitants can achieve ethical victory over state and corporation; they can critically reveal what makes the substance of authorities and being public in the nation; their heritages can be handed down to future struggles; and finally, their struggles can connect themselves on a planetary horizon by sending vibrations of the eros effect among themselves.

In the history of industrial pollution in Japan, the Minamata mercury poisoning is considered the worst instance. It was inflicted by a chemical industry backed by the state.[29] The complexity of the struggles against pollution, industry, and state are abundantly and meticulously described in the novel *Paradise in the Sea of Sorrow: Our Minamata Disease* by Ishimure Michiko (1927–2018), one of Japan's most revered novelists. This complexity entails the cosmic coexistence of tragic description of victims' suffering, detailed analysis of community life and political situations, and rich depiction of local tradition and natural environment. The novel extensively reproduces medical and legal records, interviews, statistics, and journal articles about the disease, on top of the account of Ishimure's own engagement in victims' struggle, everyday life, culture, tradition, and environment. The core is the endless battle of victims against their illnesses, their families' and offspring's illnesses, which reveals what the regime that caused the pollution ultimately signifies to the people. Ishimure's imagination often awakens the animistic spirits of Minamata—via the raw voices of victims—from local folklores living in the community. The text in its entirety thus presents a cosmology consisting of the network of natural environment and human world, as a poisonous substance travels through the food chain, symptoms appear in bodies, and victims begin their protests against the company and the government in Minamata as well as Tokyo. The world is revealed here as everything in its own complexity, which plays a part in every other complexity, composing the universe—this is a paradise in purgatory or a purgatory in paradise. With all of these implications, the Minamata mercury poisoning has been an important point of reference to understand the Fukushima radiation poisoning.

///

Fluid Underclass Struggle
Another aspect of inhabitants' struggle exists in the deterritorialized territoriality of migrant or fluid underclass workers' lives-as-struggle. Inhabitation means not only living in the same place (sedentary) but also living in one place after another (nomadic), or living the Earth as deterritorialization itself. The emphasis here is the difference of inhabitants from residents, who are citizens of a nation and behave according to their status.

In major industrial cities in postwar Japan, there are inner-city areas called *yoseba* (in translation, "gathering place"), which are populated by day laborers. These include Sanya in Tokyo, Kotobuki-cho in Yokohama, Sasajima in Nagoya, and Kamagasaki in Osaka. From there, migrant workers take day jobs in construction, dock work, road repair, heavy industries, and nuclear power plants; these were the workers who built the infrastructure for Japan's postwar democracy regime. They represent the most informal and low-paid working force. Often, they are without permanent address, social security, and health insurance. Many are not registered to vote. They make up Marx's relative surplus population.

After the militancy and militarism of the New Left gradually died down in the 1970s, some activists who continued to seek the revolutionary moment moved to yoseba, where they participated in organizing militant labor movements, including the Kamagasaki Joint Struggle Committee (Kama-kyo-to) established in 1972 and the Sanya Dispute Group (Sanya sogi-dan) in 1983.[30] Their struggles targeted issues related to day laborers, while nurturing associations with the struggles of minorities (resident Koreans, Okinawans, Ainu, and the generic social outcasts called *burakumin*) as well as armed struggle against Japanese expansionism.[31] The determination to intervene in yoseba was motivated by the realization that earlier engagements had failed to incorporate the oppressed masses. As we have seen, organized labor movements had lost their ground in Japan. In that climate, the yoseba was the only locus where the moment of radical class struggle remained. According to traditional Marxism, day workers are defined as marginal lumpen proletariat and treated as unorganizable. But along with the decline of formal labor movements, all theory based on a vanguard party of organized workers was thrown into doubt, and activists sought to grasp a new potency in the yoseba workers—more fluid, omnipresent, and rhizomatic forces, as it were, on top of the fact that they are the most tragic victims of political oppression and social inequality, existing as they do at the hierarchical bottom and outside of civil society. This intervention became the starting point or the point of starting over for the revolutionaries of following generations.

If we look at lives-as-struggle from a microscopic view, the clean-cut division between organizing and spontaneity disappears—both exist in different phases in one and the same spectrum of affective exchanges in everyday life, which is the erotic drive in molecular dimension. In other words, every aspect of everyday life in the yoseba became a stage of organizing for the post–New Left revolutionaries. The emergent uprisings of the stormy 1960s were thus followed by forms of submerged molecular organizing, where radical intervention focused more on transforming the activist's own form of life and social relations while confronting the violent power of the state manifest in the yoseba.

Through the time of the construction boom, the majority of Japanese yoseba workers were those who came to big cities from the countryside temporarily, during the farming off-season. Their home regions included those areas that are most likely to be chosen for the siting of nuclear plants. For instance, the land around Fukushima Daiichi is not particularly fertile for agriculture, and so before the plants came, the local men of age had had to go to yoseba, especially Sanya in Tokyo. Then, the nuclear plants made it possible for them to remain with their families, if and only if they took the risk of working in hazardous conditions. Thus the areas targeted by the nuclear power industry overlap with those from which a majority of day laborers come: remote locations where land is either unsuitable for agricultural production or where agricultural production is unprofitable relative to the national and global markets.

The working forces in yoseba include not only Japanese but also resident ethnic Koreans, Okinawans, and burakumin. In the postwar period, urban policy turned yoseba into monosexual zones populated almost exclusively by single males; yoseba tend to be situated next to the red-light districts where underclass women work, including migrants from Thailand, Myanmar, Korea, China, and other eastern and central Asian countries, especially since the bubble economy of the 1980s. The inner cities of yoseba and red-light districts are thus considered to be places of the trans-Asiatic underclass.

The struggle of day laborers has formed the most militant labor movement in Japan.[32] Before and after the uprisings of the 1960s, periodic riots have taken place as many as twenty-four times—especially in Tokyo's Sanya and Osaka's Kamagasaki, the two biggest yoseba. The last manifestation of these periodic riots was the Kamagasaki Riot in July 2008 during the G8 summit.[33] Because day laborers confront not only poverty and unstable living but also the violence of labor brokers (mostly yakuza/fascist organizations) as well as police brutality on a daily basis, their struggle is conditioned to be militant.[34] What is expropriated from them by the process of postwar primitive accumulation—land, local means of subsistence, family, health, dignity, permanent residence, and so on—creates the necessity and possibility of what we mean by commune as a fulfillment of commons for the dispossessed. Their living and working conditions require all aspects of reproductive care, self-organizing, and militancy, and their mutual support involves informal information exchanges for jobs and survival at bars and flop houses, free cookouts, patrols for helping homeless workers, shogi playing, seasonal festivals for empowerment, and existentially nurtured solidarity.

Now that the construction boom has passed and yoseba are in the process of aging and depopulation, organizing efforts have shifted focus toward homeless movements. The same workers are present, except that they are more nomadic, living outdoors or sleeping in one internet café or another, spreading over larger areas across the city. Losing common geographical ground, they are becoming less visible yet more omnipresent, merging with the increasing population of precarious workers throughout the country.

As the thinker and organizer of yoseba Funamoto Shuji (1945–75) emphasized, these "fluid underclass workers" have existential power precisely in their precarious status; their mobility, invisibility, solidarity, and militant networks stretch across the archipelago and beyond.[35] These are the generative conditions that allow for the emergence of the eros effect.

Yoseba such as Kamagasaki and Sanya exist in various forms in all cities across Japan, from the northern tip of Hokkaido to the southern islands of Okinawa. . . . Now in Hokkaido, monopoly capital is expropriating land for constructing the Eastern Industrial Complex around Tomakomai, and more and more peasants are turned into underclass laborers; at Usu in the Date region, Ainu fishermen are rising up against the construction of a thermal power plant for sending electricity to the Complex. Now in Okinawa, with the undisclosed slogan "men are for low wage labor commodity, women are for sexual commodity," Japanese Imperialism is expropriating land for constructing a CTS (Central Terminal Station including oil storage tanks and refineries) and the Ocean Expo Park; these projects are unequivocally turning peasants into underclass laborers. In fact, more and more peasants in Okinawa who can no longer survive by producing sugarcane are forced to migrate to Japan for subsistence. Now in South Korea, due to the importation of Japanese capital after the Treaty on Basic Relations between Japan and the Republic of Korea, the economy of agricultural communities is ruined and more and more people are forced to stow away by boat to come to Japan.[36]

As Funamoto makes clear, these fluid underclass workers are both excluded from Japanese civil society and free from its confines; they belong to a planetary territoriality divergent from that of the Japanese nation-state. Living in crises, they embody both the fragility and the power of life principles. In Japan and East Asia, they are the primary attractor and conveyor of eros effect turbulence.

Here inhabitants' struggles incorporate an alternate dimension, that is, life living without a fixed place, moving from one place to another or on the ritornello, namely, a circuity of places. The nomadic life as much as the sedentary life is a solid form of inhabiting the land (the Earth), since time immemorial. Today, immigrants and refugees—be it by war, famine, epidemic, pollution, or disaster—are amassing across the planet, and their existence embodies one epitomical or rather increasingly quintessential mode of human life. Those Who Go West and other radiation refugees are part of them. Supporting their universal rights and installing their shelters across borders are becoming the most exigent and daring projects today.

After Fukushima, some organizers of day laborers in Sanya and other types of underclass workers such as sex workers have tried to organize as well with nuclear workers, facing the post-Fukushima climate in which that class of workers, as it expands in size, is increasingly exposed to radiation. But due to the secretive and hierarchical nature of the nuclear industries as well as the placeless nature of the workers themselves, these organizing efforts are confronting difficulties. Their primary objectives are to protect workers from exposure to hazardous working conditions; to support those who have already developed symptoms; and most of all, recognizing their potency, to empower them. If empowered, nuclear workers could take over the nuclear facilities and, with the will to refuse work as their ultimate weapon, they could mobilize their technical knowledge of nuclear operation for its termination as well.

///

Mutual Aid Community Building
The late 1980s saw a flourishing of projects to build autonomous zones and mutual aid communities, initiated through the networking of young activists and precarious youth that was then accelerating across the nation. High school students' organizations formed a matrix.[37] In a manner similar to the Red Guard during the Cultural Revolution in China, groups of friends hitchhiked to various places around the country in order to meet and exchange information with other groups. In many locations in Japan, there were free spaces or autonomous zones for young activists to make extended visits and commingle (*koryū*), a term that would become an important political slogan. Komaba dormitory in Tokyo University and Yoshida dormitory in Kyoto University played such a role.[38] Aside from these public facilities, private spaces such as neighborhood community and social centers were created. This impetus surfaced along with the immiseration of youth after the bursting bubble. Contrary to the general image of 1980s youth monomindedly striving to climb the ladder of social hierarchy, activists in the late 1980s were developing a totally different mentality: not an individualistic elitism but an existential communism.

The group that took up the task of cultivating the means of communication and exchange most full-heartedly was Dame-ren (Alliance of good-for-nothings), inaugurated in 1992. With the primary slogan "Commingle!" they mainly gathered and talked. Their subjects were basically life problems, how they were good-for-nothing: unable to keep the same job, unpopular with the opposite sex, always poor, nurturing no talent, having bad features, and so on. They professed a realism of the generation of precarity. Though some of them belonged to more explicitly political organizations, the group itself did nothing that looked like a leftist political movement. In such an obscure manner, Dame-ren approached serious existential issues in Japan's post-Fordist or post-Toyota-ist society through ontopolitical strategy.

In postwar Japan, a homogeneous set of ideals—graduating from a good university, getting a permanent job, marrying at an early age, buying a car and a house in the suburbs, having two children, becoming an executive, and so on—was imposed on the whole nation. These functioned as the measure for composing social hierarchy. But in the postrecession climate, they became more and more unrealistic and absurd in the perception of commoners. Thus, by commingling and talking, the good-for-nothings challenged the value system within which they had been judged and marginalized.

Methodologically what was indispensable for the good-for-nothings was to communicate in person, not via the internet or email. Most of the members lived in the same neighborhood, along the Chuo train line (near the stations of Nakano, Koenji, Asagaya, and Kichijoji) in Tokyo. As an extension of commingling, most of them lived together in shared houses and created day-care centers for those who had kids. In these manners, they were experimenting with a new way of life for the poor, a way good-for-nothings could survive and be happy together. In 1990s Japan there were no longer Asian-type slums where people could cohabitate at ease, and there was no well-developed welfare system as in Europe. Especially at a time when society could no longer sustain the welfare system or social security, trying communal life and creating a system of hospitality was becoming more and more a matter of necessity. According to the members, talking, commingling, and sharing living space were already communism.

Dame-ren succeeded in permeation: some prominent activists and intellectuals passionately joined, and an associated group appeared in South Korea. They published several books containing discussions about pressing themes vis-à-vis precarious life as well as poignant yet self-deprecating personal experiences. All their actions were pursued with a great sense of humor and the great power of laughter, nurtured thanks to the critical distance they developed existentially from the value system of mainstream Japan. The power of laughter was important, all the more so given its absence in both radical left and moderate progressive milieus. This movement is significant because it has given the generic name "good-for-nothings" to today's youth and offered them ground for creating new anticapitalist discourses and projects. It has created a cultural paradigm where the generation of precarity can express themselves and communicate with each other. In fact, the neighborhood community Amateur Riot, which organized a series of successful antinuclear demonstrations and initiated exchanges with Asian activists after the Fukushima disaster, is an extension of the Dame-ren network, having inherited the same Koenji neighborhood in Tokyo.

///

Tackling Infrastructural Power
A theoretical project called landscape theory (*fukeiron*), which appeared in the late 1960s and developed over several years until the mid-1970s, illuminated the infrastructural mutation by multifaceted catastrophe whereupon the lives-as-struggle of inhabitants, fluid underclass workers, and precarious youth emerged. Its primary motivation was the critical scrutiny of the revolutionary movements of the 1960s, by way of cinematic, photographic, and theoretical productions.[39] Therein, landscape was employed as metaconcept to reconsider a series of concepts that had grounded the discourses on revolution: governance, economy, urbanization, community, territoriality, and subjectivity. The main object of scrutiny was the power operation based on infrastructural development that swept the entire archipelago.

Landscape theory debates were initiated by articles written by cinema critic Matsuda Masao.[40] Some of his main pieces concerned the collective production of the 1969 film *AKA Serial Killer*, a documentary consisting only of the landscapes encountered by an epitomic underclass worker, Nagayama Norio (1949–97), during his migrant life.[41] Nagayama was one of those youths collectively sent to Tokyo after graduation from junior high school, as the cheapest labor force (called "golden eggs"), by the demand of high economic growth. After having failed innumerable attempts to improve his life, he broke into the US Marines base in Yokosuka and stole a gun and bullets, with which he randomly murdered four men, including a security guard and a taxi driver. During imprisonment, he self-educated and wrote several books of essays and novels, which profoundly affected a multitude of progressive readers. In 1997 he was executed by the state of Japan, despite innumerable appeals and protests. The production group of the 1969 film was led by Japan Red Army revolutionary and filmmaker Adachi Masao. It was a collective decision to produce a landscape-only documentary, as opposed to a drama on Nagayama's "tragic" life such as Shindo Kaneto's 1970 narrative film *Live Today, Die Tomorrow.*

Matsuda had sensed the landscape-dominant mode in the new cinema of the time, especially in the so-called road movies, where traveling across landscapes was the main narrative, or else the bare presence of landscape overwhelmed the narrative structure. For him, this tendency embodied the world mutating by the new wave of the capitalist-state mode of development.

Questioning the influential propositions of leftist ideologues such as Yoshimoto Takaaki (1924–2012) and Tanigawa Gan (1923–95), Matsuda emphasized that in Japan there was no longer a united working-class subjectivity, independent critical subjectivity, or any unconsumed countryside where the base for armed revolution could be built: neither the idea of a vanguard party of workers nor that of a stronghold detached from the metropolis would work. Another target of his criticism was Terayama Shuji (1935–83), a poet, filmmaker, and theater director known for surrealist and nostalgic portrayals of his wretched homeland in the northern countryside. All this ground or home is gone, and the landscape that exists everywhere is only a horizon of power operation for endless development. Pseudo-utopia for consumers produced by the control society is everywhere. Meanwhile, Matsuda's hypothetical revolutionary subjectivity was the fluid underclass worker, like Nagayama Norio himself, wandering all over the archipelago and finally absorbed into the Tokyo metropolis only to commit crimes.

Zen-kyo-to organizer and writer Tsumura Takashi pointed out that the importance of landscape theory was its ability to read landscape as the text of state power. But if so, he continues, the text cannot be simply about the apparatus of violence. Instead, it involves many "noises" (*zatsuon*) that we are forced to live with, even beyond and after political confrontation with the state, because we are existentially entangled in them.[42] Thus noise embodies a large part of what landscape has become, that is, power: the entire network of apparatuses of capture, both physical and informational, produced by urbanization, along with what this production process entails, namely, the dynamism where the construction of space and the destruction of the environment are becoming one and the same.

The problematic of landscape also addresses the accelerating production of the representation of landscape: while the natural and rural landscape that used to be identified as Japanese has been destroyed and is disappearing, scenic images produced within the information/media society have become the primary index to teach us the way to see and admire landscapes in mutation. Wherever we travel, what we see is what we have been taught to see by innumerable tourist advertisements. Beginning in the early 1970s, Japanese National Railways started a tourism campaign called "Discover Japan," in synchronicity with "Reconstruction of the Japanese Archipelago" instigated by Prime Minister Tanaka Kakuei. Here the landscape apparatus was introduced for the expansion of the Tokyo apparatus in order to elaborate the networking of the insular apparatus. In all these senses, the landscape of landscape theory was less the environment itself than an apparatus for maneuvering and representing the environment.

Forty years after Matsuda's writings and one year before the Fukushima disaster, there appeared a book called *Genshiryoku toshi* (Atomic city) by Yabu Shiro, an anarchist activist and writer. Yabu wrote this book consciously as an extension of landscape theory, and it miraculously predicted many aspects of post-Fukushima society: "Atomic city is the city that appears in the atomic age coming after the age of steel. Atomic city does not have a boundary. Atomic city does not exist here or there, but everywhere. It is a city that expands indefinitely like ocean, beyond the spatial limit of land.... Information control of atomic city spreads lies and secrets everywhere, driving our sensibility toward total indifference. Our desires and interests are thus made controllable and manipulable."[43] Yabu categorizes capitalist development in two stages: the age of steel as that of labor and the age of nuclear as that of managerial technic. In reference to Robert Jungk's *The Nuclear State*, he points out that nuclear management with its inclination to extreme secrecy and control expands to the entire social sphere, where labor loses its grounding power and the right to strike, and where even accidents and radiation exposure are part of the managerial and technical process. And this management extends its operation to land, information, politics, community, body, and sensibility. *Genshiryoku toshi* is written as a travelogue, documenting Yabu's itinerary to many cities and towns that are more or less taken hostage both economically and environmentally by nuclear power plants. His emphasis is on the absurdity of the landscape rather than the classical landscape of misery: that is, superficial cleanliness, ostensible flourish, eventlessness, and indifference are observed in the regional places that are made through uneven development and internal colonization to serve the Tokyo metropolis with their electricity, agricultural and fishery products, and cheap labor power. His ultimate sense is that, in this manner, the entirety of Japan is now becoming an atomic city.

Seeds of crises disseminated in the 1980s germinated during the 1990s and fully blossomed with the nuclear disaster in 2011. In an ex post facto view, all events around people's everyday lives seem to have occurred in preparation for the Fukushima explosion. Such is the effect of catastrophic discontinuity, by which we are made to radically change our way of seeing the past.

Beginning from the bursting bubble of the mid-1990s, the becoming precarious of the majority crushed the dream of a democratic, peaceful, middle-class-centered society. Many men lost their storied "lifetime employment"; their patriarchal status was troubled in their families. Women took available part-time jobs, on top of their housework. Youth—sons and daughters—began the dual life of student/worker or else waged human strike in the form of social withdrawal called *hikikomori*. Men staying home after retirement or by unemployment and behaving as arrogantly as before were despised as "bulky trash." Divorce rates spiked. Women and children were liberated in a dual sense— losing the benefit of a stable home and becoming free from domestication. At the same time, there appeared signs of the decline of national procreativity.[44] Many analyses exist to make sense of it. But in the big picture, depopulation must be a psychosomatic response to the manifestations of the material limit the expansive World is bumping into. Along with the tendency of the population aging, care workers are dramatically increasing among youth. In terms of the labor force, the introduction of foreign workers is visibly swelling in many industrial sectors. What is expected in the future is the transmutation of homogenous nationhood into immigrant society. It is crucial for us to grasp the impacts of the Fukushima disaster along with this transmutation.

The Fukushima disaster gave an additional blow to the social reproduction already in crisis. The unprecedented damages to living conditions have created a conjuncture wherein there is no other choice for many but to change the course of their promised lives. People are tacitly developing ideals diverging from those promoted in the postwar regime. The value of life—happiness—needs to be rediscovered outside that which was developed along with economic growth. Some youth have been politicized in the protest movement while nurturing proactivity in projects concerning health, food and community. By women's initiative, a number of projects to defend lives from radiation have been created in both private and public sectors. The social factory came to be sustained by the extra labor of commoners—especially women and youth—without wages or public recognition. In post–nuclear disaster Japan, the invisible practices of reproductive workers have been illuminated more than ever—alongside the agonizing working conditions of nuclear workers at the crippled nuclear reactors.

In terms of political protest, the main impressions of what is happening today are weakness and self-regulation. The vigor and resoluteness of the 1960s cannot be found anywhere. Before the question of success or failure, the horizon of confrontation itself—the objective and context of opposition—seems to be forestalled by the status quo based on national integrity. Meanwhile, the struggles of inhabitants who are affected by radiation are taking the lead to create their contexts. But they have not yet materialized a horizon of opposition as a step toward the decomposition of the nuclear state. In ostensible definition, this is a "political defeat." But that is not the conclusion here.

The Fukushima disaster took place as the culmination of the process through which the lifeworld of commoners had been mutated since '68. During the period in between, their lives-as-struggle had already transmuted, as the horizon of their political engagements had been gradually stretched, thickened, and dispersed. Then, the disaster struck and delivered catastrophe for both the status quo and lives-as-struggle. The catastrophic situation seems to have been successfully normalized by the tremendous forces of social, political, and economic inertia—the apparatuses of capture—at least in mediatized representation. At the same time, however, it continues toward unknown consequences, which in a longer and wider perspective challenges not only our physical existence but also the metaphysical thinking that grounds political and scientific rationality. It is a catastrophe in the generic sense. The way peoples' lives-as-struggles respond to it, in their difficulties or internal complexity, is revealing the horizon of a battleground in formation.

What does post-Fukushima life-as-struggle contribute to the idea of changing the world? This question is the crux of this project. In the remaining pages, I provide a series of theoretical problematics that contextualize the question. These have to do with the invisible effects of radiation over the subjectivation of inhabitants' lives-as-struggle, based on their affectivities and sensitivities to radiation as well as on the way they are implicated in nuclear capitalism. Then, I explain what the universality of singular lives-as-struggle entails for affirming the present and imagining what planetary revolution could look like.

///

An international debate has long been taking place about the effects of radiation on the body. In Japan, this goes back to Hiroshima/Nagasaki. After the bomb, primary attention was paid to external radiation, which affects people via solar and cosmic radiation from the atmosphere, X-rays, or an atomic bomb, while internal radiation occurs via the intake of radioactive particles by way of breathing dust, drinking water, and eating food. The latter, which is considered nastier for its slow, long, and incalculable mutation of cells, was revealed by the sufferings of the atomic bomb victims who had not been exposed to the explosion itself but lived in the areas thereafter.[45] Many of them have gone through hardships to achieve justice and compensation from the US and Japanese governments, due to the complication in proving the effects of internal exposure.

The main point of the debate concerns two models that are used judicially for identifying the causality of radiation's effects. The International Commission on Radiological Protection (ICRP) advocates that health hazards can appear from radiation exposure no matter how small the dose. This position is based on the so-called linear nonthreshold (LNT) model. On the other hand, the Japanese government, following the Atomic Bomb Casualty Commission (ABCC), holds that there is a threshold dose for the development of health hazards. As we have seen, the ABCC is the US government organization that intervened after Hiroshima/Nagasaki for the examination (but not cure) of the bombs' effects on casualties' bodies.[46] It is this latter position that functions as a buffer for the authorities in manipulating the permissible dose. Furthermore, this debate itself is providing the process through which we all are made to get used to living with low-dose radiation. In this regard, one crucial point of divergence between struggles is whether they accept the idea of permissible dose or persist in the idea that no dose should be permissible.

Soon after the wake of the disaster, an antiradiation movement emerged in response to the new situation, overlapping with or aside from the antinuclear movement. Learning from the experiences of Hiroshima, Nagasaki, and especially Chernobyl, many people started DIY projects to confront radiation contamination. Among them, a group calling themselves zero-becquerelists sought to tackle the threats of radiation from the vantage of oppositional politics.[47] Zero-becquerelism was named for an assembly of varied voices of people who experienced the invisible and unknowable effects of radiation and fought against the attempts of governance to nationalize them. These are the voices of nuclear workers, reproductive workers, farmers, fishermen, sanitation workers, homeless people, informal workers, youth, and so on. They attest to the unevenness and complexity of radioactive contamination, according to the degrees in which they are physically affected and the ways in which they sense them.

Zero-becquerelists have been focusing on radiation monitoring and information exchange as well as advocating a mass exodus from the eastern part of Japan, on the premise that these practices constitute resistance. In that case, however, "zero-becquerel" cannot really be a goal, since radiation contamination is irreversibly expanding and we will have to live with it more or less. "Zero-becquerel" is rather an index or a political manifesto. It is supposed to be the conjunctive point at which all struggles coordinate their projects, as the possibility of radiation exposure has now become the shared condition for all, under the pronuclear governance. In order to refuse any involvement in the government's argumentation on threshold dose, zero-becquerelists declare: "We don't need a society that tells us to eat radiation."[48] Ultimately, they advocate the refusal of the subsumption of our lives and the management of our bodies by apocalyptic capitalism.

But among zero-becquerelists, a sectarianism has emerged as purism against the heterogeneous constituencies of the radioactive crowd. Some of those who held the "principle of preventative measure against radiation" moralistically accused those individuals and groups who were "still" living and active in the eastern part of Honshu, including the Tokyo metropolis, and refused to collaborate with them. By adopting the "absolute justness of avoiding radiation" as a norm, this position flattened out the singularities of inhabitants' lives in struggle. Radiation became a transcendent object; the zero-becquerelist movement created a new negative theology.

This turn of events made us reconsider the problematic complexity of radiation. At this moment, there is no absolute principle to deal with radiation, though its nastiness makes us wish it were otherwise. It is necessary to acknowledge the impossibility of calculating the precise effects of internal exposure to small doses. There is no other choice for us but to employ both models—smaller threshold number and refusal of threshold itself—according to context. Those people who monitor radiation have to speculate safety by smaller numbers. Inasmuch as administrative and judicial power operates based on the threshold model, victims are conditioned to fight for a smaller number in court and parliament. But we must refuse the government policy to spread radiation through the distribution of food and waste by manipulating the threshold number. Finally, we must accept the fact that most of the land in the world is polluted, more or less, not only by radiation but also by many other toxins. Those of us who are eager to create associations of various inhabitants on the planet must affirm varied forms of life in varied locations, including both those who choose to migrate from polluted zones and those who determine to remain in them. In other words, we must affirm different radio affectivities and sensitivities.

Radio affectivities/sensitivities are embodiments of varied existential territories, wherein two epitomes have stood out as political subjectivities to confront the pronuclear regime: nuclear worker and reproductive worker. These two modes of existence are considered the main indices of the forms of life-as-struggle in nuclear catastrophe. While they make a stark contrast in terms of social, political, and economic existence, they both are exploited by nuclear capitalism comprehensively. Nuclear workers—especially those employed by the lower stratum of subcontractors—are directly expropriated by the nuclear industry at reactors while sustaining energy production and their ultimate potency to liquidate it. Reproductive workers are most sensitively responding to the radioactive environment and protecting the health of their family members; in a larger perspective, their efforts contribute to the sustenance of social reproduction but without acknowledgments and wages. It is also they who confront the pronuclear governance most resolutely.

In terms of the opposition against the nuclear state and capitalism, a debate arose to determine whether reproductive workers or nuclear workers should be entrusted as the leading force. From the standpoint of class politics, certain Marxists define the projects of reproductive workers as petit bourgeois intervention and not revolutionary, while certain zero-becquerelists pay less attention to the existence of nuclear workers because of their moral objection to the workers' individual choice in being engaged in nuclear industries at the risk of their own radiation exposure. The feminist, antinuclear/radiation activist Mari Matsumoto critiques the polarization between nuclear worker and reproductive worker by stressing a common denominator: "These two are the forms of existence that have been made to maintain capitalist production, while being excluded out from it. They are the people who are exploited, in multiple layers, by sovereign power, productive system, and within family; they are paying off the debt of the entire society, in the invisible structure of exploitation."[49] Her point is that the post-Fukushima situation revealed nuclear capitalism's complex apparatuses of capture in which we all are implicated; these two modes of existence are certainly two epitomes, but what is crucial now is to grasp their common denominator, beyond the polarization of social movements based on old institutional categorizations.

In the older framework, while those prioritizing the nuclear worker consider the domain of production to be the main battleground, those prioritizing the reproductive worker consider it to be the domain of reproduction. Practically speaking, the former seek the abolition of nuclear power and the latter prioritize the defense of inhabitants' health and life. Finally, echoing in this division are the gendered roles of the labor movement for men and the citizens' movement for women. But while the crises of reproduction are permeating multidimensionally and everywhere, the nationalized, institutionalized, and gendered categorizations of movements are shaken by catastrophe, where their common denominator of being planetary inhabitant is coming to the surface. For instance, at the wake of the disaster, most struggles were led by women, but many commoners regardless of gender joined and developed them further. At present, the defense of life must be recognized as a project for all. As we have seen, the yoseba of day laborers / nuclear workers / homeless have sustained their projects of everyday care, whose exigency now stands out more than ever. Furthermore, foreign workers are increasingly introduced to the clean-up operations in Fukushima.[50] With the irreversible process that the radiation leak from the reactors is spreading over the planet, the catastrophe must be deemed universal.

There is no reason that one must prioritize either the defense of life from radiation or the abolition of nuclear power. Now, more than ever, we must discover ways to connect these fronts.

Here it is crucial to acknowledge an asymmetric relation: the universally shared domain of reproduction affected by nuclear production in confrontation with the specificity of nuclear production and its promoters. In this relation, all commoners on the planet are made to face nuclear catastrophe in varied manners according to their existential territories; they are also made to serve the global nuclear regime directly or indirectly, by its formal and real subsumptions, in varied manners according to their mode of subsistence. In catastrophe, all planetary inhabitants are becoming nuclear victim / nuclear worker. The way planetary inhabitants are victimized by the global nuclear regime and the way they serve it assume a class complexity that is asymmetrically confronting it transnationally. Therefore, the project to abolish nuclear power should be the technical takeover of all nuclear apparatuses for their decomposition by all those who are made to serve and who are victimized by it—laborers offering their blood (in uranium mines, transportation, processing facilities, and power plants), inhabitants whose land is expropriated by power plants, payers of taxes and electricity bills, casualties of war, and victims of radiation exposure. The abolition of nuclear power could be realized only in combination with inhabitants' projects to create and defend their autonomous zones of reproduction.

In terms of the common denominator, Matsumoto elaborates the concept of "deprived community" vis-à-vis the tangible and intangible effects of radioactive contamination: the loss of health, home, family, subsistence, and so forth. She continues: "Those which cannot be reduced to monetary value ... intangible things that are indispensable for constituting individuals and communities—places to live and act, their relations, ways and means of life—are largely destroyed."[51] And there is no prospect for recovery. There are no formulas to deal with such a situation. But there is one thing that one can and must do, and that is to "continue to record what happens, how situations change and how [the victims] feel about it." This is precisely what Ishimure Michiko did for twenty-some years in the struggle of Minamata victims, before she was finally able to begin to write *Paradise in the Sea of Sorrow*. "The power of [this] novel," according to Matsumoto, "involving actual enunciations and events of the victims and their movement, exists in [Ishimure's] persistent memorization and documentation of the everyday of endless purgatory for oceanic lives, animals, children, farmers, fishermen, etc. Only by this strategy of persisting in *unbearable temporality,* even the absurd events that refuse interpretation can spark from time to time. Fukushima nuclear disaster too is very much the event of such temporality and senses. And our strategy to confront it must be based upon recording and memorizing."[52] Thereafter, what is recorded must be shared as "collective intelligence"—as information warfare against the government's intellectual and affective manipulations.

The spatiotemporality of the Fukushima event is unbearable, after all, not only in its limitless expansion and duration but in its disarticulation of the social process that would otherwise create catharsis after the tragedy: that is, mourning for the losses, sharing rage, and collectively acting. As Matsumoto explains, "The nuclear disaster doesn't have an end, therefore healing by mourning is out of the question at this point. What unites us is rage, which is the basic weapon to organize ourselves in order to fight against the nuclear capitalism and state. . . . Mourning is solidly shared among those victims of the earthquake and tsunami, who have physically lost homes, families and means of subsistence. But in this case, where the nuclear disaster immediately followed, another spatio-temporal dimension that is unthinkable for us was imposed, spreading like a social cancer and depriving us of any cathartic solution."[53] This is why the complexity of emotions appears *simultaneously*: grief, despair, anxiety, rage, and exhilaration. The difficulty of creating a horizon of collective confrontation has to do with this derangement of event and process.

In both Minamata and Fukushima, the memorization and recording of unending catastrophe would also require enduring and meticulous observation as well as daring imagination, since pollutants are invisible, affected territories are undefinable, and effects are unmanageable. In the case of Minamata, methylmercury permeated sea water, affected ecological links, and bioaccumulated via the food chain. As depicted by Ishimure, the apocalyptic universe involves a chaotic and invisible nexus of human life, culture, history, economy, society, and politics, both in the fishing community as well as the nation. In a manner akin to the Apocalypse qua Revelation of D. H. Lawrence, Ishimure's observation, recording, and imagination reveal the invisible connectivity that makes us, our society, and the universe—as the union of spirit and body—through vital activities in tragic mutation. This is the very moment at which we discover what forces make us and what potencies we have in accepting the irreversible and engaging in survival.

But the case of Fukushima has not yet born an observer/recorder equivalent of Ishimure. Neither has it formed a united front of the radioactive crowd; nobody knows how long these projects would take. Fukushima's mushubutsu (無主物) travels a much larger territory than Minamata, via water and air, along with complex planetary movements, which nullifies our spatiotemporal senses as well as government's demarcation of administrative districts and national territory. Therefore, all the projects vis-à-vis the Fukushima catastrophe would be inexorably endless, with only processual articulations. Here comes the age of permanent life-as-struggle—the apocalypse—wherein what matters is less the realization of telos or the ultimate fulfillment of conditions that would realize human liberation than the enrichment and empowerment of the processes of life-as-struggle, in each and every phase, by its intensification and singularization. To say it differently, this life-as-struggle is destined to conceive multiple temporalities vis-à-vis existential territories: everyday routine, community, agricultural cycles, capitalist-state interventions, planetary movements, and aspiration rather than telos. Living in multiple temporalities has long been the existential horizon of inhabitants' movements asymmetrically opposing the capitalist/state mode of development across the planet: this is the ontopolitical dimension of the universality of the Fukushima catastrophe.

The ontometaphysical dimension of Fukushima's universality is elucidated in the introduction of the French book *Fukushima et ses invisibles*, by the editorial collective Les éditions des mondes à faire. The authors define the Fukushima nuclear disaster as a "metaphysical catastrophe," in a manner that is "decisively materialized in planetary existence."[54] It is metaphysical in the sense that "the collapse of authority (or authenticity) has been emphatically observed, not only that of the government but also that of the reality itself constructed by sciences and industries, which produces the everyday life of people." In other words, "the metaphysical reading of the nuclear disaster throws Western thinking into crisis: based upon the distinction between myth and reality, nature and culture, subject and object."[55] In this context, Western thinking is the thought that has grounded the endless expansion of the World. According to Les éditions des mondes à faire, "The role of the scientific laboratory has always been to make visible the invisibles and to make comprehensible the unreachable. . . . In the natural order, science takes material from the spirits; in the cultural order, political economy reduces all possible relations into commodity relations."[56] In other words, the governance of the World as expansive entity has always relied on the dual powers of becoming—our minds/bodies and naturing nature (natura naturans)—by turning them into natural resource or commodity through objectification, exploitation, and processing in the technomachinic processes. From ancient despot to feudal system to colonial expansion to modern capitalist nation-state, the World created the apparatuses that capture, orient, and manage the way we relate our bodies/minds with naturing nature.

What the catastrophe has revealed is a "nightmare" of the apparatuses that "exists less in the ecological disaster by radioactive contamination itself than in the transference of properties between the natural order and psycho-social order that this contamination involves, and 'the return of the invisibles' that it provokes."[57] Thus, the radio affectivities/sensitivities of the radioactive crowd are "seeking to confront the invisibles that transform their experience and developing techniques to negotiate with them for cohabitation." The invisibles here include not only radioactivity but also "bacteria, celestial body, poisons, and medicines as well as spell and curse, spirits and souls"—all of which "populate the animistic world."[58]

Here, in synchronicity with Ishimure's evocation of Minamata's spirits and ghosts via methylmercury, Fukushima's 無主物 functions as a catalyst or attractor that reveals and reactivates the invisible interconnectivities of all events called the Earth—erotic turbulence—in a precise manner, by which animistic attribution can connect what makes us, our society, and the universe. In this sense, the animistic world is equal to the existential horizon on which the lives-as-struggle of the planetary crowd reverberate with each other.

///

Our perceptions, sensibilities, and conceptualizations vis-à-vis our life/body, communal relations, and the environment are going through a radical transformation via the Fukushima experience. In exchange for irreversible contamination, we have achieved a moment to discover new value, happiness, and life, against those that the capitalist nation-state has long imposed on us. In other words, we are walking a step toward *affirmation* of the catastrophe and are moving beyond being passive victim to the disaster.

The primary transformation appears in our idea of life—from one based on individual interest endlessly (re)produced in capitalist economy to one of ephemeral yet singular vital activity that is part of communal relations and life chains. This is a machinic turn that acknowledges both organic and nonorganic lives and both life and death drives, in a way akin to the Buddhist notion of karmic cycle beyond individual life and death. It is a discovery of *masterless life* within ourselves. There is no life that lasts forever; there is no life that expands indefinitely; there is no life without otherness and death. But in capitalist society, we too are implicated in capital's reproduction and expansion and made to perform an indefinitely expansive life. The notions of a successful life—happiness—in our society do not originate in us but are constantly transferred to us from this capitalist drive. Our everyday anxiety and depression come from the essential impossibility of performing expansive and eternal life; every life gets wounded, gets sick and dies. And yet every life knows passion in its singularity. Precisely because of its being vulnerable and ephemeral and yet eventful, life has pure power that is essentially impersonal and universal. It is this life that we seek to nurture and protect in our efforts toward a full-hearted recommonization.

In practice, this new idea of life is materialized around the body, in the power of its affectivity and sensitivity vis-à-vis the environment in mutation. Body and life are ephemeral and limited, and for this precise reason they *know* an eroticism of solidarity outside the endlessness promoted by capitalist valorization and state sovereignty. Accordingly, an intensive form of body politic has emerged in a series of technopolitical projects by the radioactive crowd to confront radioactive chaos: for example, sharing stories about different emotions and experiences of contamination; monitoring radiation with Geiger counters as prosthetic devices; researching how to sustain health vis-à-vis radiation and other pollutants; mapping fluctuating radioactive zones; migrating to safer environments to experiment with new forms of life; naming both friends (planetary inhabitants) and enemies (proxy politicians, scientists and media personae in the nuclear village); and distributing information via independent networks.[59]

The projects of the radioactive crowd provide us with a new model for creating collective intelligence, which is an aggregate of information in the social milieu and as such realizes a common knowledge building that cannot be subsumed into individual property. Such intelligence potentializes collective decision making beyond any leadership and outside of the media network of an insular territory. It produces a magnetic field at the meeting point of vital energy (body) and electric signal (information), which collects the memories, experiences, and aspirations of planetary inhabitants and becomes an attractor for climatic reverberations among different sensibilities, corporealities, and communalities.[60]

The meeting point of body and knowledge is the *milieu*, which is drawn with rhythms in varieties/variables/variations out of chaos (entropy). The creation of milieu implies the re-creation of continuity between geographical terrain and human habitation, which includes both our minds/bodies and communal relations (local wisdom, history, and culture) as well as naturing nature—in and as planetary complexity. Therefore, the milieu provides the horizon where various lives-as-struggle seeking to create new forms of life in autonomous zones can connect and empower each other. More precisely, the practices that have appeared as a response (direct or indirect) to the Fukushima event are tacitly forming an inclusive milieu—a new horizon—for various other projects for mutual empowerment. On this new horizon, all lives-as-struggle could interact and create turbulence whose orientation would be unknown, whose battleground would be everywhere—in our bodies and minds, social relations, and environments, all constantly affected by atmospheric movements and shaken by tectonic activities. This is the horizon of the climatological politics of the Earth and the basis for communism in the apocalypse.

///

There are a number of examples of autonomous zones in Japan, which however weak, humble, and inconspicuous at the moment, are substantially empowering each other.

Within Tokyo, Amateur Riot, in the lineage of the good-for-nothings, have been actively expanding connections with collectives and communes in Asia, on top of developing their neighborhood. Also at the core of the metropolis, the homeless camp in Tokyo's Yoyogi Park has been miraculously sustaining forms of communal living outside the capitalist commodity economy. As it is their inhabitation that is threatened by the coming 2020 Tokyo Olympics most imminently, they have been organizing a broad coalition against it.[61]

In Osaka, Kamagasaki's communities of day laborers and homeless have been fighting to block accelerating gentrification against their neighborhoods and outdoor camps while enriching their mutual aid projects such as a communal kitchen in an occupied park (Triangle Park), patrols to help the sick on the street, collective movie making, outdoor film screenings, street shogi games, and so forth. Confronting depopulation, young activists are also seeking to revitalize the community by increasing shared houses and inviting like-minded people from across the country and abroad. In particular, they have been strengthening their connections across the Kansai area, for example with the Yoshida dormitory at Kyoto University. A communal living space self-managed for decades by its inhabitants, including both students and nonstudents, and independent from university administration, Yoshida has long been an important gathering place. But as of last year, it faces an eviction order; the university intends to demolish it to build a new high-rise dormitory. With one hundred inhabitants determined to stay and fight the eviction, the occupied dormitory is now attracting activists from various places who seek to reinforce and revitalize this common space.[62]

Meanwhile, in the archipelago's peripheries, evacuees' communities have been tacitly increasing, especially in Hokkaido and western Japan. In some of these, notably in Kyushu, newcomers are learning farming, hunting, carpentry, handicrafts, and other native wisdoms for living from the locals, while communally managing markets for barter trade and skill shares, in order to create new forms of life. In Okinawa, struggles against the construction of US military bases continue as people are increasingly determined to defend their local living and natural environment, including a rare preserve of coral reef where endangered dugong live. In September 2018, an anti–US military base candidate was chosen in the gubernatorial election, which encouraged many in Okinawa and abroad.[63]

These milieus of lives-as-struggle are all dealing with catastrophe in their varied existential territories and are all mutually empowering. Through their reverberation, they share the same impetus to create autonomous zones, collaborate in resistance against the subsumption of post-Fukushima governance, and develop together new rapport with the land—be it urban neighborhood or countryside community. Sharing the moment to rediscover archipelagic relations within insular territory and to reverberate with distant lives-as-struggle, these milieus are creating many worlds, as it were, out of the breaches of one World.

As we have seen, archipelagic Japan is the counternarrative to the insular Japan that is equal to the territorialization of the modern nation-state. Archipelagic relations are not equal to a geographic archipelago itself but to multilateral social relations based on heterotopic exchange, as a geohistorical derivative of the archipelago. According to the Martiniquan poet and philosopher Édouard Glissant (1928–2011), "archipelagic thinking" speaks to a resistance to integrality (totalization) and to a common horizon of absolute heterogeneity. In the post-Fukushima climate where all thoughts and movements based on national integrality have failed, we insist on the lives-as-struggle in singular places and expand our horizon of imagination by infinitely repeating "Creolization," or incessant divergence and merger, multilingualism, and so on.[64]

For Glissant, the world is inevitably Creolized but in different manners according to different regional geohistories. For instance, North America has been Creolized by slavery, colonization, and other discriminatory systems. The Mediterranean Sea is concentrated into a point, which made multinational European history. Meanwhile, the Caribbean Sea is an open and diffracted space, wherein through triangular trade, cultural elements from heterogeneous horizons encountered each other, merged in complexity, and created the absolutely unexpected and new reality of Creolization.[65] If the Caribbean Sea is the entrance to the South and North American continents, the Japanese archipelago is either an end or an appendix to the Asian continent. We do not know what the Creolization of Japan would lead to, but it is certain that, along with the rising current of an aging population and increasing foreign workers (immigrants), creolized autonomous zones would create new forms of life and social relations as embodiments of the joy of relating to the Earth, in exchange for the apocalyptic decline of the World.

At the moment, these milieus of autonomous lives-as-struggle are weak, humble, and inconspicuous in the major political theater of the World. But by the further development of their synchronicity beyond the Japanese archipelago, a horizon for *planetary revolution* could be cultivated. This horizon would be the milieu of all milieus—the in-between place—wherein climatological reverberations among all the lives-as-struggle of planetary inhabitants would take place. The attractor of reverberations is the shared sensing of that threshold that planetary inhabitants experience simultaneously based on their internalized commensurability: living the Earth. This commensurability is further activated in their common efforts to create rapport with a singular place.

As we observe in many places in the world (which I would not dare name here), the communes or milieus that have established a strong rapport with local communities and land are powerful in and of themselves, and valuable for other communes or milieus to visit and learn from. In other words, inhabitants' vertical involvement in a singular place attracts the eros effect of reverberation with other inhabitants' involvement. Due to their singular rapport with a place, these communes internalize the impetus of dispersion from and decomposition of the national integrity (or insular nationhood) facilitated by the apparatuses of capture—toward the re-creation of archipelagic relations. This dispersion, however, is not equal to atomization. It accompanies mutual visiting among communes for creating collaborative projects for collective empowerment, such as extracapitalist exchange of local products, equipment sharing, technical support, and the collective defense of territories. Physical traveling is the most substantial basis for eros effect reverberations, moving via vital energy among distant lives-as-struggle, on top of those that move via electric signals. In fact, these practices have been inconspicuously accelerated in recent years among communes across the planet. In Japan, their precedent is found among the decentralized militants of the New Left and the generation of good-for-nothings. In human history, we recall the lives of numerous revolutionaries, including anarchist geographer and communard Elisée Reclus (1830–1905), who nurtured a revolutionary theory and practice for the sake of planetary inhabitants rather than nationals. His magnum opus *L'Homme et la terre* begins with the epigraph "L'homme est la nature prenant conscience d'elle-méme" (the human is nature becoming aware of herself).[66] What grounded this pronouncement of the ontological status of humans vis-à-vis the Earth were Reclus's engagements in singular places and with singular people. Through elaborate travels across the European continent as well as the Americas, Reclus was able to create a climatological cartography for the reverberation of planetary lives-as-struggle.[67]

Now in this age of the irreversible mutation of the planetary environment, a new horizon emerges more timely than ever in the reverberation of planetary lives-as-struggle. But this horizon has not yet revealed its full picture; what we have gotten so far is only its glimpses. While we are still entrapped in and increasingly exhausted by the Politics of the expansive World, it is clear that the ontology of our lives-as-struggle can no longer be subsumed into that of the World organized by capitalist nation-state developments; the essence of revelation (apocalypse) is the asymmetricity of the former to the latter. This asymmetricity is embodied in layers of historically stratified ontological horizons of governance / ungovernable: that is, industrial production / everyday reproduction; vanguardist party / nonhierarchical groupuscule; sociopolitical movement / life-as-struggle; technology as systematic aggregate of techniques / wisdom as revolutionary arrangement of techniques; integration / dispersion; and dialectic synthesis toward the unification of the World / reverberation among singularities in the immanence of the Earth.

The age of apocalyptic communism has come. It is neither utopia nor dystopia but a set of conditions inexorably imposed on us at the beginning of the long-lasting end of the World. Revolutionary milieus today are characterized by their weakness, humbleness, and invisibility, and this we must affirm, for neither could we nor would we want to make a strong unified force to beat and take over the nation-states and American and Chinese empires, but rather we would only want to decompose them from within in synchronicity. This difference distinguishes our time from the time of the New Left, when revolution was the international taking over of capitalist regimes in the Cold War paradigm. Our cartographical strategy is no longer based on the geopolitics of the World, wherein enclaves of national territories are absorbed into or split apart from a continental empire (Europe, America, China, or whatever follows). It is one of archipelagic relations, wherein the complexity of anti-nation-state milieus creates heterogeneous relations among them. These relations are the dispersing power of the nameless and the deviation from the automatic extension of World History.[68]

If we can characterize revolution after 2011, it should be considered less a singular event (regime change) than a series of events (existential metamorphosis) toward a New Earth, even if the latter may inevitably be accompanied by the former at one time or another.[69] More than anything, our revolutionary will is to become something else *existentially*, to metamorphose existence from the national to the planetary, from *homo nationalis* to *homo terrae*. In other words, revolution today is nothing but the Copernican turn shifting our tactical and strategic attention from the World to the Earth. We know that the Earth exists as an autonomous entity that has its own dynamic process and movement or, if I may say so, subjectivity. Though we cannot touch its whole, we are part of it. We too are the Earth.

EPILOGUE / *Forget Japan*

During modernization, Japan's population increased consistently due to energy revolutions. During the 260 years of the Edo period, it remained relatively consistent, around 30 million. After the Meiji Restoration, it grew dramatically and reached 72 million by the end of World War II. In the postwar period, it further increased up until the peak of 128 million in 2010. Then, beginning from the year 2011 — Fukushima year zero — it started to shrink. The tendency of depopulation is epitomic to the decline of the World, whose expansion was equal to the development of industrial civilization based on mineral resources: fossil fuel and uranium.

Within the country, an aging population is expected to trigger the collapse of the social security system and to result in the weakening of the labor force. This will compel the nation-state to change its course drastically. Two pillars that have long sustained its power and integrity are gone: no longer the industrial and economic impetus; no longer the unity based on homogeneous nationhood. Increasing numbers of youth will be taking charge of care works instead of technoindustrial development or global financial trade. Foreign workers will be introduced more and more. The recent enthusiasm for national integrity — from both the left and the right — can be considered a desperate cry to hold onto what the postwar regime embodied, namely, what "Nippon" signified for the nation.

Now in the post-Fukushima climate, the question of revolution has to do with how to respond to and incorporate this tendency, in the most material dimension of mass corporeality. The proposition of this project is to *affirm this tendency*, by affirmatively forgetting what Japan embodies. This is neither irony nor cynicism; instead, forgetting the nation is equal to relearning ways to love people, land, history, and culture — as earthly singularities or the *masterless Earth*—which is practically realizable only by decomposing the apparatuses of capture that have long constituted Japan as a modern capitalist nation-state. This can be said of all nations in the World, but Japan seems to provide an epitomic instance for initiating this orientation.

Japanese history is a process through which an archipelago was condensed into an insular territory by the apparatuses of capture. Through this process, the nation established varied forms of constitution based on insular territory—ancient kingdom, feudal system, modern nation-state, empire, and nation-state again—as part of the expansive World. Now we find ourselves in the juncture—the beginning of Japan's decomposition. We do not know what form it will take, and it is likely that none of us will see its ultimate consequence in our lifetime, but the idea of revolution—active engagement in changing the world—must follow it on the horizon of planetary politics. Decomposition, however, does not mean a direct return to the archipelago in a geopolitical sense; rather, "archipelagic relations" would provide a guideline for our engagements in the process.

In this regard, Édouard Glissant's geohistorical conceptualizations of "Creolization" are significant in teaching us how the totality of the World internalizes an irreducible heterogeneity, which was primarily inscribed in geographical forms: in other words, how geographical forms determined the formations of human relations. The continent made possible imperial expansion and insular territory facilitated nation-state crystallization while the archipelago provided unknown possibilities to develop heterogeneous relations. Glissant rendered his view of archipelagic relations from his own experience and reading of Caribbean history, wherein he saw a seed of hope in the juncture where the geographical complexity and relationality of the archipelago intermingle with the tragic memories of the slave trade and massacres of the indigenous and create future alternatives to all the stratified layers of colonial history.[1]

In the case of Japan, archipelagic relations are in stark distinction from the dominant relation through which the apparatuses of capture were created. Historically, in opposition to insular territorialization, innumerable deterritorializing people withdrew their bodies, minds, and communities from the dominant apparatuses and created lines of flight toward the unknown horizon of "absolute deterritorialization."[2] A geophilosophical reading of Japanese history suggests that, even when it is topographically suppressed, this archipelagic relationality as deterritorialization continues to find expression in our bodies, minds, and social relations as collective memory.[3] Thus, it generates new relations along with the decomposition of the nation and the World while developing our new relationship with the Earth.

The above is the main proposition of this project. But I am well aware that in confrontation with increasing and intensifying catastrophes, the attempts to respond by relying on either national unity or international orchestrations—by the governance of the World—will continue. As recent experiences of disaster show, the real sites of rescue operation inevitably comprise the conflictual forces of both states' top-down projects and people's bottom-up actions. This project does not mean to oppose the demand of "big solution by big power" simple-mindedly; rather, it intends to show that different ways to act on catastrophes have been paved by the planetary nameless on the basis of their existential necessities. The ideal situation would be that the multitudinous lives-as-struggle become the big power for the big solution in and of themselves—at the zenith of their reverberations.

In any case, the main objective of this project is not to propose concrete programs on what needs to be done. The propositions herein remain rather hypothetical. And yet, as an inevitable inclination of our crisis-ridden existence in this age, we all are more or less imagining possible procedures to abolish nuclear power, war, and all other sources of planetary catastrophe that could lead to the end of the human world on Earth—as a race against time. So let us exemplify a couple honest responses to the haunting questions—how to abolish nuclear power/war and what to do with the end of the human world—with the condition that we would not rely on national and international politics.

While the protest movements to oppose nuclear power and war have been important and will continue to be so, their limits have been sensed among many of us. These movements may be able to create a social atmosphere opposing them; but they can rarely stop an actual nuclear plant or war; and they can never decompose their matrix—the apparatuses of apocalyptic capitalism based on the military–industrial complex, whose global nexus implicates our lives so widely and deeply.

Some Greek friends have made an imaginative yet practical proposal for a global antiwar movement.[4] The proposal envisions a situation wherein the people who are implicated differently by the nuclear/war apparatuses take them over from their life bases simultaneously across the planet: miners in mines, workers in plants, scientists in laboratories, engineers in facilities, soldiers in the military, computer security technicians everywhere, electricity consumers everywhere, and so on. These actions would be purely based on each individual's living environment or workplace, taking it over from the power and turning it under their control—whether technically liquidating it in order to materially wipe it out from the planet or decomposing and recomposing it in order to reemploy it for their benefit.

This proposal is inspiring for several reasons. First, the apparatuses of nuclear power and those of war are considered as one and the same (this is increasingly true). Second, instead of activists expressing opposition on the political theater, inhabitants would existentially fight for defending and nurturing their own living territories. Third, the action is supposed to take place simultaneously across the planet. This means that for everyone, one's own local government, industries, and nation-state would be the primary target to decompose; and all decompositions would happen everywhere at once. The fundamental premise of this global antiwar movement is that it is necessary to abandon once and for all the historically lingering debates over the left's involvement in national war—be it right or wrong, unavoidable or avoidable. It is imperative to acknowledge that for all of us, our own nation-state is the archenemy.

Certainly, the difficulty lies in sharing this conviction universally and acting on it simultaneously. Even if the conviction were shared, still the global simultaneity might be only imaginative; for making this situation possible, the planetary reverberations among inhabitants' lives-as-struggle would have to be reinforced in an unprecedented intensity. On the other hand, however, we are also sensing that, on a planetary dimension, lives-as-struggle are getting to know each other, more than ever, for intensifying reverberations to an unknown level. Finally, in terms of a real technopolitics for this movement, recently we observed a number of daring actions, for example by hackers, from within the apparatus. These provide us with the sense of possible actions.

All in all, none of us are optimistic. We are perceiving signs of civilizational decline in all kinds of disasters. We know that our living conditions will be changing for the worse and possibly the worst: the apocalypse. We feel that our struggles may be losing the race against apocalyptic time. It is hard not to imagine the end of our living environment, through apocalyptic imaginaries, scientific data, and increasing experiences of disasters. On the other hand, frankly and honestly, the reality is that we are not always thinking about the end. Even though it could come soon, we are also sustaining an ephemeral and humble happiness in everyday life, and there is no other choice for us but to continue to do so. Is this a lack of awareness of the magnitude of the problem? To face this aporia, an American anarchist friend gave me an important suggestion: even if the end of all comes tomorrow, what is important is to sustain autonomy and mutual aid relations *here and now* rather than transferring initiative to and being ruled by the state or the UN. The only thing one can say accordingly is that peoples' struggles for autonomy and the project to save the planetary environment—many small efforts and one big project—need to synchronize for decomposing the World and saving the Earth at the same time, with the inevitable risk of losing the race against time.

In a strict sense, we can do nothing if the end of the World/Earth comes as a singular event. As long as we are not transcendent and can do nothing about such occasion, the End is not our problem. We will have to live on by nurturing and sharing techniques for survival in local purgatories, in order to turn them into microparadises. We are neither ruler nor savior of the planet. We are just trying to live in a way comfortable for us and to die in a way suitable for us, with a mobility with which we can live where we want to live. We want to achieve a future that is undetermined, a future that we can create.

Inhabitants of the Earth, reverberate!

PROLOGUE: WRITING THROUGH FUKUSHIMA

1 See the *J-Fissures* website, http://www.jfissures.org.

INTRODUCTION: DISASTER/CATASTROPHE/APOCALYPSE

1 The concept of nomos is employed here in reference to Deleuze and Guattari's "nomadology" and not to Carl Schmitt's "nomos of the earth," which is equal to the Eurocentric world order. Deleuze and Guattari, *A Thousand Plateaus*; Schmitt, *The Nomos of the Earth*.

2 This notion of existential territories owes to such works as Guattari, *Schizoanalytic Cartographies*; and Guattari, *The Three Ecologies*.

3 See Katsiaficas, "Eros and Revolution"; and Thompson, "Remembering May '68."

4 What "political ontology" refers to here is not its sense in political science. Rather, it signifies the horizon or the operative dimensions of revolutionary struggles.

5 Lilly et al., *Catastrophism*.

6 Solnit, *A Paradise Built in Hell*; Klein, *The Shock Doctrine*.

7 Deleuze and Guattari, *A Thousand Plateaus*, 456.

8 Virilio, *Unknown Quantity*, 6.

9 For more on nuclear exceptionalism, see Hecht, "Nuclear Ontologies"; Hecht, "The Power of Nuclear Things"; and Hecht, *Being Nuclear*.

10 See Marx, *The Eighteenth Brumaire of Louis Bonaparte*, 15: "Hegel remarks somewhere that all facts and personages of great importance in world history occur, as it were, twice. He forgot to add: the first time as tragedy the second as farce."

11 During the fourteenth and fifteenth centuries, the idea of universal salvation that appeared as an offshoot of Dharma's decline (*mappo-shiso*) grounded the popular impetus that led to the one-hundred-year rebellion

of Ikko Shu against ruling warlords and temples. This rebellion assembled forces of peasants, fishermen, merchants, pirates, samurais, and monks and created a commune in Kaga Province on the Sea of Japan.

12 The monk Shinran (1173–1263), who initiated the True Pure Land School, stated: "Even a virtuous person can attain rebirth in the Pure Land, how much more easily a wicked person!" Yuienbo, *Tannisho*, 3.

13 Her new chant is in reference to Donna Haraway's *Staying with the Trouble*.

14 Lawrence, *Apocalypse*, 59.

15 Deleuze, "Nietzsche and Saint Paul, Lawrence and John of Patmos," 36.

16 Deleuze, "Nietzsche and Saint Paul, Lawrence and John of Patmos," 45–46.

17 Deleuze, "Nietzsche and Saint Paul, Lawrence and John of Patmos," 51–52.

18 Deleuze and Guattari, *What Is Philosophy?*, 85.

19 The attempt to read Deleuze and Guattari's ontology of immanence from the vantage point of anarchism (libertarianism) is best exemplified by Colson, *A Little Philosophical Lexicon of Anarchism*.

CHAPTER 1: TRANSMUTATION OF POWERS

1 Nixon, *Slow Violence and the Environmentalism of the Poor*, 2.

2 Kuchinskaya, *The Politics of Invisibility*, 2.

3 National Police Agency of Japan, "Damage Situation and Police Countermeasures."

4 "Parallel chain crisis" (*heikō-rensa-kiki*) was an expression used in a report by the Independent Investigation Commission on the Fukushima Daiichi Nuclear Accident (Minkan jiko cho), issued on February 28, 2012, http://park.itc.u-tokyo.ac.jp/tkdlab/fukushimanpp/minkan.html.

5 Motoyuki, "Puromeiteusu no wana" [The trap of Prometheus].

6 One example was the act of publicly sharing residents' personal information to identify those potentially unable to respond to the state of emergency because of age or physical incapacity. Risking incrimination, some local leaders shared this information in an attempt to rescue people who were left in the evacuation zone.

7 This situation is well depicted through ridicule in the 2016 film *Godzilla Resurgence*, codirected by Anno Hideaki and Higuchi Shinji.

8 Funabashi, *Kauntodaun merutodaun* [Countdown meltdown].

9 Lynne Peeples, "US Armed Forces Sickened after Fukushima Meltdown Get Help from Online Fundraising," *Huffington Post*, March 8, 2014.

10 Justin McCurry, "Fukushima Reactor Meltdown Was a Man-made Disaster, Says Official Report," *The Guardian*, July 5, 2012.

11 "Five-Year Jail Terms Sought for Ex-Tepco Executives over Fukushima Nuclear Crisis," *Japan Times*, December 26, 2018.

12 Funabashi, *Kauntodaun merutodaun*, vol. 1, 32.

13 Fukushima Nuclear Disaster News blog, accessed April 20, 2016, http://blogs.yahoo.co.jp/fukushima_nuclear_disaster_news/33788561.html.

14 "India, Japan Reach Agreement on Nuclear Cooperation," *World Nuclear News*, December 14, 2015.

15 The most graphic example is the endless failure of the Rokkasho Reprocessing Plant. See, for example, Greenpeace, "Planning for Failure: International Nuclear Safeguards and the Rokkasho-Mura Reprocessing Plant," November 2002, http://www.greenpeace.org/international/Global /international/planet-2/report/2002/11/planning-for-failure-internat.pdf.

16 Funabashi, *Kauntodaun merutodaun*.

17 See, for example, Mina Pollman, "Japan's Controversial State Secrets Law: One Year Later," *The Diplomat*, December 9, 2015; Ayako Mie, "Security Laws Usher in New Era for Pacifist Japan," *Japan Times*, March 29, 2016; and Daisuke Kikuchi, "Controversial Conspiracy Bill Approved by Abe Cabinet," *Japan Times*, March 21, 2017.

18 Michiyo Nakamoto, "Plight of Fukushima Farmers Takes Its Toll," *Financial Times*, March 29, 2011.

19 World Health Organization, "FAQs: Japan Nuclear Concerns," September 2011, http://www.who.int/hac/crises/jpn/faqs/en/index7.html.

20 "Nuclear Watchdog Questions Environment Ministry's Plans to Reuse Radioactive Soil," *Mainichi Shimbun*, January 9, 2017.

21 The campaign "Eat and Support Fukushima" (tabete ōen shiyō) was instigated by the Ministry of Agriculture, Forestry and Fisheries and still continues today, involving a number of fast-food chains, supermarkets, restaurants, and consumers. According to the ministry's website, "Tabete ōen shiyō" [Eat and support Fukushima], accessed February 5, 2015, http:// www.maff.go.jp/j/shokusan/eat: "We call for a wide cooperation for the campaign, in order to support the reconstruction of the disaster-stricken areas by actively consuming food products from the areas." All translations are mine unless otherwise noted.

22 The number of forced evacuees from Fukushima Prefecture is recorded by the government's Reconstruction Agency, but this does not include the number of voluntary evacuees from the Tohoku and Kanto regions. See Reconstruction Agency, "Efforts for Reconstruction of Tohoko," accessed April 10, 2014, http://www.reconstruction.go.jp/english. For the distribution of forced evacuees across Japan, see "Situation of the Evacuees," *Fukushima on the Globe*, accessed April 10, 2014, http://fukushimaontheglobe .com/the-earthquake-and-the-nuclear-accident/situation-of-the-evacuees.

23 In a water purification plant for Tokyo residents, iodine-131 was detected at 210 becquerels per liter. In terms of Japanese government regulations, the maximum yearly intake of radioactive substance that can be considered safe is 300 becquerels for adults. For infants the maximum is 100 becquerels, or one-third that of the standard for adults, while in the United States and Europe this ratio is as small as one-tenth, due to infant susceptibility.

24 Hiroko Tabuchi, "Citizens' Testing Finds 20 Hot Spots around Tokyo," *New York Times*, October 14, 2011.

25 For more on Amateur Riot, see the Submedia website, accessed October 2, 2015, https://submedia.tv/amateur-riot.

26 The penetrating power of radiation varies according to the type of particles: alpha radiation can be stopped by a sheet of paper, beta radiation penetrates paper but not metals, gamma radiation penetrates metals but with varied intensities according to the types of nuclides (cesium and cobalt), and neutron radiation penetrates almost all material.

27 Alexievich, *Voices from Chernobyl*, 495.

28 See, for example, "Nihon zenkoku hōshanō osen mappu" [Map of radio-contamination across Japan], accessed May 23, 2018, http://www.imart.co .jp/fukushima-genpatu-houshasen-osen-zenkoku-map.html. For mappings of soil contamination, see "Shinkokuna seshiumu dojō osen mappu" [Map of serious cesium contamination], accessed May 23, 2018, https://matome .naver.jp/odai/2131468288290995401.

29 For example, Rokusaisha Reporters, *Toden oikake mappu* [TEPCO and nuclear power plants]; and Rokusaisha Reporters, *Tabū naki genpatsu jiko chōsho* [Records of nuclear accidents, without taboo].

30 "Obituary: Shuntaro Hida, Doctor Who Survived A-Bomb," *Sunday Times*, April 9, 2017.

31 Hida and Kamanaka, *Naibu hibaku no kyoi* [The threat of internal radiation exposure].

32 Hida Shuntaro, "Naibu hibaku wo norikoete ikiru tame ni" [For surviving internal radiation], April 25, 2012, http://www.magazine9.jp/interv/hida2 /index1.php. In this interview, Hida proposes "Seven Items to Live by in the Post 3/11 World": "(1) recognize the impossibility of evading internal exposure; (2) make efforts to strengthen immunity; (3) sleep early and wake early; (4) have three meals a day regularly; (5) chew food well, so that the intestine can fully absorb nutrients; (6) decline anything that is harmful to the body; (7) cherish your one and only life in the world with care."

33 Kimura, *Radiation Brain Moms and Citizen Scientists*.

34 For more on the activities of radiation-monitoring groups in Japan, see Schanen, "Radiation Monitoring Group."

35 For more on the concepts of minor science and royal science, see part 12 of Deleuze and Guattari's *A Thousand Plateaus*.

36 Yabu and Ikegami, *Genpatsu o tabero to iu nara, sonna shakai ha iranai* [We don't need a society that tells us to eat radiation].

37 Hapax, *Ikata hōki no tame no danshō* [Fragments for the Ikata insurrection], 13.

38 The idea is taken from the tradition of Marxist feminism. See, for instance, Federici, *Revolution at Point Zero*.

39 This is a pun: the Japanese word for radioactivity (*hōshanō*) sounds the same as the phrase "radioactive brain."

40 For more on women's status and engagements in the post-Fukushima situation, see Kimura, *Radiation Brain Moms and Citizen Scientists*.

41 Matsumoto, "Rages of Fukushima and Grief in a No-Future Present."

42 Tarachine, accessed August 25, 2013, https://tarachineiwaki.org/?fbclid =IwAR3q4TcDhPScW796sjtxS6zaG7r4nIRd5JEY-JdzxSJorzI1w7ktE9 ClDrU.

43 On yakuza, see Suzuki, *Yakuza to genpatsu* [Yakuza and nuclear]. For examples of memoirs, see Horie, *Genpatsu jipushii* [Nuclear migrancy]; and the 1995 documentary "Nuclear Ginza," directed by Nicholas Röhl, YouTube, August 17, 2013, http://www.youtube.com/watch?v=mJTuWVDjarg.

44 Kodama, "Tsunami-tendenko and Morality in Disasters."

45 Yamashita, *Tsunami tendenko*.

46 In the case that voluntary evacuees were able to receive housing support, it was always tenuous, as reported in "Fukushima 'Voluntary' Evacuees to Lose Housing Support," *Straits Times*, January 17, 2017.

47 According to the standards of the International Commission on Radiological Protection (ICRP), 20 mSv (millisievert) is the occupational dose limit for radiation workers, while 1 mSv is the limit for the public.

48 The official number of evacuees was published as 65,300 from Fukushima Prefecture and 45,395 from other prefectures (as of July 1, 2015). Kansai University, *Genpatsu hinansha hakusho* [Nuclear evacuees white paper]. This number does not include voluntary evacuees.

49 For instance, in 1970, responding to people's rage against the polluting industries that insisted on their innocence and their disappointment in a legal system that failed to come to victims' aid, monks organized the movement Jusatsu kitō sōdan (Monks for deadly curses) to curse the polluting industries directly. See footage of this movement's actions in "20150827 UPLAN," YouTube, August 27, 2015, https://www.youtube.com/watch?v =Kbto4mWuyjE.

50 For English-language testimonies of comfort women, see Asian Women's Fund, "Testimonies of the Victims," accessed June 30, 2015, http://www .awf.or.jp/e3/oralhistory-00.html.

51 Nasubi, "Challenging the Issues."

52 Quoted from a zine produced by the organizers of the action, Okyupai Oi no ran (Riot of Occupy Oi).

53 "Japan's Sole Operating Reactors Allowed to Be Online Until September," *Mainichi Shimbun*, July 3, 2013.

54 For one example from the populist movement, see the Coalition Against Nukes website, accessed March 23, 2017, http://coalitionagainstnukes.jp/en/.

55 For instance, Shibaki-tai, a group claiming to be antiracist, forcibly controlled and excluded actions that the official organizers of the demonstration considered disorderly, acting precisely as a mercenary for liberal/ progressive political parties or movements. This was a new phenomenon of nationalist antiracism, claiming that true Japanese must not discriminate against foreigners.

56 This phrase is taken from a critique of the antinuclear movement published in 1979: Midnight Notes Collective, *Strange Victories*.

57 For an extensive interview with Koide, see Hirano and Kasai, "'The Fuku-shima Nuclear Disaster Is a Serious Crime.'"

58 Yabu, "Before and after 3/11."

59 Azuma, *Fukushima-daiichi-genpatsu kankōchika keikaku* [The plan to make Fukushima Daiichi a tourist site). For English-language material, see the project's website, accessed September 7, 2016, http://fukuichikankoproject.jp/project_en.html.

60 For English-language reporting on J-Village, see a list of articles on the website of the *Japan Times*, accessed September 7, 2016, http://www.japantimes.co.jp/tag/j-village.

61 Iguchi, "Depopulation and Mura-Okoshi (Village Revival)."

62 For creating tourist sites across the nation, the Japanese public broadcasting corporation NHK has produced annual TV dramas about historical heroes from various regions, and in orchestration with the programs, Japan Railways has instigated tourist campaigns targeting regions across Japan. This collaborative project persists without end.

63 For the most thorough analyses of the postmodern representation of Japan, see Miyoshi and Harootunian, *Postmodernism and Japan*.

64 See the website of the International Commission on Radiological Protection, accessed October 15, 2015, http://www.icrp.org.

65 For English-language reporting on ETHOS, see "ETHOS in Fukushima," *Citizen Perth* (blog), August 3, 2014, https://citizenperth.wordpress.com/2014/08/03/ethos-in-fukushima/; and dunrenard, "Project ETHOS: Living in the Nuclear Garden, a Crime against Humanity," *Fukushima 311 Watchdogs* (blog), November 13, 2015, https://dunrenard.wordpress.com/2016/11/13/project-ethos-living-in-the-nuclear-garden-a-crime-against-humanitypart-i.

66 "NHK: ICRP," *ETHOS in Fukushima* (blog), July 9, 2012, http://ethos-fukushima.blogspot.fr/2012/07/nhk-icrp.html.

67 See, for example, the website of the Center for Marine and Environmental Radiation, accessed October 23, 2012, http://ourradioactiveocean.org/results.html; and Behrens et al., "Model Simulations on the Long-Term Dispersal."

68 Deleuze and Guattari, *What Is Philosophy?*, 85.

69 Motoyuki, "Puromeiteusu no wana."

70 See the website of Whitefood, "Sekai kakkoku ni okeru yūnyū kisei ni tsuite" [Import restrictions by country], accessed July 2, 2017, https://news.whitefood.co.jp/radioactivitymap/forign-government/3419/.

71 See the website of Fukushimaken nōminren, accessed March 5, 2015, http://www.f-nou.com.

72 For more on Fujino Denryoku, see "About Fujino and Fujino Life," *Fujino Life*, accessed September 12, 2018, http://www.fujinolife.com/about/; and Carol Smith, "Transition Town Fujino Goes for Local Energy Independence," *Our World*, October 26, 2012, https://ourworld.unu.edu/en/transition-town-fujino-goes-for-local-energy-independence.

73 See the website of Zenkoku gotōchi enerugii kyōkai, accessed September 12, 2018, http://communitypower.jp.
74 This attitude is attested to by a recent publication edited by Umi Soya, *Designing New Ways of Life, Beginning from the City.*
75 Motoyuki, "Puromeiteusu no wana."
76 "Fukushima oki gyokairui" [Fukushima offshore fishing], *Asahi Shimbun,* March 7, 2016.

CHAPTER 2: CATASTROPHIC NATION

1 The mysterious concept of Urstaat internalizes an essential simplicity: "the State itself has always been in a relation with an outside and is inconceivable independent of that relationship." Deleuze and Guattari, *A Thousand Plateaus,* 360.
2 This is the state of desire that functions as affirmation of life, when it is not territorialized by power and retroactively wanted as lack. See Deleuze and Guattari, *Kafka.*
3 See Watsuji, *Sakoku* [Closed nation], for a more detailed account of sakoku policy.
4 Amino, *Rethinking Japanese History.*
5 See, for instance, Okakura, *The Book of Tea.*
6 Okakura, *The Ideals of the East,* 5.
7 Okakura, *The Ideals of the East,* 8.
8 Nishida, "Zettai mujunteki jikodōitsusei" [The self-identity of absolute contradictions], 7.
9 Kobayashi, "Nishida no shisō to nihongo no mondai" [Nishida's thought and the problematics of the Japanese language]; Tokieda, *Kokugogaku genron* [Principles of national language study].
10 For illustrations of such propaganda, see Orr, "A 1942 Declaration for Greater East Asian Co-operation."
11 But Barthes carefully differentiated between the "real" Japan and the Japan he wanted to write. See Barthes, *Empire of Signs.*
12 For the most thorough analyses of the postmodern representation of Japan, see Miyoshi and Harootunian, *Postmodernism and Japan.*
13 Harootunian, *The Empire's New Clothes,* 8
14 Jungk, *Children of the Ashes,* 241.
15 "Radiation Research Foundation to Apologize for Studying but Not Treating Hibakusha," *Mainichi Shimbun,* June 17, 2017.
16 Eto, *1946 kenpō* [The 1946 constitution].
17 Muto, "The Buildup of a Nuclear Armament Capability."
18 One of these men was Nakasone Yasuhiro (1918–2019), who served as prime minister of Japan from 1982 to 1987.
19 Monnet, "A Chaosmos of Condivision," 243.
20 It can be asserted that a certain number of Japanese congressmen, bureau-

crats, chief executive officers (CEOs), and commentators in the media are agents of the CIA. The CIA has an annual budget prepared to have them operate—this has long been an ordinary practice. This information has been widely circulated since the publication of Arima Tetsuo's *Genpatsu, Shoriki, CIA* [Nuclear power, Shoriki, and the CIA].

21 Here it is imperative to remind us of the fact that the victimization of Marshall Islanders has been consistently neglected in the discourses on the incident in both America and Japan.

22 Gensuikyo website, "Gensuibaku kinshi undo no rekishi" [History of antinuclear bomb movement], accessed July 8, 2015, https://www.antiatom.org/profile/history.html.

23 Muto, "The Buildup of a Nuclear Armament Capability."

24 Kurihara, "Genbaku taiken kara" [From the experience of a nuclear bomb], 107.

25 According to Koide's *Genshiryoku: sono mirai* [Nuclear: Its future], the construction of nuclear plants was disrupted in the following regions: Hamamasu (Hokkaido), Taisei (Hokkaido), Taro (Iwate), Namie (Fukushima), Odaka (Fukushima), Maki (Niigata), Suzu (Ishikawa), Ashihama (Mie), Miyama (Mie), Kumano (Mie), Nachikatsuura/Taiji (Wakayama), Koza (Wakayama), Hikigawa (Wakayama), Hidaka (Wakayama), Kohama (Fukui), Kumihama (Kyoto), Kasumi (Hyogo), Hamasaka (Hyogo), Aotani (Tottori), Tamagawa (Yamaguchi), Hagi (Yamaguchi), Hohoku (Yamaguchi), Anan (Tokushima), Kubokawa (Kochi), Saga (Kochi), Tsushima (Ehime), Kamae (Ohita), and Kushima (Miyazaki). Meanwhile, struggles continue in Kaminoseki (Yamaguchi) and Oma (Aomori).

26 Muto, "The Buildup of a Nuclear Armament Capability."

27 Yamamoto, *Kindai Nihon hyakugojūnen* [150 years of Japan's modernity], v.

28 For instance, the anarchist activist and theorist Osugi Sakae (1885–1923) was assassinated by a group of army officers, along with his lover and comrade Ito Noe and his nephew.

29 It is said that one-tenth of all deaths from the earthquake were by massacre, in rough estimation between six thousand and ten thousand.

30 Kon, "Shinsai barakku no omoide" [Memory of earthquake shacks], 322.

31 Shiba, *Tochi to Nihonjin* [Land and the Japanese], 282–83.

32 Here I am thinking of the 1970 "Discover Japan" campaign by the Japanese National Railways (Kokutetsu). See Kikuchi, "Discover, Discover Japan."

33 See the language used by the IMF on its website, "2012 Tokyo Annual Meetings," accessed February 2, 2013, http://www.imf-wb.2012tokyo.mof.go.jp/english/.

34 International Bank for Reconstruction and Development, "Address by the Prime Minister of Japan, Hayato Ikeda."

35 Debord, *Comments on the Society of the Spectacle.*

36 On this point, see Wark, *The Spectacle of Disintegration,* 3.

37 Deleuze and Guattari, *A Thousand Plateaus,* 432–33.

38 *Endnotes,* "Misery and Debt."

39 In terms of the post-Olympics situation in Athens, see Ross Domoney's 2014 film, *Future Suspended,* available at https://vimeo.com/86682631.

40 See the website of No Olympics 2020 (Hangorin no kai), accessed November 15, 2014, at http://hangorin.tumblr.com.

41 Hangorin no kai, accessed November 15, 2014, https://hangorin.tumblr.com.

CHAPTER 3: APOCALYPTIC CAPITALISM

1 Debates around this question have involved such intellectuals as Slavoj Žižek, Fredric Jameson, and Mark Fisher.

2 Caffentzis, "The Work/Energy Crisis and the Apocalypse," in *In Letters of Blood and Fire.*"

3 Goodchild, *Edward Teller.*

4 Mitchell, *Carbon Democracy.*

5 On the Manhattan Project, see Jungk, *Brighter than a Thousand Suns.*

6 Hecht and Oldenziel, "Islands."

7 Tiqqun, "The Cybernetic Hypothesis."

8 Hecht, "Nuclear Ontologies," 6.

9 The IAEA was an international mediator for the trade of enriched uranium before becoming an inspector for the Treaty on the Non-Proliferation of Nuclear Weapons (NPT). Finally, after the first Gulf War in 1991, it became a subordinate to the United Nations Security Council as an inspector of weapons of mass destruction.

10 Mumford, *The Myth of the Machine,* vol. 1.

11 Koide, *Genpatsu no uso* [The lies of nuclear power].

12 Koide, *Genpatsu no uso.*

13 For more on the nuclear village, see Kingston, "Japan's Nuclear Village"; and Kingston, "Power Politics."

14 The ten main electric power companies are Hokkaido, Tohoku, Tokyo, Chubu, Hokuriku, Kansai, Chugoku, Shikoku, Kyushu, and Okinawa.

15 Anders, *L'Obsolescence de l'homme,* 261; and Röhrlich, "'To Make the End Time Endless,'" 55.

16 Jungk, *The Nuclear State,* vii.

17 Jungk, *The Nuclear State.*

18 Mumford, *The Myth of the Machine,* vol. 2; Deleuze and Guattari, *Anti-Oedipus,* 142, 156.

19 Mumford, *The Myth of the Machine,* 2:258.

20 Massumi, *Ontopower.*

21 Massumi, *Ontopower,* 20–21.

22 Massumi, *Ontopower,* 131.

23 Hecht, *Being Nuclear.*

24 Caffentzis, "Against Nuclear Exceptionalism."

25 Caffentzis, "Against Nuclear Exceptionalism."

26 Midnight Notes Collective, *No Future Notes.*

27 For more on the vampire lives of nuclear power, see "Waste Storage 'in Perpetuity,'" *Ground Truth Trekking,* August 28, 2012, http://www.ground
truthtrekking.org/Issues/OtherIssues/perpetual-waste-storage
-perpetuity.html; and "Bad Choices—Video for the Stop Rokkasho Project," YouTube, August 1, 2016, https://www.youtube.com/watch?v
=h2guFrnqAoI.

28 Briefly, the victims (and perpetrators) of nuclear bomb testing are Marshall
Islands and Nevada (United States); Semipalatinsk, Kazakhstan (Soviet
Union); Montebello Islands and Maralinga, Australia (United Kingdom);
Reggane, Algeria and Fangataufa, Polynesia (France); and Lop Nur, Xinjiang (China).

29 Motoyuki, "Puromeiteusu no wana."

30 This point is addressed in both Caffentzis, "Against Nuclear Exceptionalism"; and Mies and Bennholdt-Thomsen, "Defending, Reclaiming and Reinventing the Commons."

31 Ironically, the word *sōzō* means "complete restoration of the body, soul and
spirit; to save, heal and deliver; to be made whole."

32 Muto, "Fukushima genpatsu kokuso-dan no hōkoku" [Report of the Fukushima nuclear prosecution team], 181.

33 There are two types of plutonium: weapons-grade and reactor-grade. It is
unclear whether the reactor-grade variety produced in Japan can be used to
create atomic bombs, which require at least 92 percent pure Pu-239. Bombs
made with larger amounts of reactor-grade plutonium would be unstable,
unpredictable, and dangerous to their creators.

34 Statista website, "Number of Operable Nuclear Reactors as of June 2019, by
Country," accessed March 9, 2020, https://www.statista.com/statistics
/267158/number-of-nuclear-reactors-in-operation-by-country/.

35 Heidegger, "The Age of the World Picture."

36 Morton, *Hyperobjects,* 1.

37 Deleuze and Guattari, *What Is Philosophy?,* 300.

38 Deleuze and Guattari, *What Is Philosophy?,* 240.

CHAPTER 4: CLIMATE CHANGE OF THE STRUGGLE

1 In the terms used by Deleuze and Guattari, this is a disjunctive or distributive synthesis, akin to desiring machines. See Deleuze and Guattari, "Body
without Organs," in *Anti-Oedipus.*

2 Thompson, "Remembering May '68."

3 Kohso, "Mutation of the Triad."

4 Katsiaficas, "Eros and Revolution," 498.

5 The major strikes at the Miike mines in northern Kyushu took place in 1953
and 1959–60. The direct impact of this local opposition on the New Left
was conveyed via the Sākuru mura undō (Circle village movement) by

connecting the miners' strikes in the countryside to the struggles against the US-Japan Security Treaty (Ampo) concentrated in Tokyo. Sākuru mura undō was originally organized in 1958 by feminist poet Morisaki Kazue (b. 1927) and poet/political activist Tanigawa Gan (1923–95) in order to connect the various struggles of workers and their communities across Kyushu through the production of a DIY publication (also called *Sākuru mura*).

6 The National Diet Building has since been the main target for any large mobilization against the government, including the post-Fukushima demonstrations.

7 Hirai, *Ai to nikushimi no Shinjuku* [Love and hatred of Shinjuku].

8 Performers included the art performance group Zero jigen (Zero dimension) and Kara Juro's theater group Jokyo gekijo (Situation theater). On the events in the station, see the films of Jonouchi Motoharu, especially *Shinjuku Station* (1974).

9 The main coordinators were Chukaku-ha of the Kakumeiteki kyosanshugisha domei (Core Faction of the Revolutionary Communist League), Marukusu-reninshugisha domei (Marxist-Leninist League), and Daiyon intanashonaru (Fourth International).

10 One of the targets was Nagoya's Towa factory on October 19, 1966.

11 See Adachi Masao and Koji Wakamatsu's 1971 film, *The Red Army/PFLP: Declaration of World War*. It is important to distinguish the Japan Red Army from the United Red Army that committed the 1972 massacre of its own members.

12 On the way struggles within the university were dispersed into the "sea of people," see Noriaki Tsuchimoto's 1969 film, *Prehistory of the Partisans*.

13 Notorious examples surfaced after the last big joint struggle in June 1970 against the US-Japan Security Treaty (Ampo) renewal. For instance, the 1972 United Red Army (Rengo sekigun) affair, during the groupuscule's attempt at guerrilla war against the Japanese government, saw fourteen people killed as disciplinary punishment, and there was escalating strife among three sects: the Core Faction (Chukaku-ha) of the Revolutionary Communist League, the Revolutionary Marxist Faction (Kakumaru-ha) of the Revolutionary Communist League, and the Liberation Faction (Kaiho-ha) of the Socialist Youth League of the Revolutionary Workers' Association.

14 *Uchigeba* is a compound word formed from the Japanese *uchi* (intra) and the German *Gewalt* (violent struggle).

15 Only one full account of intrasectarian uchigeba has been published: the well-known journalist Tatehana Takashi's 1975 *Chukaku tai kakumaru* (Chukaku vs. Kakumaru) detailed the divergence and violence between those two factions of the Japan Revolutionary Communist League (Kakukyodo). Then, in 2002 a series of symposia on uchigeba was organized, but sadly one of the participants was victimized by an uchigeba attack and seriously injured. Since then, public scrutiny has stopped.

16 Marcuse, *Eros and Civilization*, 91; Katsiaficas, "Afterword"; Deleuze and Guattari, *A Thousand Plateaus*, 236–37.

17 Kant, "To Perpetual Peace: A Philosophical Sketch"; Hegel, *Phenomenology of Sprit*; Marx and Engels, *Capital*.

18 Moore, *Anthropocene or Capitalocene?*

19 See, for example, Federici, *Caliban and the Witch*; and Federici, *Revolution at Point Zero*.

20 Deleuze, "Postscript on the Societies of Control," 3–7.

21 Yamamura and Murakami, "Ie Society as a Pattern of Civilization."

22 One such instance was the group Kichi to guntai o yurusanai kodosuru onnatachi no kai (Active women's group against the bases and military). For Japanese-language analyses of the Okinawan situation from a feminist standpoint, see Urashima, *Yutakana shima ni kichi ha iranai* [An abundant island does not need bases].

23 Ui, *Kōgai genron* [Principles of environmental pollution], 17–22.

24 These four "pollutions" are Minamata disease in Kumamoto, Niigata Minamata disease in Niigata, Itai-Itai disease in Toyama, and asthma in Yokkaichi.

25 Ui, *Kōgai genron*, 8.

26 Nakata, "Jūmin undō no naka no kukai jōdo to Minamatabyō tōsō" [The inhabitants' movement in *Paradise in Purgatory* and the Minamata struggle], 110.

27 Hirabayashi, "Genpatsu okotowari chiten to hangenpatsu undō" [Locations refusing nuclear plants and the antinuclear movement].

28 Nakata, "Jūmin undō no naka no kukai jōdo to Minamatabyō tōsō," 110.

29 For decades, the Chisso Corporation let organic mercury flow into the Sea of Yatsushiro. Now renamed Japan New Chisso (JNC), this company today is a global enterprise, supplying one-third of the liquid crystals used worldwide for LCD displays. In its leading role in the chemical industry, Chisso has been unwaveringly sponsored by the state and has collaborated fully with state policy. In the prewar period, it produced plastic; in the early postwar period, as the nation was facing a severe food shortage, the state prioritized agriculture and supported the company's production of fertilizers. Between 1932 and 1968, Chisso's chemical factory in Minamata released large quantities of industrial wastewater contaminated with highly toxic methylmercury. The entire Minamata Bay was affected: first plankton absorbed the poisonous substance, and then the bioconcentration was intensified up the food chain from plankton to fish to animals to humans. As of March 2001, the contamination inflicted by this state-supported industry has been recorded in the cases of 2,265 individuals, 1,784 of whom have died.

30 Concerning the struggles in Sanya and other yoseba, see the texts concerning the 1985 documentary *Yama: Attack to Attack* by Mitsuo Sato and Kyoi-

chi Yamaoka at the Bordersphere website, accessed January 15, 2013, http://www.bordersphere.com/events/yama2.htm.

31 The militant group Higashi ajia hannichi busō sensen (East Asia Anti-Japan Armed Front) attacked a number of targets that drove Japan's expansionism before and after World War II, including the emperor system, big enterprises, police, and nationalist monuments. One of these, the 1974 bombing of Mitsubishi Heavy Industries headquarters, killed eight people. Afterward it was revealed that the bomb had been set to explode earlier, so that it would affect only the empty building.

32 See Haraguchi, "Notes on the 4.5 Great Kamagasaki Oppression."

33 On the relationship between the 2008 Kamagasaki riot and the anti-G8 protest, see Kohso, "Climatology of the Eros Effect."

34 On the day laborers' struggle, see the film *Yama: Attack to Attack*.

35 For more on Funamoto Shuji, see Yang, "Man on Fire."

36 Funamoto, *Funamoto Shuji ikkō-shū* [Posthumous writings of Funamoto Shuji], 168–69.

37 The network Zenkoku kokosei kaigi (National Council of High School Students) was established in 1989.

38 After a long dispute that began in 1984, Komaba dormitory was forcibly evicted in August 2001 by the university administration.

39 In terms of photography, the works and writings of Nakahira Takuma are considered to have pioneered this current. I would also like to acknowledge here that the cinema historian Go Hirasawa's writings, curations, screenings, and personal conversations have been an indispensable reference for my understanding of landscape theory in relationship to the militant movements in the 1960s. See also Furuhata, *Cinema of Actuality*; and Toscano and Kinkle, *Cartography of the Absolute*.

40 Matsuda, *Fukei no shimetsu* [Extinction of landscape].

41 "AKA Serial Killer," YouTube, May, 15, 2015, https://www.youtube.com/watch?v=2t4ztcQnLdA.

42 An overview of Tsumura's concept of zatsuon can be found in Matsuda, *Fukei no shimetsu*, 48.

43 Yabu, *Genshiryoku toshi* [Atomic city], 4–5.

44 Olga Garnova, "Japan and Its Birth Rate: The Beginning of the End or Just a New Beginning?," *Japan Times*, February 10, 2016.

45 Jungk, *Children of the Ashes*.

46 Jungk, *Children of the Ashes*.

47 Yabu and Ikegami, *Genpatsu o tabero to iu nara, sonna shakai ha iranai*.

48 Yabu and Ikegami, *Genpatsu o tabero to iu nara, sonna shakai ha iranai*.

49 Matsumoto, "Rages of Fukushima and Grief in a No-Future Present," 155.

50 Murai, "At Least Four Firms."

51 Matsumoto, "Rages of Fukushima and Grief in a No-Future Present," 145.

52 Matsumoto, "Rages of Fukushima and Grief in a No-Future Present," 145.

53 Matsumoto, "Rages of Fukushima and Grief in a No-Future Present," 146.

54 Les éditions des mondes à faire editorial collective, "Introduction," in *Fukushima et ses invisibles* [Fukushima and its invisibles], 29.

55 Les éditions des mondes à faire editorial collective, "Introduction," in *Fukushima et ses invisibles*, 30.

56 Les éditions des mondes à faire editorial collective, "Introduction," in *Fukushima et ses invisibles*, 32.

57 Les éditions des mondes à faire editorial collective, "Introduction," in *Fukushima et ses invisibles*, 31.

58 Les éditions des mondes à faire editorial collective, "Introduction," in *Fukushima et ses invisibles*, 31.

59 On the nuclear village, see Rokusaisha Reporters, *Toden oikake mappu*.

60 The theory collective Hapax accounts for the archival of stories by the radioactive crowd as follows: "The issue at stake is not which story is right and which one is wrong. Insofar as it is a story of this body, everything is equally respected. . . . Embodying the possibility of collective intelligence against radioactive socialization by gathering voices from below, this collection is the fruit of resistance to the intellectual globalization laundered through English. . . . what such efforts generate most fundamentally is a plane of anarchic coalition whereupon innumerable narratives coexist and interact. . . . The data collected by the radioactive crowd cannot be detached from their narrativity. This coalition of stories can be called a 'data strike.'" Hapax, *Ikata hōki no tame no danshō* [Fragments for the Ikata insurrection], 12–13.

61 No Olympics 2020, accessed April 14, 2018, https://hangorin.tumblr.com.

62 For more on the Yoshida dormitory, see "Kyoto University Students Protest Closure of Yoshida Dormitory," *Throw Out Your Books* (blog), February 16, 2018, https://throwoutyourbooks.wordpress.com/2018/02/16/kyoto-university-students-oppose-campus-signboards-closure-yoshida-dormitory/. Searching for images with the keywords "Kyoto University Yoshida dormitory" is also illustrative.

63 Motoko Rich, "U.S. Marine's Son Wins Okinawa Election on Promise to Oppose Military Base," *New York Times*, September 30, 2018.

64 Glissant, *Traité du tout-monde*.

65 Glissant, *Introduction á une poétique du divers*.

66 Reclus, *L'Homme et la terre*.

67 For more on Reclus's life, see Clark and Martin, *Anarchy, Geography, Modernity*.

68 On this concept, see Zibechi, *Dispersing Power*.

69 The concept of "new earth" can be found in Deleuze and Guattari's *A Thousand Plateaus*, wherein it also indicates "absolute deterritorialization": "Deterritorialization is absolute when it conforms to the first case and brings about the creation of a new earth, in other words, when it connects lines of flight, raises them to the power of an abstract vital line, or draws a plane of consistency" (510).

1 For "Creolization," see Glissant, *Poetics of Relations.*
2 Deleuze and Guattari, *A Thousand Plateaus,* chapter 12.
3 For "geophilosophy," see Deleuze and Guattari, *What Is Philosophy?,* chapter 4.
4 Kohso and two Greek anarchists, *Girisha no anakizumu 2018* [Greek anarchism 2018].

Alexievich, Svetlana. *Voices from Chernobyl*. Translated by Keith Gessen. London: Dalkey Archive Press, 2005.

Amino, Yoshihiko. *Rethinking Japanese History*. Translated by Alan S. Christy. Ann Arbor: University of Michigan Press, 2012.

Anders, Günther. *L'Obsolescence de l'homme: Sur l'ame de l'époque de la deuxieme revolution industrielle*. Paris: Éditions de L'Encyclopédie des Nuisances, 2002.

Arima Tetsuo. *Genpatsu, Shoriki, CIA* [Nuclear power, Shoriki, and the CIA]. Tokyo: Shincho-Shinsho, 2008.

Azuma Hiroki, ed. *Fukushima-daiichi-genpatsu kankōchika keikaku* [The plan to make Fukushima Daiichi into a tourist site]. Shisō chizu bēta 4-2. Tokyo: Genron, 2013.

Barthes, Roland. *Empire of Signs*. Translated by Richard Howard. New York: Farrar, Straus and Giroux, 1982.

Behrens, Erik, Franziska U. Schwarzkopf, Joke F. Lübbecke, and Claus W. Böning. "Model Simulations on the Long-Term Dispersal of ^{137}Cs Released into the Pacific Ocean off Fukushima." *Environmental Research Letters* 7, no. 3 (2012): 1–10.

Caffentzis, George. "Against Nuclear Exceptionalism with a Coda on the Commons and Nuclear Power." Presentation, Crisis and Commons: Prefigurative Politics after Fukushima, Tokyo University, December 2, 2012.

Caffentzis, George. *In Letters of Blood and Fire*. Oakland, CA: PM Press, 2013.

Clark, John, and Camille Martin, eds. *Anarchy, Geography, Modernity: Selected Writings of Elisée Reclus*. Translated by John Clark and Camille Martin. Oakland, CA: PM Press, 2013.

Colson, Daniel. *A Little Philosophical Lexicon of Anarchism from Proudhon to Deleuze*. Translated by Jesse Cohn. New York: Minor Compositions, 2019.

Debord, Guy. *Comments on the Society of the Spectacle*. Minneapolis: University of Minnesota Press, 1997.

Deleuze, Gilles. "Nietzsche and Saint Paul, Lawrence and John of Patmos." In

Essays Critical and Clinical, translated by Daniel W. Smith and Michael A. Greco, 36–52. New York: Verso, 1998.

Deleuze, Gilles. "Postscript on the Societies of Control." *October*, no. 59 (1992): 3–7.

Deleuze, Gilles, and Félix Guattari. *Anti-Oedipus: Capitalism and Schizophrenia*. Translated by Robert Hurley, Mark Seem, and Helen R. Lane. Minneapolis: University of Minnesota Press, 1983.

Deleuze, Gilles, and Félix Guattari. *Kafka: Toward a Minor Literature*. Translated by Dana Polan. Minneapolis: University of Minnesota Press, 1986.

Deleuze, Gilles, and Félix Guattari. *A Thousand Plateaus: Capitalism and Schizophrenia*. Translated by Brian Massumi. Minneapolis: University of Minnesota Press, 1987.

Deleuze, Gilles, and Félix Guattari. *What Is Philosophy?* Translated by Hugh Tomlinson and Graham Burchell. New York: Columbia University Press, 1994.

Les éditions des mondes à faire editorial collective. *Fukushima et ses invisibles* [Fukushima and its invisibles]. Vaulx-en-Velin: Les éditions des mondes à faire, 2018.

Endnotes. "Misery and Debt: On the Logic and History of Surplus Populations and Surplus Capital." *Endnotes* 2 (2010).

Eto Jun. *1946 kenpō: sono kōsoku* [The 1946 constitution: Its bind]. Tokyo: Bungei Shunjyu, 2015.

Federici, Silvia. *Caliban and the Witch: Women, the Body and Primitive Accumulation*. New York: Autonomedia, 2004.

Federici, Silvia. *Revolution at Point Zero: Housework, Reproduction and Feminist Struggle*. Oakland, CA: PM Press, 2012.

Funabashi Yoichi. *Kauntodaun merutodaun* [Countdown meltdown]. 2 vols. Tokyo: Bunshun Bunko, 2016.

Funamoto Shuji. *Funamoto Shuji ikkō-shū* [Posthumous writings of Funamoto Shuji]. Tokyo: Renga Shobo Shinsha, 1985.

Furuhata, Yuriko. *Cinema of Actuality: Japanese Avant-Garde Filmmaking in the Season of Image Politics*. Durham, NC: Duke University Press, 2013.

Glissant, Édouard. *Introduction á une poétique du divers*. Paris: Éditions Gallimard, 1996.

Glissant, Édouard. *Poetics of Relations*. Translated by Betsy Wing. Ann Arbor: University of Michigan Press, 1997.

Glissant, Édouard. *Traité du tout-monde*. Paris: Éditions Gallimard, 1997.

Goodchild, Peter. *Edward Teller: The Real Dr. Strangelove*. Cambridge, MA: Harvard University Press, 2004.

Guattari, Félix. *Schizoanalytic Cartographies*. Translated by Andrew Goffey. New York: Bloomsbury, 2013.

Guattari, Félix. *The Three Ecologies*. Translated by Ian Pindar and Paul Sutton. New York: Continuum, 2008.

Hapax. *Ikata hōki no tame no danshō* [Fragments for the Ikata insurrection]. Hapax 1. Tokyo: Yakosha, 2013.

Haraguchi, Takeshi. "Notes on the 4.5 Great Kamagasaki Oppression and Nuclear Power Industry." *J-Fissures*, April 14, 2011.

Haraway, Donna. *Staying with the Trouble: Making Kin in the Chthulucene.* Durham, NC: Duke University Press, 2016.

Harootunian, Harry. *The Empire's New Clothes: Paradigm Lost and Regained.* Chicago: Prickly Paradigm, 2004.

Hecht, Gabrielle. *Being Nuclear: Africans and the Global Uranium Trade.* Cambridge, MA: MIT Press, 2012.

Hecht, Gabrielle. "Nuclear Ontologies." *Constellations* 13, no. 3 (2006): 320–31.

Hecht, Gabrielle. "The Power of Nuclear Things." *Technology and Culture* 51, no. 1 (2010): 1–30.

Hecht, Gabrielle, and Ruth Oldenziel. "Islands: The United States as a Network Empire." In *Entangled Geographies: Empire and Technopolitics in the Global Cold War,* edited by Gabrielle Hecht, 13–41. Cambridge, MA: MIT Press, 2011.

Hegel, Georg Wilhelm Friedrich. *Phenomenology of Sprit.* Translated by A. V. Miller. Oxford: Oxford University Press, 1977.

Heidegger, Martin. "The Age of the World Picture." In *The Question Concerning Technology and Other Essays,* translated by William Lovitt, 115–54. New York: Garland, 1977.

Hida Shuntaro, and Kamanaka Hitomi. *Naibu hibaku no kyoi* [The threat of internal radiation exposure]. Tokyo: Chikuma Shinso, 2005.

Hirabayashi Yuko. "Genpatsu okotowari chiten to hangenpatsu undo" [Locations refusing nuclear plants and the antinuclear movement]. *Ohara shakai mondai kenkyūjo zasshi* 661, no. 3 (2013): 36–51. http://oisr-org.ws.hosei.ac .jp/images/oz/contents/661-03.pdf.

Hirai Gen. *Ai to nikushimi no Shinjuku* [Love and hatred of Shinjuku]. Tokyo: Chukuma Shobo, 2010.

Hirano, Katsuya, and Hirotaka Kasai. "'The Fukushima Nuclear Disaster Is a Serious Crime': Interview with Koide Hiroaki." Translated by Robert Stolz. *Asia-Pacific Journal* 14, no. 6.2 (March 2016): 1–27.

Horie Kunio. *Genpatsu jipushii* [Nuclear migrancy]. Tokyo: Gendai Shokan, 2011.

Iguchi, Takashi. "Depopulation and Mura-Okoshi (Village Revival)." In *Forestry and the Forest Industry in Japan,* edited by Yoshiya Iwai, 259–77. Vancouver: University of British Columbia Press, 2002.

International Bank for Reconstruction and Development. "Address by the Prime Minister of Japan, Hayato Ikeda." In *1964 Annual Meetings of the Boards of Governers.* http://documents.worldbank.org/curated/en /591861468167659630/pdf/534000BRoboard10B0x345609B01PUBLIC1.pdf

Ishimure, Michiko. *Paradise in the Sea of Sorrow: Our Minamata Disease.* Translated by Livia Monnet. Ann Arbor: University of Michigan Press, 2003.

Jungk, Robert. *Brighter than a Thousand Suns.* Translated by James Cleugh. New York: Harcourt, 1958.

Jungk, Robert. *Children of the Ashes*. Translated by Constantine Fitzgibbon. New York: Harcourt, 1961.

Jungk, Robert. *The Nuclear State*. Translated by Eric Mosbacher. London: John Calder, 1979.

Kansai University, ed. *Genpatsu hinansha hakusho* [Nuclear evacuees white paper]. Institute of Disaster Area Revitalization, Regrowth and Governance. Kyoto: Jinbun Shoin, 2015.

Kant, Immanuel. "To Perpetual Peace: A Philosophical Sketch." Translated by Ted Humphrey. In *Perpetual Peace and Other Essays*. 107–43. Indianapolis: Hackett Publishing Company, 1983.

Katsiaficas, George. "Eros and Revolution." *Radical Philosophy Review* 16, no. 2 (2013): 491–505. doi:10.5840/radphilrev201316238.

Katsiaficas, George. "Afterword: Marcuse as an Activist: Reminiscences of His Theory and Practice." In *The New Left and the 1960s: Collected Papers of Herbert Marcuse*, vol. 3, edited by Douglas Kellner, 192–203. New York: Routledge, 2005.

Kikuchi, Daisuke. "Discover, Discover Japan." *Japan Times*, September 11, 2014.

Kimura, Aya Hirata. *Radiation Brain Moms and Citizen Scientists: The Gender Politics of Food Contamination after Fukushima*. Durham, NC: Duke University Press, 2016.

Kingston, Jeff. "Japan's Nuclear Village." *Asia-Pacific Journal* 10, no. 37.1 (September 2012): 1–23.

Kingston, Jeff. "Power Politics: Japan's Resilient Nuclear Village." *Asia-Pacific Journal* 10, no. 12.4 (March 2012): 1–11.

Klein, Naomi. *The Shock Doctrine: The Rise of Disaster Capitalism*. Toronto: Alfred A. Knopf Canada, 2007.

Kodama, Satoshi. "Tsunami-tendenko and Morality in Disasters." *Journal of Medical Ethics* 41, no. 5 (2015): 361–63.

Kobayashi Toshiaki. "Nishida no shisō to nihongo no mondai" [Nishida's thought and the problematics of the Japanese language]. September 2016. http://www.nihontetsugaku-philosophie-japonaise.jp/wp-content/uploads/2016/09/nihontetsugakushi12-1.pdf.

Kohso, Sabu. "Climatology of the Eros Effect: Notes from the Japanese Archipelago." In *Spontaneous Combustion: The Eros Effect and Global Revolution*, edited by A. K. Thompson and Jason Del Gandio, 211–33. Albany: State University of New York Press, 2018.

Kohso, Sabu. "Mutation of the Triad: Totalitarianism, Fascism, and Nationalism in Japan." *e-flux*, no. 56 (June 2014).

Kohso, Sabu, and two Greek anarchists. *Girisha no anakizumu 2018* [Greek anarchism 2018]. Hapax 10. Tokyo: Yakosha, 2018.

Koide Hiroaki. *Genpatsu no uso* [The lies of nuclear power]. Tokyo: Fuso Sha, 2011.

Koide Hiroaki. *Genshiryoku: sono mirai* [Nuclear: Its future]. Tokyo: Hon-no-izumi-sha, 2011.

Kon Wajiro. "Shinsai barakku no omoide" [Memory of earthquake shacks]. In *Kon Wajiro shū*, vol. 4, 320–28. Tokyo: Domesusha, 1971.

Kuchinskaya, Olga. *The Politics of Invisibility: Public Knowledge about Radiation Health Effects after Chernobyl*. Cambridge, MA: MIT Press, 2014.

Kurihara Sadako. "Genbaku taiken kara" [From the experience of a nuclear bomb]. In *Hangenpatsu jiten*, vol. 2, 105–15. Tokyo: Gendai Shokan, 1979.

Lawrence, D. H. *Apocalypse*. New York: Penguin Books, 1995.

Lilly, Sasha, David McNally, Eddie Yuan, and James Davis, eds. *Catastrophism: The Apocalyptic Politics of Collapse and Rebirth*. Oakland, CA: PM Press, 2012.

Marcuse, Herbert. *Eros and Civilization*. Boston: Beacon Press, 1974.

Marx, Karl, and Friedrich Engels. *Capital: A Critique of Political Economy, Vol. 1*. Translated by Ben Fowkes. London: Penguin Books, 1990.

Marx, Karl. *The Eighteenth Brumaire of Louis Bonaparte*. New York: International Publishers, 1963.

Massumi, Brian. *Ontopower: War, Powers, and the State of Perception*. Durham, NC: Duke University Press, 2015.

Matsuda Masao. *Fukei no shimetsu* [Extinction of landscape]. Tokyo: Tabata Shoten, 1971.

Matsumoto, Mari. "Rages of Fukushima and Grief in a No-Future Present." In *Rebellious Mourning: The Collective Work of Grief*, edited by Cindy Milstein, 123–59. Oakland, CA: AK Press, 2017.

Midnight Notes Collective. *No Future Notes: The Work/Energy Crisis and the Anti-Nuclear Movement*. Brooklyn, NY: Midnight Notes Collective, 1980.

Midnight Notes Collective. *Strange Victories: The Anti-Nuclear Movement in the U.S. and Europe*. Brooklyn, NY: Midnight Notes Collective, 1979.

Mies, Maria, and Veronika Bennholdt-Thomsen. "Defending, Reclaiming and Reinventing the Commons." *Canadian Journal of Development Studies* 22, no. 4 (2001): 997–1023.

Mitchell, Timothy. *Carbon Democracy: Political Power in the Age of Oil*. New York: Verso, 2011.

Miyoshi, Masao, and H. D. Harootunian, eds. *Postmodernism and Japan*. Durham, NC: Duke University Press, 1989.

Monnet, Livia. "A Chaosmos of Condivision: Radiation Aesthetics in the TV Anime Series *Coppelion* (2013)." In *Ecocriticism in Japan*, edited by Hisaaki Wake, Keijiro Suga, and Yuki Masami, 239–66. Lanham, MD: Lexington Books, 2018.

Moore, Jason, ed. *Anthropocene or Capitalocene? Nature, History, and the Crisis of Capitalism*. Oakland, CA: PM Press, 2016.

Morton, Timothy. *Hyperobjects: Philosophy and Ecology after the End of the World*. Minneapolis: University of Minnesota Press, 2013.

Motoyuki Maeda. "Puromeiteusu no wana" [The trap of Prometheus]. *Asahi Shimbun*, November 15–27, 2011. http://digital.asahi.com/articles/list/prometheus.html?ref=comr_cnt_pr.

Mumford, Lewis. *The Myth of the Machine*. Vol. 1, *Techniques and Human Development*. New York: Harcourt, Brace and World, 1967.

Mumford, Lewis. *The Myth of the Machine*. Vol. 2, *The Pentagon of Power*. New York: Harcourt Brace Jovanovich, 1970.

Murai, Shusuke. "At Least Four Firms Used Foreign Trainees to Clean up Radioactive Contamination from Fukushima Nuclear Plant: Ministry." *Japan Times*, July 13, 2018.

Muto, Ichiyo. "The Buildup of a Nuclear Armament Capability and the Postwar Statehood of Japan: Fukushima and the Genealogy of Nuclear Bombs and Power Plants." *Inter-Asia Cultural Studies* 14, no. 2 (2013): 171–212.

Muto Ruiko. "Fukushima genpatsu kokuso-dan no hōkoku" [Report of the Fukushima nuclear prosecution team]. In *Posuto-Fukushima no tetsugaku*, 178–83. Tokyo: Akashi Shoten, 2015.

Nakata Norihito. "Jūmin undō no naka no kukai jōdo to Minamatabyō tōsō" [The inhabitants' movement in *Paradise in Purgatory* and the Minamata struggle]. Bungei: Tsuitō Ishimure Michiko, 2018.

Nasubi. "Challenging the Issues around the Radiation-Exposed Labor That Connects San'ya and Fukushima: Toward a Revival of the Underclass Workers' Movement." *J-Fissures*, August 30, 2012.

National Police Agency of Japan. "Damage Situation and Police Countermeasures." https://www.npa.go.jp/news/other/earthquake2011/pdf/higaijokyo_e.pdf. December 10, 2019.

Nishida Kitaro. "Zettai mujunteki jikodōitsusei" [The self-identity of absolute contradictions]. In *Nishida Kitaro tetsugaku ronshu III*, edited by Ueda Shizuteru, 7–84. Tokyo: Iwanami Bunko, 1989.

Nixon, Rob. *Slow Violence and the Environmentalism of the Poor*. Cambridge, MA: Harvard University Press, 2013.

Okakura, Kakuzo. *The Book of Tea*. New York: Putnam, 1906.

Okakura, Kakuzo. *The Ideals of the East with Special Reference to the Art of Japan*. London: John Murray, 1905.

Orr, James. "A 1942 Declaration for Greater East Asian Co-operation." *Asia-Pacific Journal* 6, no. 3 (2008): 1–5.

Reclus, Elisée. *L'Homme et la terre*. 6 vols. Paris: Librairie Universelle, 1905–8.

Röhrlich, Elisabeth. "'To Make the End Time Endless': Günther Anders' Fight against Nuclear Weapons." In *The Life and Work of Günther Anders: Émigré, Iconoclast, Philosopher, Man of Letters*, edited by Günther Bischof, Jason Dawsey, and Bernhard Fetz, 45–57. Innsbruck: StudienVerlag, 2014.

Rokusaisha Reporters. *Tabū naki genpatsu jiko chōsho* [Records of nuclear accidents, without taboo]. Tokyo: Roskusaisha, 2012.

Rokusaisha Reporters. *Toden oikake mappu* [TEPCO and nuclear power plants]. Tokyo: Rokusaisha, 2011.

Schanen, Naomi. "Radiation Monitoring Group Formed during Fukushima Nuclear Disaster Now a Source of Global Data." *Japan Times*, March 9, 2018.

Schmitt, Carl. *The Nomos of the Earth*. Translated by G. L. Ulmen. New York: Telos Press, 2006.

Shiba Ryotaro. *Tochi to Nihonjin* [Land and the Japanese]. Tokyo: Chuko Bunko, 1980.

Solnit, Rebecca. *A Paradise Built in Hell*. New York: Penguin Books, 2010.

Soya, Umi, ed. *Designing New Ways of Life, Beginning from the City: Urban Permaculture Guide*. Mino City, Japan: MM Books, 2015.

Suzuki, Tomohiko. *Yakuza to genpatsu* [Yakuza and nuclear]. Tokyo: Bungei Shunju, 2011.

Tatehana Takashi. *Chukaku tai kakumaru* [Chukaku vs. Kakumaru]. Tokyo: Kodansha, 1975.

Tent for Disrupting the Oi Nuclear Plant Restart. *Okyupai Oi no ran: 6/30–7/2* [Riot of Occupy Oi], August 15, 2012.

Thompson, A. K. "Remembering May '68: An Interview with George Katsiaficas." *Upping the Anti 6*, October 26, 2009.

Tiqqun. "The Cybernetic Hypothesis." May 29, 2010. theanarchistlibrary.org/library/tiqqun-the-cybernetic-hypothesis.

Tokieda Motoki. *Kokugogaku genron* [Principles of national language study]. Tokyo: Iwanami Bunko, 2007.

Toscano, Alberto, and Jeff Kinkle. *Cartography of the Absolute*. Washington, DC: Zero Books, 2015.

Ui Jun. *Kōgai genron* [Principles of environmental pollution]. Tokyo: Aki Shobo, 1988.

Urashima Etsuko. *Yutakana shima ni kichi ha iranai* [An abundant island does not need bases]. Tokyo: Impact Shuppan Kai, 2002.

Virilio, Paul. *Unknown Quantity*. London: Thames and Hudson, 2003.

Wark, McKenzie. *The Spectacle of Disintegration*. New York: Verso, 2013.

Watsuji Tetsuo. *Sakoku* [Closed nation]. Tokyo: Chikuma Shobo, 1951.

Yabu, Shiro. "Before and after 3/11." *J-Fissures*, February 14, 2012.

Yabu Shiro. *Genshiryoku toshi* [Atomic city]. Tokyo: Ibunsha, 2010.

Yabu Shiro, and Ikegami Yoshihiko. *Genpatsu o tabero to iu nara, sonna shakai ha iranai* [We don't need a society that tells us to eat radiation]. Tokyo: Shin Hyoron, 2012.

Yamamoto Yoshitaka. *Kindai Nihon hyakugojūnen: kagakugijutsu soryokusen taisei no hatan* [150 years of Japan's modernity: Failure of the total war regime of technoscience]. Tokyo: Iwanami Shinsho, 2018.

Yamamura, Kozo, and Yasusuke Murakami. "Ie Society as a Pattern of Civilization: Introduction." *Journal of Japanese Studies* 19, no. 2 (1984): 279–363.

Yamashita, Fumio. *Tsunami tendenko: Japanese Modern History of Tsunami*. Tokyo: Shin Nihon Shuppansha, 2008.

Yang, Manuel. "Man on Fire." *CounterPunch*, July 9, 2014.

Yuienbo. *Tannisho: Passages Deploring Deviations of Faith*. Translated by Shojun Bando and Harold Stewart. Berkeley, CA: Numata Center for Buddhist Translation and Research, 1996.

Zibechi, Raul. *Dispersing Power*. Translated by Ramor Ryan. Oakland, CA: AK Press, 2010.

Black Bloc, 41
blogs, 32–33
Bonaparte, Louis-Napoleon, 12, 13
bubble economy (1980s–1990s), 48,
    127, 128
Buddhism, 8, 9, 154, 167–68n11, 168n12
Bund (Communist League), 119
burakumin outcasts, 135, 136
Bure movement, 133
Bush, George W., 100

Caffentzis, George, 90, 101
Canada, xii, 92
capital, 13, 23, 75; accumulation of, 125;
    capital/state conglomeration, 85,
    89; concentrated in Tokyo, 76, 80;
    crisis and recomposition of, 125; lib-
    eral politics and, 46; nuclear power
    plants as fixed or constant capital,
    83, 88, 104; self-reproduction and
    expansion of, 8, 85; state-regulated
    flows of, 74; variable capital (labor
    power), 88, 104
capitalism, ix, xi, xii, 6, 12, 109, 134;
    accumulation process of, 111; "di-
    saster capitalism," 5; end of, 87, 88;
    formation and restructurings of, 4;
    "good capitalism," 79; immanence
    and, 15; immortalized by nuclear
    power, 87–89; integrated spectacle
    and, 82; management of human
    bodies by, 147; military-industrial
    complex and, 44; nuclear industry
    and, 16, 25; radiation as premise of,
    81; reterritorialization of, 116; state
    merged with, 93–98; state sov-
    ereignty and, 89, 154; survival in
    permanent crisis, 101–2; totalizing
    project of, 14, 15, 87, 124; uneven de-
    velopment on global scale, 117. *See
    also* nation-state, capitalist
Capitalocene, 125
capture, apparatuses of, 45, 55, 64, 88,
    94, 145, 149; decomposition of, 162;
    forged in response to catastrophe,
    5; insular territoriality as, 56, 162;

interventions in post-disaster Ja-
    pan, 48; naturing nature and, 153
Carbon Democracy (Mitchell), 90
catastrophe, 4, 15, 111, 127, 130; affirma-
    tion of, 153; encounters with the
    Other and, 55–56, 57; migrants cre-
    ated by, 74–75; "recovery" from,
    45
Center for Environmental Creation
    (Kankyo Sōzō Senta), 108
cesium, 28, 33, 40, 170n26
chaos, 13, 111, 155
Chemical Biological Incident Response
    Force, US, 24
Chernobyl (1986), xi, 6, 21, 32, 106; ef-
    fects of radiation on human body
    and, 147; ETHOS Project and, 48
Chiapas movement, 133
Chidaism blog, 33
children, ix, 29, 144; in contaminated
    areas, 48; evacuated from radiation
    zones, 33, 35; susceptibility to radia-
    tion, 41
China, 54, 118, 176n28; Belt and Road
    Initiative, 109; Cultural Revolution,
    122, 139; imperialism of, 159
Chinese, resident in Tokyo, 77
Chisso Corporation, 41, 178n29
Christianity, 7–8, 11, 56
Chukaku tai kakumaru [Chukaku vs
    Kakumaru] (Tatehana, 1975),
    177n115
CIA (Central Intelligence Agency), 68
"citizens' movement" (*shimin undō*),
    130
Citizens' Nuclear Information Center
    (CNIC), 32
civil war, 3
civilization, 115, 161; Asiatic, 60; capital-
    ism and, 4, 8; decline and end of,
    72, 164; Western, 56
class struggle, 90, 125, 135
climatology, 15, 117
cobalt, 170n26
Cold War, 66, 92, 100, 102, 107; model
    of revolution during, 159; nuclear

Enlightenment, 124
environment, 6, 103, 124; commons and, 105; defense of living environment, 130–35; destruction of, xii, 142; radionuclides in, 5
Eros and Civilization (Marcuse), 115
"eros effect," 3, 115
eschatology, 4, 7, 126
ETHOS Project, 48–49
evacuation zones, 108, 168n6
everyday life, 42, 44, 113, 144, 165; erotic drive in molecular dimension, 136; politics of, 114
exodus (mass evacuation), 27, 28, 37, 38, 51

farmers, 26, 29, 35, 50; in Japanese history, 58; Narita airport construction resisted by Sanrizuka farmers' struggle, 121, 132, 133; products wasted by radioactive contamination, 51
fascism, 12, 39, 63; fascist labor brokers, 137; microfascism, 124
fatalism, 4, 8, 9
feminism, 14, 36, 46, 129, 149, 178n22
feudal system, 153, 162
Fisheries Cooperative Association, 53
fishermen, 26, 35, 50
fission, nuclear, xii, 31, 83, 88, 98, 103; as absolute anti-spectacle, 85; deadly effects on human body and the environment, 99; Janus face of, 7
food safety, 36
fossil fuel, 95, 161
Foucault, Michel, 55
"Fourth Comprehensive National Development Plan" (1987), 80
France, xii, 48, 109; La ZAD struggle, 121, 133; as nuclear state, 92
Freud, Sigmund, 115
fukoku kyōhei ("wealthy nation and strong soldiers"), 26, 45, 56, 58, 64; persistence in postwar regime, 94; scientific/technological progress and, 71

Fukushima Daiichi Nuclear Power Plant, 24, 37, 38, 99, 136; total blackout and meltdown at, 21; "tourization" of disaster site, 47–48
Fukushima et ses invisibles (Les éditions des mondes à faire), 152
Fukushima Kanko Project, 47, 48
Fukushima nuclear disaster (2011), xi, 1, 81, 106; atomic world history and, 93; as catastrophe, 6; disaster phase, 21–27; dual role of, 3; earthquake and tsunami precipitating, 5, 15, 18–19, 37, 151; emotions provoked by, 7, 18, 32, 151; as endless event, 111; as epitome of dystopian world, ix; as eschatological sign, 8–9; evacuations following, 27–28, 169n22; as repetition and continuation of Hiroshima/Nagasaki, 31; singularity of, 4, 17; social reproduction crisis and, 144–45
Fukushima Prefecture, 22, 26, 107; number of evacuees from, 40, 171n48; quality of food products associated with, 29–30
Funamoto Shuji, 137, 138

Genshiryoku: sono mirai [Nuclear: Its future] (Koide), 174n25
Genshiryoku toshi [Atomic city] (Yabu), 143–44
Gensuikin (Japan Congress Against Atomic and Hydrogen Bombs), 69
Gensuikyo (Japan Council Against Atomic and Hydrogen Bombs), 69
geology, 15, 58, 117
geophilosophy, 55
geopolitics, 51, 91
Glissant, Édouard, 157, 162
global nuclear regime, 16, 91, 92, 100, 112; driven by power contestations, 93; formal and real subsumptions of, 150
global warming, 95, 109
Go Hirasawa, 179n39
"good-for-nothings". *See* Dame-ren

governance, 4, 6, 32, 63, 74, 107, 111; economic growth as, 66; empowerment associated with, 108; localities absorbed into national governance, 131; of ordered territories of the World, 115; planetary, 109; post-disaster, 27; pronuclear, 112, 147

Great East Asia Co-Prosperity Sphere, 60

Greece, xii, 42

green zones, 29

Guattari, Félix. *See* Deleuze (Gilles) and Guattari (Félix)

Gulf War, first (1991), 175n9

Hamai Shinzo, 68

Hapax theory collective, 34, 180n60

Harootunian, Harry, 64

Hecht, Gabrielle, 91, 100

Hegel, Georg W. F., 124, 167n10

Hibakusha Counseling Center, 33

Hida Shuntaro, 33, 170n32

Higashi ajia hannichi busō sensen (East Asia Anti-Japan Armed Front), 179n31

hippies, 120

Hirohito, Emperor, 13, 66

Hiroshima/Nagasaki atomic bombings, xi, xii, 7, 16, 67, 118; advent of new epoch and, 61; antinuclear discourse defined by, 107; collective memory and, 78; effects of radiation on human body and, 146, 147; end limit of conquest and, 94; eyewitnesses to, 33; Japan's surrender in World War II and, 57; nuclear power plant in Hiroshima, 68; as ongoing events, 63; survivors of, 31, 62, 70

Hitler, Adolf, 13

homeless people, 46, 84, 129, 137, 149, 155

Homme et la terre, L' (Elisée), 158

Hong Kong, 54, 86

human rights, 124

Hungarian Revolution (1956), 119

hyperobjects, 109–10

IAEA (International Atomic Energy Agency), 23, 91, 108, 175n9

ICRP (International Commission on Radiological Protection), 48, 49, 68, 146, 171n47

IMF (International Monetary Fund), 80, 81

immanence, ontology of, 14, 114, 168n19

immigrants, 14, 45, 144, 161

imperialism, 90, 92, 118, 120

India, 25

indigenous movements/peoples, 14, 44, 126

Indo-China, 118

industrial reserve army, 75

infrastructure, 2, 22, 83; landscape theory and, 141–44; reconstruction of, 45, 83

"inhabitants' movement" (*jumin undō*), 69, 114; defense of living environment, 130–35; fluid underclass struggles, 135–39; landscape theory and, 141–44; mutual aid of precarious youth, 139–41

integrated spectacle, 82, 85

internationalism, 120, 121

International Olympic Committee (IOC), 82

Iran, 100

Ishimure Michiko, 134, 150, 151–52, 153

Israel, 92

Ito Noe, 174n28

Japan, xii, 11, 92; archipelagic versus insular, 55–61, 156–57, 162; Buddhism in, 8, 9, 154, 167–68n11, 168n12; collective soul of, 7; de-Tokyo-ization of, 86; as earthquake-prone archipelago, 16, 17–18; economic troubles of, 26; evacuation policy, 40; household (*ie*) society, 129; hyperconsumerism of, 21; imperialist expansion into Asia Pacific, 39, 42, 56–57, 59; Kansai area versus Tokyo, 75; modernization of, 26, 55, 58, 71, 132, 161;

Japan (*continued*)
    as museum of Asiatic civilization,
        59, 60; national bond (*kizuna*), 7,
        25; National Diet Building, 118, 121,
        177n6; occupation by US forces,
        64–65; population growth and de-
        population, 161; postwar constitu-
        tion, 46, 47, 63, 118; postwar regime,
        x, 6–7, 16, 161; radioactive zones, 5;
        Self-Defense Forces, 24, 67; upris-
        ings of 1960s, 114, 117–24; as US cli-
        ent state, 16, 24
Japan Atomic Energy Agency, 108
Japan Communist Party (JCP), 46, 69,
    119, 123
Japan Railways, 48, 172n62
Japan Red Army, 122, 141, 177n11
Japan Revolutionary Communist
    League (Kakukyodo), 177n115
Japan Socialist Party, 69
JATEC (Japan Technical Committee to
    Aid Anti-War GIs), 122
Jeju Island, 54, 59, 67
Jokyo gekijo (Situation theater), 177n8
Jonouchi Motoharu, 177n8
Jordan, 25
Judeo-Christianity, 9
Jungk, Robert, 98–99, 143
Jusatsu kitō sōdan (Monks for deadly
    curses), 171n49

Kamagasaki Joint Struggle Committee
    (Kama-kyo-to), 135
Kamagasaki Riot (2008), 137
Kamikaze fighters, death mission of, 30
Kan Naoto, 24, 105
Kant, Immanuel, 124
Kara Juro, 177n8
Katsiaficas, George, 3, 115, 116, 124
Kazakhstan, 92, 176n28
KEPCO (Kansai Electric Power Com-
    pany), 43, 97
Kichi to guntai o yurusanai kodosuru
    onnatachi no kai (Active women's
    group against the bases and mili-
    tary), 178n22

Klein, Naomi, 5
Kōgai genron [Principles of environ-
    mental pollution] (Ui), 130
Koide Hiroaki, 47, 174n25
Koizumi Shinjirō, 26
Kokutetsu (Japanese National Rail-
    ways), 127, 143
Komaba dormitory, Tokyo University,
    139, 179n38
Kon Wajiro, 77–78
Korea, South, xii, 25, 54, 138, 140
Korean peninsula, 58, 59, 67, 118
Koreans, resident in Japan, 45, 77, 118,
    135, 136
Korean War, 66, 118, 121
Kuchinskaya, Olga, 21
Kurihara Sadako, 70
Kyoto, city of, 75
Kyoto School, 60

labor power, 83, 93; disposable, 74, 75;
    irradiated, 92; as masterless object,
    104; as variable capital, 88, 104. *See
    also* working class
labor unions, 28, 69, 133
landscape theory (*fukeiron*), 141–44,
    179n39
Lawrence, D. H., 11, 151
La ZAD struggle (France), 121, 133
Leviathan, Hobbesian, 4
Liberal Democratic Party, 23, 25, 67
liberal politics, ineffectiveness of,
    46–47
linear nonthreshold (LNT) model,
    146
lives-as-struggle, xii, xiii, 5, 13, 43, 44;
    anarchy in the apocalypse as ho-
    rizon of, 112; bridge from global
    1968 to today, 130; climatic politics
    of the Earth and, 117; confronted
    by global nuclear regime, 92; dual
    battle of, 34; eroto-politics of de-
    sire and, 116; as main battleground,
    14; milieus of, 155, 156; ontological
    asymmetricity and, 126, 133–34;
    political ontology and, 3; politics of

national unity narrative, 18

nation-state, capitalist, 1, 16, 20, 126, 162; apparatuses of capture and, 153; beginning of the end of, 114; decline of, 38; expansion of the World and, 62; geopolitics of, 95; insular form of, 59; necessity to decompose, 54; response to catastrophe, 5; territorialization of, 156–57; territorial wars of, 14; Tokyo as laboratory for, 75; World as *logos* and, 2. *See also* capitalism; World, the

naturing nature (*natura naturans*), 10, 11, 153, 155

Navy, US, 24, 56

necropolitics, 13

neoliberalism, 26, 42, 47, 128

New Left, 46, 115, 119, 158, 176n5; Cold War paradigm of revolution and, 159; JCP in conflict with, 123; Shinjuku Riot and, 120

New Testament, 7

NGOs (nongovernmental organizations), 37

NHK [Nippon Hōsō Kyōkai] (Japan Broadcasting Corporation), 45, 76, 172n62

Nietzsche, Friedrich, 11

Niger, 92

9/11 terrorist attacks, 100

Nippon Television Network Corporation, 68

Nishida Kitaro, 60

Nixon, Rob, 20

Noda Yoshihiko, 25, 42

No Olympics 2020 (Hangorin no kai), 85

North, Global, 2–3, 126

North Africa, 2

No TAV struggle (Italy), 121

nothingness, ontology of, 59, 60

NPT (Nonproliferation Treaty), 175n9

Nuclear and Industrial Safety Agency (NISA), 23, 24

nuclear exceptionalism, 91, 92, 100, 101

nuclear power, xii, 47, 57, 82, 164; abolition of, 149, 150, 163; atomic world history, 89–93; beneficiaries of, 19; capitalism and state merged by, 93–98; capitalism immortalized by, 87–89; critics of, 47; difficulty of abolishing, 89, 93; export of, 25; formation of postwar regime in Japan and, x; global prevalence of, 25; intellectuals' positions on, 70; Janus face (weapon and energy) of, 63, 67, 89, 98; petroleum-dominant economy and, 91, 100; privileged position in capitalist/state apparatuses, 44

nuclear power plants, 70, 143, 163; construction of plants stopped by protests, 132; decommissioning of, 88; geopolitics and siting of, 95–96, 102–3; hierarchical organization and secrecy of, 37–38; proliferation in Japan, 16; shutting down of, 43; workers in, 38, 42–43, 99. *See also* Fukushima Daiichi Nuclear Power Plant

nuclear proliferation, xi, 25, 33

Nuclear Regulatory Commission (United States), 23

Nuclear Safety Commission, 22, 23

Nuclear State, The (Jungk), 99, 143

nuclear warfare, 62, 69, 106

nuclear warheads, 70, 91

nuclear workers, 43, 138, 139; agonizing conditions of, 145; commonality and polarity with reproductive workers, 148–49; deaths by radiation exposure, 70; as generalized condition for planetary inhabitants, 150; as most susceptible to radiation, 35; as "saviors" and "martyrs," 99; subcontracted, 37, 38, 42, 102; zero-becquerelism and, 147

Occupy Wall Street (OWS), 1

Oceanographic Research Project, 36–37

Oe Kenzaburo, 70

oil shock (1973), 127

Oi Nuclear Power Plant, 43, 45
Okakura Kakuzo, 59–60
Okinawa, 54, 59, 67, 121, 123, 130; defense of environment, 156; Okinawans as yoseba day laborers, 135, 136; rape of schoolgirl as catalyst for anti-base movement, 129
ontologies, political, 3, 11, 46, 51, 125, 130, 167n4; of commons, 106–7; life-as-struggle and, 3, 36; shift from dialectics to immanence, 14, 16, 114; of the World and of the Earth, 50, 103
ontometaphysics, 21, 59, 100, 101, 111, 152
Osaka, city of, 75, 137, 155
Osugi Sakae, 174n28

pacifism, 123
Pan-Asianism, 60
Paradise in the Sea of Sorrow: Our Minamata Disease (Ishimure), 134, 150
"parallel chain crisis" (*heikō-rensa-kiki*), 21, 27, 168n4
patriarchy, 20, 35, 36, 144
peace, 67, 68, 69; "atoms for peace," 31, 55, 99; Japan's postwar constitution and, 46, 63, 66, 67
peripheries, underdeveloped, 20
permaculture, 52
PFLP (Popular Front for the Liberation of Palestine), 122
Philippines, 54
planetary becoming, 9, 10, 13
planetary crowd, 1, 10, 42, 133, 153
plutonium, 30, 91, 108, 176n33
police, 1, 42, 137
pollution, industrial, 113, 131–32, 178n24
populism, nationalist, 12, 44–45
populism, progressive/liberal, 45–46, 171n55
postmodernism/postmodernity, 61, 117
Potsdam Declaration, 57
precariat/precarity, 126, 139
"preemption" doctrine, 100
Prehistory of the Partisans (film, 1969), 177n12
primary (immediate) impacts, 18–19

primitive accumulation, 74, 84, 137
proletariat, in Marxist theory, 124, 125

Radiation Effects Research Foundation (RERF), 65
radiation/radioactivity, ix, 2, 19, 27; double invisibility of, 21; effects on human body, 146–47; invisible threat of, 29, 146; in soil, 108; threshold of contamination levels, x, 41, 171n47
"radioactive brain" (*hōsha-nō*), 35, 170n39
radioactive crowd, 2, 5, 10, 49, 111; creation of collective intelligence and, 154–55, 180n60; new political ontology and, 11; technopolitics of, 154; united front of, 152
radionuclides, 5, 9, 14, 72; accumulation of, 19, 51; half-lives of, 30, 103; heterogenesis of, 34; levels of exposure to, 31, 170n26; mutation by, 17; in soil, 26; virtual flow beyond Japan's borders, 49
radiosensitive crowd, 49, 50, 111
rationality, politics of, 32
Reclus, Elisée, 158
Red Army/PFLP Declaration of World War, The (film, 1971), 177n11
"Remodeling of the Japanese Archipelago" plan (1972), 80
reproduction, social, 17, 125, 144–45
reproductive workers, 20, 145, 147, 148–49
reterritorialization, 75, 82, 116
revelation, 7, 9, 11, 55, 158
revolts/uprisings, 10, 42, 45–46, 113; crushing and quelling of, 3; curse character and, 41; of Fukushima mothers, 41; interconnectivity of, 3; millennialist, 4; self-organization of, 117
revolution, x, 81, 110; anti-Stalinist, 119, 120; Arab Spring, 1; global revolution (1968), 114, 115, 117; Japan's 1968 movements, 117–24; as metamorphic series of events, 159; planetary, 146, 157; as religious war, 8; scientific, 90; uprisings of 1960s, xii

Revolutionary Communist League: Core Faction, 177n9, 177n13; Revolutionary Marxist Faction, 177n13

Ring of Fire, 18

Rio de Janeiro, city of, 84

Rojava, 133

Rokkasho Reprocessing Plant (Aomori Prefecture), 108

Russia, 109

sakoku (national enclosure), 56

Sākuru mura undō (Circle Village Movement), 176–77n5

Sanriku tsunami (1933), 39

Sanrizuka farmers' struggle, 121, 132, 133

Sanya Dispute Group (Sanya sogi-dan), 135

Satō Eisaku, 69

Sato Mitsuo, 178n30

science, 6, 34, 56, 71, 111

SEALDS (Students Emergency Action for Liberal Democracy), 46

secondary (collateral) impacts, 19

sensibility, politics of, 32

Seoul, city of, 86

seppuku (ritualistic suicide), 30

sexism, 124

sex workers, 138

Shibaki-tai, 171n55

Shiba Ryotaro, 78–79

Shindo Kaneto, 142

Shinjuku Riot (1968), 120

Shinjuku Station (film, 1974), 177n8

Shinkansen, 72

social democracy, 14

socialism, 14, 133

Soeda Takashi, 33

Sohyo (General Council of Trade Unions of Japan), 69, 127

Solnit, Rebecca, 5

South, Global, 2, 76, 126

Soviet Union, 57, 69

Spain, 42

spectacle, political and media, 3, 11, 32, 73; Debord's "society of the spectacle" theory, 82, 117; information war against, 85–86; life-as-struggle and, 36; Olympics and, 81, 82–86; street demonstrations and, 10

SPEEDI (System for Prediction of Environment Emergency Dose Information), 22

Standing Rock movement, 133

state of emergency, 17, 22, 168n6

Strike for Recovering the Right to Strike [Suto-ken-suto] (1975), 127

strikes, union and wildcat, 120–21

student movement (1960s), 71, 119, 120, 122–23

Sunfield Nihonmatsu Golf Course, 104

surplus value, 92, 102

Taipei, city of, 86

Taiwan, 54

Taketani Mitsuo, 70

Tanaka Kakuei, 80, 143

Tanigawa Gan, 142, 177n5

Tarachine (radiation-monitoring station), 36–37, 49

Tatehana Takashi, 177n115

technology, 2, 6, 56, 71, 105

technopolitics, 10, 32, 93, 100, 111, 154, 164; lives-as-struggle and, 21; nuclear exceptionalism and, 101; nuclear technology as epitome of, 64, 88; ontology (becoming) of the Earth, 50

tectonic plates/activities, 5, 9, 18, 58, 155

Teller, Edward, 90

TEPCO (Tokyo Electric Power Company), 18, 19, 22, 24, 53, 132; evacuation policy and, 40; farmers' efforts to seek compensation from, 51; hierarchical organization of, 23, 38; lawsuits against, 25, 36; monopoly capital status of, 97; negligence of, 33; on radiation as masterless object, 104; self-exemption from responsibility, 105, 110; workers evacuated from site, 23

Terayama Shuji, 142

territorialities, 14, 45, 53, 54, 56

Thanatos drive/death drive, 30, 45, 57, 124

thermodynamics, 90

Third World, 121

Those Who Go North activists, 37, 38

Those Who Go West activists, 37, 54, 86

Thousand Plateaus, A (Deleuze and Guattari), 180n69

Three Mile Island (1979), xi, 101, 106

Tiqqun collective, 55

Tokieda Motoki, 60

Tokugawa Shogunate, 56, 75

Tokyo, city of, 30, 37, 72; antinuclear actions in, 41; as apparatus and machine, 72–81; businesses centered in, 132; countryside in service to, 96; destroyed by US bombing in World War II, 77; destroyed in Kanto earthquake (1923), 39, 77; end of, 72; growth in response to catastrophes, 39, 57; history of, 75–76; homeless camp in Yoyogi Park, 155; hyperconsumerist society in, 61; "Memorial Museum" proposal for, 48; migrants to, 73, 74–75, 76; pollution and overcrowding, 73; radioactive contamination in tap water, 28, 169n23; sarin gas subway attack (1995), 129; Shinjuku Riot (1968), 120

Tokyo Gaikan Expressway, 80

Tokyo Olympics (1964), 73, 81

Tokyo Olympics (2020), x, 45, 48, 81; coalition organized against, 155; spectacle and, 82–86

Tokyo Sunaba Project, 33

topography, 117

Toshiba, 23

totalitarian society, 82

totality, 87, 110, 113, 124, 125, 162

tourism, 44, 47–48, 61, 80, 172n62; Japanese National Railways "Discover Japan" campaign, 143; tourization of Tokyo Olympics (2020), 86

Toyotomi Hideyoshi, 79

Trans-Pacific Partnership, 51

Treaty of San Francisco (1952), 65

Trotskyist League, in Japan, 119

Truman, Harry S., 99

Trump, Donald, 13, 99

Tsuchimoto Noriaki, 177n12

Tsumura Takashi, 142

tsunamis, 39, 58

tsunami tendenko (tsunami escape plan), 38–40

Turkey, xii, 25

uchigeba (violence internal to New Left sects), 123, 177nn13–15

Ui Jun, 130–31, 132

underclass struggle, fluid, 135–39

United Arab Emirates, 25

United Nations (UN), 91, 124, 126, 165, 175n9

United Red Army (Rengo sekigun), 177n11, 177n13

United States, xii, 7, 31, 55, 92, 109; counterculture and protest movements (1960s), 120; as dominant power in the Pacific, 91; Fukushima radiation in Pacific Northwest, 49, 53; global strategy of, 16, 64; imperialism of, 118, 120, 159; military bases in Japanese archipelago, 62, 70, 121, 122, 156; Occupy movement, 1

uranium, 68, 88, 109, 161, 175n9; depleted uranium weapons, 92, 102; mining of, 92, 95, 102, 150

urbanization, 13, 142

Urstaat ("original state"), 55, 173n1

US-Japan Security Treaty (Ampo), 69, 118, 177n5; action against renewal of (1970), 122, 123, 177n13; uprising against (1960), 119

utopias, 9, 68, 101, 126; capital's utopia as dystopia, 25; dream of sublime energy for the future, 89

vanguardism, 46, 123, 124, 142, 159

Vietnam, 25

www.ingramcontent.com/pod-product-compliance
Lightning Source LLC
Chambersburg PA
CBHW070327270326
41926CB00017B/3792